Pelican Special
The Whores of War

W9-CYB-155

Wilfred Burchett was born in 1911 in Australia and is
recognized as a specialist in Asian affairs. He spent
nineteen years in South-East Asia and in China.
During the war he was war correspondent for the
Daily Express, reporting for the Asian and Pacific
theatres. In 1955 the Australian government revoked
his passport because of his opinions on the Korean and
Vietnam wars. Wilfred Burchett is a freelance
journalist and author of twenty-three books which
have been translated into thirty languages and sold all
over the world. *My War with the C.I.A.* (with Prince
Norodom Sihanouk, 1973) and *China: The Quality of
Life* (with Rewi Alley, 1976) have been published in
Pelicans. Wilfred Burchett speaks six languages and
now lives in Paris with his wife and three children.

Derek Roebuck was born in Stalybridge, Cheshire, in
1935 and was educated at Manchester Grammar School
and Hertford College, Oxford. After general practice
as a solicitor in the north of England and some years
as a lecturer in commercial law in the Victoria
University of Wellington, New Zealand, he is now a
professor of law in the University of Tasmania.
Author and co-author of sixteen books on commercial
and comparative law, he has been a member of a
number of international commissions of inquiry into
United States war crimes in Vietnam, into the
reunification of Korea and now into mercenaries.

Wilfred Burchett and
Derek Roebuck

The Whores of War
Mercenaries Today

Penguin Books

Penguin Books Ltd, Harmondsworth,
Middlesex, England
Penguin Books, 625 Madison Avenue,
New York, New York 10022, U.S.A.
Penguin Books Australia Ltd, Ringwood,
Victoria, Australia
Penguin Books Canada Ltd, 2801 John Street,
Markham, Ontario, Canada L3R 1B4
Penguin Books (N.Z.) Ltd, 182–190 Wairau Road,
Auckland 10, New Zealand

First published 1977

Made and printed in Great Britain by
Cox & Wyman Ltd, London, Reading and Fakenham

Set in Monotype Times

Contents

Preface

In June 1976, the authors attended the trial in Luanda of thirteen British and American mercenaries. Wilfred Burchett was there as a journalist, Derek Roebuck as a member of the International Commission of Inquiry on Mercenaries. The Commission asked the authors to write the truth about the present activities of mercenaries, their recruiters and those who pay them. This book is the result.

The title shows no male insensitivity to the causes of prostitution or the unhappiness it brings to women. But the analogy of the mercenary and the prostitute is apt. In each case economic power is abused to hire human bodies with the specific intentions of avoiding public association with them and responsibility for their welfare, and using money to exploit moral weakness. It was Gus Grillo, the captured American mercenary, who first coined the metaphor. As a former Mafia enforcer, he knew enough about both trades. In the mercenary business, too, it is the recruiters, the pimps of war, who deserve the greater blame. And if it were not for those who pay the money, the trade would not exist. It is to stop all their activities that this book is committed.

The authors have shared the work. When we use the words 'we' or 'the authors', we mean both or either of us. All material in square brackets is the authors' comment.

W.B.
D.R.

Introduction

For three thousand years and more there have been rulers who have seen advantages in hiring their soldiers from abroad. For almost as long there have been critics who have emphasized the drawbacks or the immorality of such action. For a long time, too, there have been writers and apologists who have seen in the mercenary's job a romantic quality often assumed by the mercenary himself, though never apparent to his victim.

The present resurgence of the use of mercenaries is caused by the need of governments to carry on military operations, without the support or even sometimes the knowledge of their electorates, against those who have taken up arms to free themselves from colonial or other oppression. But the older reasons for hiring mercenaries still have some influence.[1] Their primary function has been to supply tyranny with a fighting force without the risks involved in arming the people, who might turn their arms and training on the tyrant.

In feudal times, the nobles were jealous of their role as the recruiters of the king's army. The feudal obligation to provide the king with armed men, though usually seen as a burden, was a weapon which the nobles used to great political advantage and were loth to give up. Magna Carta extracted from John a covenant not to employ foreign troops. This has not stopped every British monarch since then from including mercenaries in their army, from the Welsh who conquered Scotland for Edward I, to the Hessians who helped George III to lose the American War of Independence,

1. For the history of mercenaries, see V. G. Kiernan, 'Foreign Mercenaries and Absolute Monarchy', *Past and Present*, April 1957, pp. 66–86; A. Mockler, *Mercenaries*, Macdonald, 1969; M. Mallett, *Mercenaries and their Masters: Warfare in Renaissance Italy*, Military Book Society, 1974; and the sources they cite.

to the Gurkhas now in the Gulf. As only the king could afford them, mercenaries were seen as one means of ensuring the success of the king's attempts to replace feudalism by absolute monarchy. Moreover, foreign troops can be trusted to have no soft sympathies with the subjects, which might relax their iron-fisted firmness in suppressing revolt. They leave behind no widows and orphans to be supported after their deaths. They do not hang about, unemployed and troublesome, when the war is over, though the possibility of their changing sides to a higher bidder has always been a danger. Traditionally, in their training and in their ability to handle the latest weapons and tactics, they have been professionals. The Flemish and German mercenaries who fought in the Wars of the Roses were the first soldiers in an English army to use hand guns. Let Raleigh or Machiavelli rail against mercenaries as untrustworthy or debilitating. Despots from Xerxes to Mobuto can't all be wrong! Mercenaries have turned the tide of battle often enough through the centuries to perpetuate a market for their services.

The modern mercenary seeks the same rewards as his forerunners. Loot is never far from his mind. There are rich pickings to be had, or so his masters and the recruiters tell him. The disasters of his own emotional inadequacy can perhaps be forgotten with the women he is promised or in the special relations he has with his close comrades of war. For an unemployed soldier, cast off by the army of his own country, the pay of a mercenary seems a fortune. He may attain a rank – for honours are cheap for his master to bestow – which he could only covet in a regular army. He usually expects to be armed with weapons superior to those of his enemy, whom he is led to believe is inferior, perhaps simply because of race. He may enjoy fighting, particularly when the odds are greatly in his favour.

And so, from the inadequate, the discarded, the cruel, the bully, the unimaginative, the fantasist, the racist, and above all the greedy, are recruited the human resources to make the war machine work. They are, like the arms they use, available to anyone who can afford them. No longer from the poverty of subsistence farming in Nepal or Baluchistan but from the unemployed of Camberley and California they go to fight in wars about political issues they rarely understand. In the Luanda trial Wiseman, the sadly misnamed

British proletarian casualty, on being asked whether it was for money or ideology that he willingly went to fight in Angola, replied 'I can't answer that question' and for many reasons he was right.

In this book we try to show how mercenaries are being used now. The Luanda trial was a dramatic and moving concentration of effort to stop their future use. The political initiatives taken there can lead to worldwide action to outlaw them. While many of our points are exemplified by the mercenaries who were tried in Luanda or have returned to England, we show that mercenaries are a universal phenomenon, that there is a loose but effective association of mercenaries, recruiters and their masters, and that there are principles of general application which govern their use.

Our book has a purpose which we openly state: to relate what is really happening, to draw together as much of the disparate information as we can gather, to present it as best we can, and to enlist the readers' support in the campaign to show up the use of mercenaries for the scourge it is.

The tawdry and sinister image of the mercenary must be contrasted with that of the liberator: the man or woman who takes up arms only when convinced that all else has failed and when the unbearable oppression of others compels the moral decision to use retaliatory force. The inadequate bully stands against the ordinary man, not just the prepared revolutionary but the ordinary worker in field or factory for whom fighting is a horrifying intrusion into his life. Look at our cover and see the whole story! Sende Isabel and Andrew Gordon McKenzie: the pregnant peasant woman and her brutal unwanted intruder. May Sende Isabel's child grow up in a world in which the mercenary monster has no place!

Part One

Angola and Beyond

1 Why Mercenaries Now?

The present revival in the use of mercenaries was dramatized by the execution of four of them in Luanda, Angola, on 10 July 1976, and the sentencing of nine others to long prison terms. Why did the captors not shoot the captives on the battlefield – usual enough in such circumstances – instead of preserving them for public trial? By burying the subject together with the bodies, recriminations would have been avoided. One would have thought that – apart from the captives – everyone would have been relieved!

One reason was that the captors were disciplined, revolutionary forces who could not be expected to use the methods of fascist armies or colonialist expeditionary corps. Also, if the People's Republic of Angola – just seven months old on the day the trial opened – decided to arraign thirteen mercenaries before a People's Revolutionary Tribunal, it was because its leaders were convinced that a new phase had started in the armed independence struggles of the peoples of southern Africa. The treatment of captives and the legitimacy of the trial were matters of principle for the MPLA. The fact that it was held in the presence of eminent jurists and outstanding personalities of some forty countries stressed the desire not only to establish the legitimacy of the Luanda trial but also to alert world public opinion to this new danger, as the first step towards having it removed.

Not that there was anything new in the use of mercenaries to put down national liberation struggles in Africa or anywhere else. But the context in which mercenaries were used in Angola was new and opened up the prospects of a more generalized use of such 'soldiers of fortune' in the area. This was because of the limitation on the use of direct intervention by governments traditionally interested in ensuring that the West holds on to what is richest and best and most important to their global interests and strategies. The Korean war, in which sixteen nations engaged their troops on the southern side against those of North Korea and their allies, the Chinese 'People's Volunteers', was the last occasion on which an international expeditionary corps could be used. The United States tried to rally the same participants to help them in the Vietnam war – but failed. The United States in Vietnam was reduced to subsidizing – at a very high price – the troops of a few client states, South Korea, the Philippines and Thailand, and mobilizing the loyalties of Australia and New Zealand to furnish token units to give some façade of 'international support'.

Repetitions of the Vietnam strategy as a means of saving the remnants of Portugal's empire in Angola, or the illegal South African occupation of Namibia, or the illegal racist régime in Rhodesia, or even that bastion of *apartheid* – South Africa itself – were unacceptable, not because of moral inhibitions, but because of the facts of life. The direct use of force and threats of force had been seriously devalued by the American debacle in Vietnam. 'Gunboats up the Congo' methods had been discredited, to say the least, and more sophisticated variants of that old imperialist formula even more so. The most promising of the latter had come to grief in Vietnam. 'Special war', designed by the late President John Kennedy as a rich power's gadget to put down national liberation struggles without committing their own combat troops, had been a disaster. The concept of teleguided wars in which the United States would put up the arms, the dollars, the instructors – 'advisers' who would actually direct strategy and tactical operations – air and naval support, everything short of the actual cannon fodder, came to grief in the jungle and paddy-fields of South Vietnam. The United States had to move up one more rung of the strategy ladder and go over to 'limited war' – all-out war with everything except nuclear weapons thrown in. Use of the latter would mean that the top rung of 'global nuclear war' had been reached.

The failure of 550,000 of the best infantrymen the United States could field, together with unlimited air and naval support, to halt the national liberation struggle in Vietnam – and the various associated scandals culminating in Watergate – traumatized US public opinion to the extent that further US overseas military adventures were ruled out – at least for a decade or so! And if not the USA – who could take over the white man's burden of ensuring that Angolan oil, coffee, diamonds and other riches did not fall into black hands? Apparently Red black hands at that! South Africa? A clear possibility – there was no lack of zeal on the part of her racist leaders. South African troops, with the complicity of Portuguese generals, had been acquiring experience in anti-guerrilla operations in Mozambique and Angola for years past.

Vorster at least seems to have believed he would have discreet US support for an interventionist role if things got tough for US-backed forces in Angola. But South Africa's armed forces were thin on the ground and would themselves have to be reinforced from other sources. Because of increasing pressures inside South Africa itself – which reached flash-point in the Soweto massacres starting 16 June 1976 – and in Namibia (South West Africa), where SWAPO[1] guerrillas were stepping up their activities, South Africa was forced to call home its armed police forces sent to prop up the Smith régime in Rhodesia. But until the end of 1975, South Africa seemed the most hopeful and competent guarantor that southern Africa would be kept safe for white rule and multinational investors.

Rhodesia (Zimbabwe to its African population) was however a source of worry to those hoping to preserve the status quo – 280,000 whites battling to maintain colour-of-skin privileges against 9,000,000 blacks! White males of military age were showing an ever-increasing interest in one-way 'holiday' trips to South Africa and elsewhere. There was a steady increase in departures over arrivals, a net loss of 2,280 in the first half of 1976, compared to a net gain of 1,590 (mainly Portuguese quitting Angola and Mozambique) for the same period of 1975, and a gross loss of 12,000 for 1976, with net monthly losses in December twice that of January. Defence Minister Reg Cowper resigned on 14 February 1977, after the business community claimed the economy would be ruined if his extended call-up plans for males between 38 to 50 was put into effect! Symptomatic of reasons for the funk-flight was the sen-

1. South West Africa Peoples Organization (SWAPO) is recognized by the UN, the OAU (Organization of African Unity) and other international organizations as the sole legitimate representative of the people of Namibia.

tencing on 28 July 1976 of fifty-six Africans to ten years of prison each for failing to report the presence of guerrillas on their boss's farm!

By the end of 1975, it was clear that the Smith régime was going to be in urgent need of military muscle. Where could it come from? Exhortations to young white Rhodesians to defend the land where they were 'born and bred' fell on ears that became increasingly hard of hearing. The days of automatic response to the waving of flags and banging of drums had gone for ever. The only hope lay in imported cannon fodder. But again – from where? Any overt help would be in direct and flagrant violation of UN resolutions, which had outlawed the Smith régime. The Rhodesia of Ian Smith was in a state of 'rebellion' as far as Britain was concerned. But the inner core of the British Establishment was at one with its counterparts on the other side of the Atlantic in their determination to ensure that Rhodesian chrome, copper, tobacco and other profitable products should not fall into black hands – even if these were not yet as Red as those in Angola (and Mozambique) were suspected to be.

The problem was to find new ways of waging war without the governments concerned appearing to be directly involved. This was particularly true of the two major powers, the United States and Britain, normally quickest off the mark in defending what the establishments in those countries considered their 'vital interests'. It needs to be kept in mind that Britain – through its traditional ties with Portugal – had long been a major investor in the Portuguese colonies, with the United States fast overhauling it, especially in Angolan oil and diamonds. But public opinion in those countries would not tolerate open involvement in what would have been an old-fashioned imperialist enterprise. What to do? As far as Angola was concerned, it looked as if the problem could be solved by enlisting the services of two willing neighbours – South Africa, from its bases in illegally occupied Namibia, which had a common frontier with Angola in the south, and Zaire, which bordered on Angola in the north. But Rhodesia? The most obvious fireman – South Africa – had a common cause but not a common frontier, not to mention the growing problems at home and on its front and back doorsteps.

For Rhodesia, the use of mercenaries was the obvious answer — that millennia-old device for protecting wealth, power and privilege by which the owners, or would-be owners, lacking strength or stomach for the fight, hired others to fight for them.

To 'save' Rhodesia, mercenaries were the only answer. They were neo-colonialism's last card and eventually would be for South Africa as well – a faceless and bottomless reserve of cannon fodder, not identifiable with governments and their policies, immune to public criticism and debate. The perfect substitute for the expeditionary forces.

It was the perception of this that led the leaders of the People's Republic of Angola to stage the Luanda trial before the world press and a forty-two-member International Commission. The intention was to burn that last card before it could be used; to bring the whole question of the use of mercenaries into the forefront of public opinion and to stimulate international action to ban this odious practice once and for all.

An interesting question is why a recruiting machinery originally intended as a fairly leisurely operation for Rhodesia suddenly had to be thrown into top gear for Angola. What was going on in Angola?

As part of the decolonization process sparked off by the victories of the national liberation movements and the April 1974 'Captains' coup' in Portugal, an agreement had been signed (15 January 1975) between the Portuguese government and the three Angolan independence movements, the MPLA, FNLA and UNITA,[2]

2. Popular Movement for the Liberation of Angola, headed by Dr Agostinho Neto, National Front for the Liberation of Angola, headed by Holden Roberto, and National Union for the Total Independence of Angola, headed by Dr Jonas Savimbi, respectively. To the great chagrin of the Portuguese counterparts of the racist white Rhodesians, smaller movements, such as FLEC (Liberation Front for the Cabinda Enclave), PCDA (Angolan Christian Democratic Party) and a dozen others, were excluded from the negotiations. Of the three recognized movements, only the MPLA, the first to be formed (in December 1956), had a deep-rooted, nation-wide organization and all-Angolan concepts. The FNLA was tribal-based, with its influence restricted to the northern areas adjoining Zaire. UNITA was also tribal-based and, according to official Portuguese sources, when the coup took place in Portugal it had no more than three hundred badly equipped men!

recognized as 'the only legitimate representatives of the people of
Angola'. This accord, known as the Algarve (or Alvor) Agreement,
provided for the setting-up of a three-member 'presidential
college' in the Angolan capital, Luanda, presided over by each of
the three movements in turn. A transitional government of thirteen
ministers formed by three each from the movements and four
nominated by Portugal would also be set up. It was intended that
the transitional period would end, by 31 October 1975, with
nation-wide elections, to form an all-Angolan government, with
independence to be declared by 11 November 1975, followed by
a phased Portuguese withdrawal to be completed by February
1976.

On paper it was a good agreement, with strict equality between
the three movements in all spheres and parity between Portugal
and the three movements in matters of joint concern during the
transitional period. It never worked, partly because it accorded the
FNLA and UNITA a status far beyond that merited by their
respective contributions to the national liberation struggle. And
this was used by them to continue what was really a war of
aggression against the Angolan people, which had started from the
founding of these two movements, in 1962 and 1966 respectively,
and in which the MPLA, and not the Portuguese, was regarded as
the main enemy. This war was carried on in a concentrated form
after delegations of the three movements entered Luanda in
November 1974, each having signed cease-fire accords with the
Portuguese. The FNLA brought in substantial military forces.
The MPLA entered Luanda without a single soldier or weapon.
Assassinations, arbitrary arrests and torture of MPLA cadres
built up to direct attacks on 23 March 1975, against MPLA in-
stallations at Cazegna and Vila Alice, in Luanda.

These provocations reached their climax on 24 March with the
massacre at Kifangondo, about twenty kilometres north of
Luanda, of fifty-one unarmed members of the MPLA, who were
simply rounded up in their homes and places of work – mainly in
Luanda – by FNLA armed bands, taken off in trucks and
machine-gunned. At the end of that month the FNLA brought
into Luanda a motorized column comprising five hundred troops.

According to Comandante 'Juju', spokesman of the General

Staff of FAPLA[3] at the time he was interviewed by the authors, the fighting in Luanda:

... really started in March, when Zaire regular troops and Zaire-based FNLA troops infiltrated from the north, occupying Ambriz, Carmona and other places. Some of our forces then entered Luanda. During March, there were three or four incidents every day. We made various ceasefire agreements, but each was followed by an escalation of the attacks. There was virtually continuous fighting throughout June and early July, culminating with FNLA shelling of a funeral ceremony for an MPLA woman cadre, Lilia Celina, on 9 July.

Three days later, the FAPLA attacked and destroyed the FNLA headquarters in Luanda and, within a few days, with the support of the Luanda masses, led by MPLA militants, the FNLA–UNITA forces were driven out of the capital. The transitional government composed of the three movements and Portugal virtually came to an end, although the MPLA never abdicated its government functions.

Repeated attempts by the FNLA forces to retake the capital were repulsed. The country seemed to be settling into a three-way partition, with the FNLA controlling large tracts of territory in the north, the MPLA the north-centre and east and UNITA the centre-south. The MPLA political infrastructure was either arrested or underground in the areas controlled by FNLA–UNITA. On the other hand, the MPLA permitted all FNLA–UNITA cadres to withdraw safely from Luanda and other MPLA-controlled centres where three-way administrations had been installed.

At the beginning of August 1975, South African troops occupied two Angolan towns, Calueque and Pereira de Eça, fifty kilometres and forty kilometres (by road) respectively from the Namibian border. Reports of this were strenuously denied by Pretoria until 26 January 1976 when, replying to a motion of no confidence in the

3. FAPLA (Angolan People's Liberation Armed Forces) were the armed forces of the MPLA, ELNA (Angolan National Liberation Army) were those of the FNLA, and FALA (Armed Forces for the Liberation of Angola) were those of UNITA. Almost all FAPLA commanders used *noms de guerre*, some of them borrowed from such legendary revolutionary leaders as Ho Chi Minh and 'Che'.

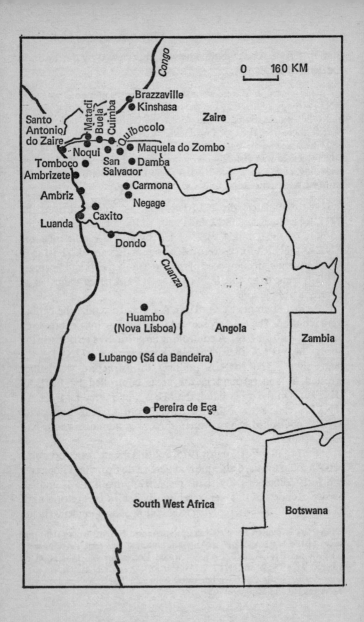

South African Parliament because of the debacle in Angola, Defence Minister Pieter Botha admitted that Calueque had been occupied in early August 'because South African troops had been fired on'.

Comandante Farrusco, who commanded guerrilla groups in that area at the time, told the authors that as soon as the South African troops came in they started building up for the famous 'drive north', which started on 23 October 1975. In Sá da Bandeira (now Lubango), the capital of Huila province, the first target of the South African invasion, the authors interviewed Angolans and a Portuguese school teacher, captured by the South Africans on the first day of the invasion!

The grand FNLA–UNITA strategy soon became clear. Zaire–FNLA troops pushing down from the north, and South African–UNITA troops pushing up from the south would converge on Luanda, capturing it before 11 November, so that FNLA–UNITA would be the powers to whom the Portuguese would hand over independence. That was the maximum plan. The minimum was that between them the two forces would make the city of Luanda untenable by cutting off water and electricity supplies. Zaire–FNLA forces would occupy and put out of action the pumping station on which Luanda's water supply depended, at Kifangondo, less than twenty kilometres north of the capital. South African–UNITA forces would occupy and put out of action the Cambambe hydroelectric station, which supplied Luanda with electricity, over 160 kilometres south of the capital.

The Zaire–FNLA column did manage to get within eighteen kilometres of Luanda by 7 November, and after being repulsed got to the same spot again on the morning of 10 November, putting the Kifangondo pumping station temporarily out of action by artillery fire before they were driven back. But the South Africans fell far short of even the minimum targets. Although they advanced just over 1,600 kilometres in less than a month – the FAPLA having no heavy weapons to counter their armoured cars and artillery – they were stopped – already well behind schedule – 400 kilometres south of Luanda and 240 kilometres short of their minimum target of Dondo and the Cambambe hydroelectric complex. On 30 January, at the end of the no-confidence debate mentioned earlier,

the South African Prime Minister, Balthazar Vorster, admitted
that South African troops had penetrated a 'very long way' into
Angola, and on 3 February Defence Minister Botha revealed that
between 4,000 and 5,000 South African troops were 'patrolling a
buffer zone about thirty-five kilometres deep inside Angola . . .' to
where they had been forced to retreat.[4] The fact that the MPLA,
by then firmly in control in Luanda, had presented four South
African POWs to the press in mid-December – captured deep
inside Angolan territory – accounted for some limited South
African candour on the subject!

It is worthy of note that both southern and northern drives on
the capital were halted exclusively by FAPLA forces using –
except for Soviet multiple rocket-launchers in defence of Luanda –
shoulder-fired weapons. This was at the cost of heavy casualties,
especially on the central-southern front, where the Spinolist ELP
(Portuguese Liberation Army) followed the South African troops
to attack the FAPLA forces in the rear.

The MPLA were however in complete control of Luanda on the
afternoon of 11 November 1975 when the Portuguese flag was
lowered and High Commissioner Admiral Leonel Gomes Cardoso
and his staff stepped aboard a frigate to sail out of Luanda harbour, marking the formal end of almost 500 years of Portuguese
rule in Angola.

At midnight, the President of the MPLA, Agostinho Neto,
proclaimed the country's independence and the establishment of
the People's Republic of Angola with Luanda as its capital. A few
hours later – in the small hours of the morning of 11 November –
veteran resistance leader Lucio Lara, acting in the name of the
MPLA's central committee and in his capacity as secretary of its
political bureau, invested Agostinho Neto as President of the
People's Republic. Later that day, the FNLA–UNITA declared
the establishment of the Democratic People's Republic of Angola
with its capital at Huambo (formerly Nova Lisboa), the country's
second largest city, 600 kilometres south-east of Luanda. One of
the first acts of the People's Republic – with the South African

4. On 26 January, the London *Guardian* quoted Defence Minister Botha as
stating that twenty-nine South Africans had been killed in action and fourteen in accidents 'from 14 July 1975 to 23 January 1976'.

armoured column still advancing towards the capital and the Zaire–FNLA forces licking their wounds at Caxito, about forty kilometres north-east of Luanda – was to ask Cuba for combat troops and the Soviet Union for heavy weapons and instructors in their use. Weapons started to arrive almost immediately – Cuban troops by the end of November. By the end of 1975, Pentagon sources were claiming that there were some 4,000 Cuban troops serving with the FAPLA, and a chart issued by the Pentagon on 29 January 1976 listed about 200 Soviet military advisers in Angola.

'We could have dealt with Zaire forces entirely on our own,' said Comandante 'Juju', discussing the request for Cubans. 'We could have dealt with the combination of Zaire–FNLA–UNITA forces on our own. We were well on the way to taking Huambo when the South Africans invaded in force. But we could not cope with 5,000 to 6,000 South Africans with armoured cars, artillery, helicopters and spotter planes directing their artillery fire.'

On 22 November, FAPLA forces, still operating on their own, captured Caxito, which was the FNLA logistics headquarters town, together with hundreds of tons of equipment. They pressed slowly northwards, the rate of advance dictated by the speed with which they could repair bridges blown up by the retreating Zaire–FNLA forces.

Meanwhile, as the FAPLA and their new Cuban allies prepared to take on the South Africans, something happened which brought mercenaries to the fore. On 19 December, the US Senate, by fifty-four votes to twenty-two, approved an amendment to the Defense Appropriations Bill banning the Ford Administration from continuing undercover military aid to the FNLA–UNITA forces and their allies. No less than thirty-three million dollars were said to have been earmarked for CIA operations in Angola. On the two previous days and by far larger majorities, the Senate had voted to ban the employment of US combat personnel in Angola or any US assistance to any groups there 'without the full authorization of Congress'.

The senators, especially sensitive to public opinion with an election year coming up, were doubtless influenced by articles by Leslie Gelb, formerly of the State Department, in the *New York*

Times of 25 September, and by Gelb together with Walter Pincus in the *Washington Post* of 8 and 9 November, exposing the deep involvement of the CIA in the Angolan war. *Intelligence Report*, published by the Washington-based Center for National Security Studies, in its first issue at the end of December 1975, followed up the Gelb–Pincus reports by quoting US official sources to the effect that the CIA was 'now spending fifty million dollars on the Angolan war and has already sent five artillery spotter planes piloted by Americans into the Angolan battle zones'. Shades of Vietnam! To the horror of Vorster in Pretoria, Mobuto in Kinshasa, Holden Roberto and Jonas Savimbi, it looked as if both overt and covert funds were going to dry up.

Vorster was especially hurt and felt Kissinger had lured him into a trap, as the following dialogue with *Newsweek*'s senior editor, Arnaud de Borchgrave, makes clear:

Would it be accurate to say that the US solicited South Africa's help to turn the tide against Russians and Cubans in Angola last fall?

I do not want to comment on that. The US Government can speak for itself. I am sure you will appreciate that I cannot violate the confidentiality of government-to-government communications. But if you are making the statement, I won't call you a liar.

Would it also be accurate to say you received a green light from Kissinger for a military operation in Angola and that at least six moderate Black African presidents had given you their blessings for the same operation?

If you say that of your own accord, I will not call you a liar.[5]

The only flaw in de Borchgrave's premise was that South African troops were 1,200 kilometres deep into Angola before there was any question of Russian and Cuban presence. But what counted for Vorster was that the US Congress had suddenly switched off the 'green light'; the promise of tens of millions of dollars and unlimited military equipment suddenly evaporated into thin air. Small wonder that, at the first serious FAPLA thrust at South

5. *Newsweek*, 17 May 1976. It is generally understood that the six African states referred to were Zaire, Zambia, the Ivory Coast, Senegal, Liberia and Tunisia.

African forward positions, Vorster's troops did a quick turn-about and went racing down the north–south highway even faster than they had advanced, pausing only to blow all bridges behind them.

On the morning of 4 January 1976, the Zaire army command in Carmona received a rude shock. FAPLA troops were advancing in a two-pronged operation that threatened very swiftly to completely encircle the city. Treason! What had happened to the FNLA forces that were supposed to have been guarding the flanks? They were mainly non-existent and those that were there faded out at the sound of the first artillery rounds. The Zaire troops pulled out fast and did not pause until they were safely back across the border into Zaire.[6] Holden Roberto's forward headquarters fell with hardly a shot fired – except the shooting by furious Zaire troops of any ELNA elements they encountered, considering them traitors and deserters to be shot on sight.

It was then that urgent signals went to Mr John Banks in London and his counterparts in New York, to mobilize all available mercenaries to stop the rot in Angola. And it was soon evident that, despite what seemed like watertight bans imposed by the US Senate, the CIA 'dirty tricks' department, with the complicity of the British and other governments, would have no difficulty in financing the recruitment and dispatch of mercenaries to Angola.

About the time the non-involvement debate was reaching its climax in the US Congress, a former British paratrooper of Greek-Cypriot origin, Costas Georgiou, alias Tony Callan, left London and, after a few days spent with Holden Roberto in Kinshasa, Zaire, went on to Angola to make an assessment of the military situation and mercenary requirements.

6. Information on the Zaire debacle at Carmona was collected by the authors in visits to the area and from eye-witness accounts from civilian and military participants in the action.

2 How to Become a Mercenary

In the 2 June 1975 issue of the London *Daily Express*, there was a tiny four-line advertisement tucked away at the bottom of one of the inside pages:

> EX-COMMANDOS, Paratroopers,
> SAS troops wanted for interesting work
> abroad. Ring Camberley 3356

This was one of the first of many such advertisements in the British press which between them lured about a hundred young Britons to their death in Angola and a handful of others to long terms of imprisonment.

After my sister Lesley Ann Ryan had seen an advertisement in the *Sunday People* (if I remember correctly) towards the end of January [1976] which advertised for ex-soldiers in the British Army to work for a period of six months in Zaire at a salary of £300 per fortnight [related Kevin John Marchant, in a hand-written statement made shortly after his capture], I decided to telephone the newspaper for more information on ways and means of contacting the person advertising, since this was not mentioned in the advertisement. The newspaper gave the telephone number . . .

A male voice answered and asked if I was a soldier in the British army and what my qualifications were . . . On the following Saturday – I think it was the 27 January – I received a telephone call from a man whose voice I identified as being the same as the first one that I had spoken to. He said to me: 'Mr Marchant, I heard that you would like to work abroad.' I replied 'Yes' and he asked if I was prepared to leave the following Tuesday. I replied in the affirmative and he told me that the only necessary thing to take along with me was toilet articles . . .

With that, Kevin John Marchant had taken the first step towards a gaol sentence of thirty years, pronounced just six months later.

On 18 January, the *Sunday People* had published the following article, signed by Trevor Aspinall, under the title:

JAIL SOLDIER SIGNS UP ARMY

An ex-soldier who was jailed for gun-running has recruited a squad of British mercenaries for Angola.

Their task: to help fight the Communist take-over of the former Portuguese colony on the side of the FNLA.

The twenty-five men have been recruited by a young Briton who has become one of the FNLA President Holden Roberto's top military advisers.

He is ex-British Army private Nicholas Hall, twenty-four, who in 1972 was jailed for two years at a court-martial for selling arms to Ulster Loyalists.

Hall arrived in Britain with £12,000 in American dollars and access to almost unlimited funds and quickly made contact with men who could recruit mercenaries.

These agents are being paid £200 for every man they recruit.

The first twenty-five will receive £200 a week for their services as 'military advisers'. A further contingent is being sought and will be paid £150 a week.

At the London hotel where he is staying with his wife, Hall said: 'The only chance we have left is to recruit trained white mercenaries. The bulk of our army has deserted and we are left with about 300 loyal troops, some of them only twelve and thirteen years old.'

Hall, who was President Roberto's personal driver before being promoted to major, said the first twenty-five men would fly from London tonight on the first stage of their journey to Angola. He added: 'We urgently need help from any country in the West against the Eastern-backed MPLA.

'I just can't understand how nations can stand by and watch this brutal Communist take-over.'

The talk of massive desertions and child soldiers was hardly the best way to boost recruiting! Thus, the *Daily Telegraph* on 30 January 1976 quoted Mr Frank Perren, another leading recruiter, as saying:

Mr Norman Hall, who came to London as Roberto's personal representative, is not working with us any more, because of certain errors he made in the last few days.

He's given us a lot of adverse publicity, caused us a lot of problems, and, well, just about screwed up everything . . .

The garrulous 'Major' Hall returned to Zaire, where the *Guardian* of 9 February reported he had been 'killed, reportedly shot, for failing to deliver reinforcements and for wasting money . . .' This report was apparently planted to indicate the repudiation by the other recruiters of Hall's conduct. In fact he continued to be a trusted aide of Holden Roberto.

The effect of the advertisements and articles such as that in the *Sunday People* can be seen by the hand-written testimony of Malcolm McIntyre, alias Wright:

On about 20 January 1976, a very close friend, John Cook, asked me if I was well, and informed me that I had a chance to work again as a nurse, but in Africa. He showed me a cutting of a newspaper advertisement in which nurses were required for work in Zaire, in Africa . . . John replied to the advertisement for me and sent the letter to London . . . A week later, more or less, my father told me he had received a telephone call for me from a Frank, and that if I was still interested in the job I should go to the Park Court Hotel in Paddington, London, and say that I had an interview arranged with Frank Hall. This happened on 27 January 1976 . . . At about 8 p.m., John Banks, accompanied by a tall man, came to fetch me to another room on the ground floor. In the room where we entered were Frank Hall and another man, tall – about 1·80 m, fair-haired, wearing a blue anorak, and with a strong American accent. There were air tickets on a table. The man in the blue anorak was called Aspinall. A little while before I had already seen the article in the *Sunday People* signed by Trevor Aspinall. I thought this was a strange coincidence . . .

In fact it was not Trevor Aspinall, but Leslie Aspin, whom McIntyre described – and who affected an American accent. But it is clear that the *Sunday People* article had made a big impression on him.

The press advertisements cropped up in the case history of most of the accused. John Lawlor for instance:

On about 15 January 1976, I saw in a newspaper [*Evening Standard*] an advertisement asking for ex-servicemen for work abroad. It gave a telephone number in the Camberley area. I phoned and a woman's voice asked me to leave my phone number. They phoned me that same night and later on I recognized the voice. It was that of a man who, in the hotel where we were put, went by the name of Barry. He had a beard. On the phone, he asked me to go by his house and told me how to get there. The house was in Sandhurst Road, Little Sandhurst, Camberley, Surrey. When I got there, I found it was a few metres from Sandhurst College, or rather, from its back gate. On about 20 January, I went to the office of John Banks: Barry had given me his name on the phone. When I got there, Barry opened the door for me and Banks appeared. They asked me about my military background . . .

The telephone number mentioned in the *Daily Express* advertisements was that of a John Banks. They elicited some 300 responses, according to reports culled from the British press, photocopies of the relevant parts of which constituted an important part of the evidence produced at the Luanda trial. At that time – mid-1975 – Banks pretended he was interested in volunteers to fight *against* the Smith régime in Rhodesia! It will be shown in Chapter 5 that he was really concerned to make contacts for a quite different expedition.

On 14 August 1975, John Banks founded the firm of Security Advisory Services. The initials SAS coincide with those of one of the organizations from which Banks was seeking recruits in his *Daily Express* advertisement, but the SAS in that case referred to the Special Air Service regiment,[1] a para-commando unit which specialized in rough-and-tumble, no-questions-asked anti-insurgency operations like those in Northern Ireland. Another coincidence – the firm's headquarters in Camberley, Surrey, were above a laundry, just opposite Britain's most prestigious military establishment – the Sandhurst Staff College! Malcontents, drop-outs or those made redundant – the British army was cut back by 8,000 in 1975 – only had to cross the street!

Still another coincidence: one of Banks's three partners was Frank Perren, a former Royal Marine who claimed to have served

1. The *Daily Telegraph* reported on 29 January that among the first group of Angola-bound mercenaries were 'six ex-Special Air Services men'. A fertile recruiting ground for mercenaries was around SAS bases, a number having been signed up from among drop-outs at the SAS base at Hereford. Another favourite recruiting centre was Aldershot, which houses one of Britain's largest military establishments.

with another 'dirty tricks' organization, the Special Boats' Service, described as an 'underwater commando unit'. Perren was credited with having recruited 'more than seventy old comrades in and around Plymouth last week'.[2]

Another partner in Security Advisory Services was Leslie Aspin, who has quite a story to tell. He had been up to his neck in the March 1973 *Claudia* affair – a gun-running venture for the IRA in Northern Ireland. The *Claudia* was a West-German-owned freighter, registered in Cyprus. (The director of the company which owned the vessel, Herr Gunther Leinhäuser, was later to deny that he was engaged in recruiting mercenaries for Rhodesia, but named the party which had contacted him on the matter.) He told journalists in Hamburg on 2 April 1973 that he had acted as a 'middleman' in a deal to ship arms to the IRA. The vessel was seized off the Irish coast, with five tonnes of arms aboard. Herr Leinhäuser was scandalized because there should have been 100 tonnes and he wanted to know what had happened to the missing ninety-five. Perhaps Aspin had the answer. According to Tony Geraghty's article in the *Sunday Times*, quoted above:

> The Security Advisory Services' top brass include the redoubtable Leslie Aspin, former smuggler and double agent who negotiated the *Claudia* arms consignment, before he tipped off British security ...

The fourth director was Norman Mervyn 'Nick' Hall – former parachutist dismissed in disgrace from the British army and sentenced to two years in prison for having sold weapons to the ultra-rightist, para-military Protestant Ulster Volunteer Force in Northern Ireland.

What sort of services does SAS offer? One has the answer in a ten-page pamphlet, normally available only to prospective clients. Page 1 informs clients that:

> The organization was formed in 1970 as a direct result of international demand. The initial operations group was administered by four ex-British army officers and since its inception has acted for international groups, individual countries and single clients.
>
> At any one point in time the organization has at least one squadron group in a high state of readiness. A second squadron is available at

2. *Sunday Times*, 25 January 1976.

twenty-one days' notice. Current operations include the following:
   Security Guards (un-uniformed)
   Personal Protection Officers
   Intelligence and Sabotage Teams
   Counter Insurgency Team (Fully Operational)
   Training Officers (Military)
   Training Officers (Personal Protection)
All personnel employed by the organization are fully trained in the role for which they are employed.

Page 2 deals with methods of payment and page 3 the specific types of operations that can be undertaken:

Our military operations are reputed to be beyond comparison. Our service is fully comprehensive and includes the following aspects of tactical warfare:
   Squadron operations
   Small group penetration
   Demolition deployment
   The uplifting of individuals from hostile territory or captivity
   Counter kidnapping procedures
   Single operative assignments (worldwide)
   The protection of property, valuables and personnel
   The training of defence forces (army)
   Training in psychological warfare techniques
   Interview and interrogation techniques

The pamphlet, which has no printer's name on it, maintains that the organization's 'intelligence services' are in touch with 'most countries of the world' and maintain a 'constant watch on the movements of known assassination units, political agitators and agents'. Its personnel are 'instructed in the manufacture and use of guerrilla-type explosive devices. It goes without saying that our men can locate, defuse and destroy these weapons. Demolition includes the installation and tactical demolition methods plus counter demolition activity.' No details of 'interview and interrogation techniques' are given, but these became clear in the accounts of several witnesses at the Luanda trial and from mercenaries who returned to England.

Although this list of SAS 'services' was intended for the gullible with millions of dollars to waste, rather than reflecting their real capacities, as proved by their debacle in Angola, it also reflected what the directors were prepared to offer if enough financial backing was available. They were prepared to be involved in any sort of activities if the money was there. It was apparently with such people and services in mind that the then Prime Minister, Harold Wilson, in a statement to the House of Commons on 10 February 1976, referred to 'small-time crooks [who] have become possessed of vast sums of money beyond the wildest sums they could ever earn in other ways, honest or dishonest, and have been getting access to lists of names of former soldiers, SAS and the rest, and signing them up as mercenaries in conditions which I would hope the whole House would regard as utterly abhorrent to our system of standards in this country.' Challenged as to the epithet 'small-time crooks' to characterize mercenaries, Wilson continued: 'When I referred to small-time crooks – I did not want to flatter them – I was talking about the people who organized mercenary operations.' It was a laudable statement, except that it is difficult to square the definition of 'small-time crooks' with people who were dealing in tens of millions of dollars in an attempt to hijack a nation! And it was even more difficult to accept that, although there are laws to deal with both 'small-time' and 'big-time' crooks, neither the government of Harold Wilson, nor that of his successor James Callaghan, made any attempt to invoke those laws and halt the activities of John Banks and his band.

The youngest of the 'Luanda Thirteen' was a twenty-year-old Irishman, John Nammock, whose parents had emigrated to England seeking work. A tall, lean youth, with one leg in plaster, he had a cheery smile on his face throughout the trial, as if he had little idea of the seriousness of it all. How to become a mercenary? It was ridiculously simple, as he explained in his written statement, repeated with embellishments to the court:

My friend Andy Holland, who came to Angola with me and was killed in the ambush in which I was wounded, asked me if I wanted to join the mercenaries in Angola. I told him that I didn't want to fight and that I would go to Angola if I could work in hospitals. My friend phoned the newspaper called the *Sun* [in which there had been the usual type of advertisement] where they gave him the phone number of the organization that was recruiting mercenaries, Security Advisory

Services. We phoned and a woman's voice told us to be at Fenchurch Street Station between 6 p.m. and 7 p.m. on Tuesday, towards the end of January 1976, where a bus would be waiting for us, marked St George's Club.

On the Tuesday indicated, we went to Fenchurch Street Station, the bus was waiting for us. We were about 25 to 35 mercenaries in the bus, we set off towards a pub. On the way the bus was intercepted by the police. I think they were looking for arms. We were taken to a police station for identification. After leaving the police station and stopping in a pub, we went to St George's Church. We went to the cellar of the church. There were about 200 mercenaries there. It was the first time I saw John Banks, who spoke to us about the war . . .

Nammock's British defence lawyer, Mr Peter Warburton-Jones, made a valiant effort to save his client, dwelling on the misfortunes of an innocent in the hands of official and non-official crooks:

When you decided to go, what did you do?
I phoned the *Sun*.
You are telling me that a national newspaper told you how to go?
Yes. They gave all necessary information.
Did you give your age?
No.

Among the documents submitted to the People's Revolutionary Tribunal, which help to explain the largesse displayed by John Banks at various bars, was an article by David Martin in the 1 February 1976 edition of the London *Observer* dealing with some aspects of SAS financing. The article was based on Martin's interview with a Security Advisory Services' spokesman, a 'burly, red-haired East Ender, who gave his name as John Best' and who said that:

The recruiting was being financed with American money and that his main job was to ensure the safety of the large sums SAS was receiving in cash.

He also provided a team of bodyguards at the London hotel where the mercenaries stayed last week before leaving for Zaire. The fee for the bodyguards was £1,000.

Best was quoted as stating that SAS dealt with a liaison officer at the US Embassy in London and, although Best declined to name him, David Martin wrote that Leslie Aspin had named Major James E. Leonard, Assistant Army Attaché, as the contact man. Dealing with a routine Embassy denial, the article continues:

> Despite this denial, people connected with the SAS insist that there is a liaison officer in the American Embassy. And Mr Best gave details of £282,000 the firm has received in the past three weeks.
>
> He said the money had been received in four ways: through couriers from Zaire, through a Leeds doctor, by bank transfers from Belgium and from the Zaire Embassy in London. One transfer from Belgium, he said, was of 500,000 dollars.
>
> Mr Best said £60,000 had been spent on the air tickets for 128 mercenaries who were flown to Zaire from Belgium last week. A further £5,000 had been spent on hotel accommodation in London, £1,000 for bodyguards' services, £60,000 in advance wages, £12,000 for vehicle spare parts and £50 to a London barber for military haircuts . . .
>
> For their services SAS are being paid £200 for each man they recruit, plus a servicing fee for handling the mercenaries' affairs in London. Privates in the mercenary unit receive £150 a week and NCOs and officers from £200 a week . . . An SAS spokesman said each man was being offered a bonus of £25,000 for any Russians they captured . . .

The reference to a 'Leeds doctor' was later clarified in an interview Banks gave to Ann Morrow of the *Daily Telegraph*[3] in which Banks, 'a lean, pale man with a gaunt face', explained that he had temporarily given up recruiting mercenaries for Angola, complaining that money had been dissipated, some of it 'to a bunch of East End heavies'. Banks also referred to a 'Don Belford of Leeds' as being, 'one of the paymasters for the FNLA'.

> He just gives me a suitcase full of dollars and when I ask where it come from, he says: 'Your business is to recruit soldiers and my business is to pay money . . .'

Time magazine of 23 February 1976, calculating that the target figure of 500 mercenaries at 300 dollars a week for twenty-six weeks would amount to four million dollars, noted:

3. It was published on 10 February 1976, a few days after the execution of the British mercenaries had been revealed.

In Africa, it was taken for granted that some government was picking up this hefty payroll and most of the money paid out has been fresh-from-the-printer American currency, normally still in the wrappers and bound together in sequential serialization. Reported *Time* Correspondent Lee Griggs last week: 'There are more big-denomination US bills floating around Kinshasa's black market than ever before, and mercenary sources there insist the money is coming from the US via Zaire president Mobutu Sese Seko . . .'

In his statement to the Tribunal, Derek John Barker, a tough-looking individual with lines of bitterness deeply etched into his face, said:

When we got our pay, it was in brand-new dollar notes. We were told by Banks to mix them up so as to break up the sequences . . . We were told they were from the CIA which could be why they were new . . .

There was another reference to the CIA and money in his hand-written statement after capture – for the first four hours he had pretended to be a journalist from the London *Daily Mirror*! He wrote that two days after his arrival at Santo Antonio do Zaire:

A small plane flew in with some Americans who gave us anti-malaria tablets. These we were told was CIA who supplied the money we was to get. They then flew away – to where I do not know . . .

Among the personal effects found on Callan when he was captured was an address book with, among others, two interesting addresses, one marked 'FNLA contact, M. D. Belford, 46 Bailey's Lane, North Parkway, Leeds 4' (with telephone no.), the other, 'Colin, FNLA rep., Stratford St, 177, Leeds'. In his statement to the Tribunal, Callan had refused to answer any questions, except to state his name and age and to make a short statement to the effect that he accepted full responsibility for 'the actions of the men under my command'. However, at the bottom of a hand-written statement made about one month after his capture, he wrote: 'The people which recruited me in London, which I mentioned before, were FNLA members, Mr Colin Taylor and Dr Belford.'

In the same statement he said that he had come to Zaire about 9 December and to Angola a few days later. It appears that at some stage 'Dr' Belford was working in a hospital at Negage, forty

kilometres south-east of Carmona, which was also where Callan
first made for after crossing into Angola. Among other names in
the address book was that of Nick Hall, at 33 Rosen Lane, Lincoln.
Callan further alleged that he was first contacted in London in
November 1975, by Taylor and Belford, with a view to his taking
command of FNLA troops in northern Angola. This was after
the Zaire–FNLA forces had failed to capture Luanda and after
the Chinese had stated that they were withdrawing their instructors
on the grounds that Angola's independence from Portugal had
been achieved. At the London meeting, it was agreed that, to prove
good faith, Belford should take Callan with him to his base at the
Negage hospital, while Taylor would make contact with Holden
Roberto to find out how many men would be required. Callan
assumed command of the FNLA forces in January 1976 – probably just after the debacle at Carmona.

A news item in the London *Guardian* of 9 February, under the
title 'FNLA MAY HAVE BASE IN LEEDS', stated that West York-
shire police were 'thought to be investigating reports that a semi-
detached council house in Leeds' was being used as the unofficial
headquarters of the FNLA:

> The tenant of the house in Bailey Lane, Seacroft, is Mr MacDonald
> Belford, an ex-serviceman and former hospital worker . . .
> He is also thought to be a close friend of Holden Roberto, leader of
> the FNLA.
> Together with Mr Colin Taylor of Stratford Street, Beeston, Leeds,
> he had been trying to recruit mercenaries for work in Angola. Mr
> Taylor recently placed an advertisement in a local evening paper, asking
> ex-servicemen to contact either himself or Mr Belford. He booked a
> hotel room in Leeds and eventually eight men were interviewed . . .

The report went on to state that Mr Belford was also in the market for a light aircraft.

The role of the press in the recruitment of British mercenaries
was very considerable indeed. Apart from the activities of individual journalists, most of the mass-circulation daily and Sunday
papers carried advertisements and articles likely to stimulate
interest in recruitment. One might ask whether it would have been
considered ethical by the same newspapers to accept advertise-

ments for recruits to hijack a plane. The answer would be a shocked 'No'. But surely an attempt to hijack a country is far worse! For that is what it amounted to. The People's Republic of Angola had been proclaimed on 11 November 1975 and had been recognized by over forty countries by the time Banks had shipped the first lot of mercenaries to Angola. For those who would argue that a rival government had been set up in Huambo at the same time, it should be noted that not a single country – not even Zaire or the United States or South Africa – ever recognized the so-called 'Democratic People's Republic of Angola' with its 'capital' in Huambo – liberated on 8 February 1976.

Certain sections of the US press and media – and certain journalists in the United States – played similar roles, not to mention that of Mr Banks's opposite number in the USA, David Bufkin. In his hand-written statement, Gary Martin Acker, twenty-two years old and ex-US Marine veteran of the Vietnam war, testified as follows:

I first found out about recruiting mercenaries for Angola through a newspaper article concerning a man named David Bufkin. The article describes the type of person and qualifications required. It stated that the pay would be 1,200 dollars per month. The article listed an address at the *Fresno Bee* [newspaper] at which this man could be contacted . . .

After reading the article I wrote a letter to David Bufkin explaining to him my qualifications. I also acquired his telephone number from the Information Operator . . . I called him and explained my qualifications and he said that he would get back to me. A few days later he called and said that I was alright but that I would have to pay my own way over. He said that I would be reimbursed in Kinshasa. This was approximately the end of November . . .

Later there was a meeting at Fresno, California, at which Bufkin explained that Acker would be going to Angola to be his 'personal assistant', that there were already 250 British troops there and many more from various countries in Western Europe. From Fresno, they flew to Los Angeles, where Acker was introduced to Bufkin's right-hand man, Lobo del Sol, in whose apartment the three of them recorded a TV interview with Frank Mariano of the American Broadcasting Company. Regarding the interview, Acker told the presiding judge:

Frank Mariano did the interviewing. He asked if the money was coming from the CIA. Bufkin replied: 'There's no CIA stamp on it.'

So you suspected that the money was coming from the CIA?

David Bufkin inferred that the money was coming from the CIA when Mariano asked if that was where it was coming from. A month or so previously the government had been giving money to the FNLA, but it had been stopped.

It was not important to you if you were getting money from the CIA?

It would not have made any difference.

In another statement Acker said that he realized the TV interview was 'used by Bufkin as a publicity stunt, using Lobo and I as publicity bait'. As a publicity stunt it paid off. Argentinian-born Gustavo Marcelo Grillo, one of the three Americans on trial, owner of the firm of 'G and G Guard Dogs Inc.' and one of the few politically conscious personalities among the thirteen accused, explained how he had been recruited.

In mid-January 1976, I was at home when I received a phone call from a friend of mine called Vincente Russo, who told me that three mercenaries had been interviewed on ABC's Channel 7, and that I would certainly be interested because it was about recruiting men with military experience to fight in Angola . . . [All three Americans on trial and others killed in Angola had served in Vietnam.]

The next morning I phoned Channel 7 for them to give me all necessary information. They gave me the number (209) 846-9152 and the name Dave Bufkin . . . That same day I contacted Dave Bufkin and he asked me to send him an account of my military experience, also 35 dollars. This I did . . . Then he sent me a newsletter on mercenary forces . . .

Grillo was soon on his way to a thirty years' prison sentence in the People's Republic of Angola.

The third American on trial, Daniel Francis Gearhart, a square-headed man of medium height and ramrod-stiff, drill-parade bearing, made a bad mistake in lying to his captors and lying to the Tribunal.

On 4 February 1976, Dave Bufkin telephoned me [Gearhart told his captors]. I don't know how he got my telephone number. Perhaps he had seen some advertisements that I had sent to various publications and succeeded in getting my telephone number through the name and address, contacting the information service of the telephone companies. Bufkin mentioned the salary which would be 1,200 dollars a month . . .

In his hand-written statement he stated merely that:

On 5 February, Dave called and wanted to know if I wanted a job. I said yes and he said to meet him at the Skyway motel in New York . . .

At the Tribunal, asked to state how he became a mercenary, Gearhart gave substantially the same explanation. The clear impression that Gearhart tried to create was that it had been Bufkin who had taken the initiative. Unfortunately for Gearhart, between interrogation and court proceedings, a copy of the Spring 1976 number of *Soldier of Fortune* – a very special sort of magazine – had come into the hands of the Luanda court. In the classified advertisements section on page 75, there was the following:

> WANTED: EMPLOYMENT AS MERCENARY
> on Full-Time or Job Contract
> basis. Preferably in South or Central
> America, but anywhere in the world,
> if you pay transportation. Contact
> Gearhart, Box 1457, Wheaton, MD 20902.

'How was that first contact made?' asked Texeira da Silva, Attorney-General of the People's Republic of Angola and presiding judge of the Revolutionary Tribunal.

I believe that it was through Pierre Walt, who had an Information Agency, and had sent me a circular stating what jobs were available.

On the same page of *Soldier of Fortune*, there was another advertisement:

> Wanted! MILITARY TECHNICIANS and
> Professional Adventurers. Overseas
> countries use and need these experts.
> To know who and where to write, send 5
> dollars for one, 9 for two, or 16 for
> three to: Pierre Walt, World Wild Geese
> Association, Box 33, Newark, OH 43055.

There was also evidence among Gearhart's personal belongings that he was a member – he admitted only to applying for membership – of the Wild Geese Club,[4] in Johannesburg. It is a well-known centre for mercenaries and is run by Major 'Mad Mike' Hoare, who achieved notoriety as a mercenary leader in the Congo in the 1960s. Gearhart tried to convince the Tribunal that his only interest in contacting the Wild Geese Club was to have authentic information about Africa. It was at a moment when 'Mad Mike' Hoare was boasting that he could put several hundred 'battle-hardened' mercenaries into Angola at the drop of a hat if the price was right!

Among other advertisements in this publication was one from 'El Kamas Enterprises' which, under a bold-type heading 'MERCENARIES NEEDED NOW', announced that 'persons with military or intelligence skills for rewarding and high paying work in overseas areas' could get minimum one-year contracts and that the agency was 'taking placement applications NOW'. Books advertised for the magazine's obviously red-blooded readership included titles like *Silencers, Snipers and Assassins, The Complete Book of Knife Fighting, How to Kill, C I A Explosives for Sabotage*. For specialized shoppers, catering – as an advertisement explained – to 'The Professional Adventurer and other Qualified Purchasers', a firm offered machine-guns, automatic weapons, 'nothing but the finest weapons in stock for immediate transfer'. One half-page advertisement offered 'WEAPONRY FOR MEN OF ACTION', including automatic weapons, silencers and 'special warfare devices'.

In the name of 'freedom of the press' the facts show that individual journalists and publishers, editors, newspapers and magazine proprietors bear a heavy responsibility in directly and indirectly promoting the use of mercenaries in Angola and are continuing to do so in the employment and recruitment of mercenaries elsewhere in Africa, and in the Middle East. Banks and Aspin still have access to the mass media and potential mercenaries know where to contact them. The contracts are now for Smith's army in Rhodesia and the rightists in the Lebanon.

4. 'Wild Geese' was the name adopted by bands of Irish noblemen who, in the seventeenth and eighteenth centuries, roamed Europe offering their services to any king or prince who could put up an attractive offer for their military talents.

3 Assisted Take-Off

As we were going through the passport control, Major Peters gave a form with our photographs on it to the passport officer, who said that the form was rubbish. Major Peters said something to him that I didn't hear and the passport officer then picked up a phone, talked to someone for about a minute and said it was OK, we could go through . . .

This, explained ex-paratrooper and bricklayers' labourer Derek John Barker, one of the second batch of mercenaries, was how he came to leave London's Heathrow airport on Sunday, 18 January 1976, as a member of the 'Manchester Social Club' football team. That it was not only certain sections of the press that were being co-operative in speeding mercenaries on their way to Angola was evident from the statements of all – except Callan – who were to relate their experiences some five months later in the Luanda court-room. Barker must have heaved a deep sigh of relief that everything passed off so smoothly. Two days earlier he had been drinking with four ex-servicemen pals in the bar of the Queen's Hotel, Aldershot, when his old comrade-in-arms John Banks turned up and, after buying a round of drinks, signed them all up for service in Angola. The following day, in room 332 of the Tower Hotel in London, Barker and the others were issued with small cards marked SAS (Security Advisory Services) to which were affixed passport-size photos, taken in the hotel room with a Polaroid camera. It was these that the passport officer described as 'rubbish'. They were in fact as phoney as the 'Manchester Social Club' football team!

The reason why I could not use my passport was because I was on bail from an English court and had to report daily to the police station, so that I could not renew my passport. I have a bit of a police record, having spent three years in a Borstal reformatory school from the age of 17 to 20, and I have had two prison sentences since I came out from the army, one in 1969 for 9 months, and the other in 1971, for 6 months . . .

– not to mention an offence perpetrated just two months earlier which required his daily report to the local police station. On 18 January 1976, Barker was a bail-jumper and on the police 'wanted' list; denied a passport because of a long record of crime and thus forbidden to leave the country.

With me on the plane was a young lad, Wainwright, who told me he had never been in the army and was also going to Angola to get away from the police, and others whose names I don't know. There was eighteen of us altogether. There were supposed to have been twenty, but two absconded in Brussels. RSM [Regimental Sergeant-Major] Copeland was also on the plane. McAleese and Copeland were introduced to us by Banks in the London hotel as 'Captain' and 'RSM'. Banks said that I would be a 'Captain' when we got there and that most of us would receive ranks when we got to Angola . . .

Also with Barker in the Queen's Hotel bar and on the Kinshasa-bound plane was ex-paratrooper and building-worker Andrew Gordon McKenzie, who stated that he had been told by Banks that he was to take part in the training of an army of '120,000 Angolans'. Asked by the presiding judge what he knew about the 'Manchester Social Club' football team, McKenzie replied:

It was the name we travelled under. Banks took care of all formalities at the London airport. We were told if anyone asked any questions to say we knew nothing. We were travelling as the Manchester Social Club football team and if any questions were asked we should just say that . . .

Questioned as to what was 'Security Advisory Services', he said:

I had an English passport so I don't know. It is concerned with travel, but I don't know what for. It was only for people who didn't have passports . . .[1]

Apart from the tiny advance party of Callan and a few others,

1. Eleven of the original twenty in Barker's group were either without passports or were on the police 'wanted' list!

the group of which Barker and McKenzie formed part was the first to concede that they 'slipped through' official controls without any impediments. Nine days later, a second group left Heathrow airport in two batches, for the same destination. In between these two departures, there had been considerable publicity in the press and on radio and TV so that one could suppose – if later statements by the British government sternly condemning the dispatch of mercenaries, but bewailing its impotence to prevent this odious practice, had been sincere – that some tighter controls would have been introduced, at least to prevent anyone on the police 'wanted' list from leaving the country. In fact because of the bothersome publicity the airport authorities were even more co-operative. In his hand-written statement Colin Clifford Evans describes what happened:

We arrived at Heathrow airport to find a lot of press in there. We were asked not to speak to them. The airport officials got on the bus and gave us all an aircraft boarding card.

We then got off the bus and went through immigration and passport control. Them of us who hadn't got a passport had to wait a little while. We had to fill in a form, then hand it back in. We were allowed to go into the departure lounge, where I spent some of my £25 on cigarettes and a bottle of whisky. We had a few drinks at the bar and then boarded the aircraft for Brussels . . .

The second group had been divided into two batches, those who had valid passports leaving on the first flight to Brussels, those like Evans who had no valid passport being delayed by the time it took to fill in some forms, the nature of which were not specified, but which were probably the forms of indemnity which travellers without passports are normally required to complete. Neither group, it appears, was subject to anti-hijacking controls. They met again in Brussels and continued together to Kinshasa. Michael Douglas Wiseman, who was in the same group as Evans, described his first meeting with Banks at the Park Court Hotel in London, at which Banks introduced him to

a man with greying hair, fattish, medium height: a Belgian sergeant-major called André, who I think stayed in Belgium when we passed there on the way to Kinshasa . . .

On 28 January, there was another meeting. It was chaired by a man in a blue anorak. It was about the distribution of tickets. We were told there would be two flights. We were divided into two groups and I went into the first group . . . At the airport were photographic reporters who tried to take photos of John Banks. We got out of the bus, went into the airport lounge without any kind of passport control. The mercenaries who had no passports stayed behind for the second flight. Around 10 a.m. we left for Brussels. In Brussels we stayed waiting for the second group. Banks met a short man, whose name I don't know, but who was wearing dark glasses and a raincoat . . .

Also in the same group was Cecil Martin Fortuin, who described how he was given a rendezvous at Paddington station, where he was given a reservation card for a hotel room at the Park Towers:

The card didn't have my name on it, but the name of John Ford. Everybody was together in the hotel – they all received these cards, all with false names. Later I asked Banks where he had gone to find the false names and he said: 'In the phone book . . .'

Fortuin left with the first group to Brussels, on 28 January, together with Wiseman. He also had reason to be apprehensive of airport formalities. There was a conviction against him for non-payment of alimony which made it illegal for him to leave the country.

Asked during the trial about formalities on leaving England, he replied:

There was no passport control. We went straight through the departure lounge and then on to the plane.

Is it normal that there are no controls?

Banks assured us that: 'Everything is okay. We have help from above. Everything is taken care of.'

As for formalities at Brussels, Fortuin, in his capacity as the bodyguard of Banks, was well informed:

We got to Brussels and stayed waiting for the second group. We went to the airport bar. There was a lot of journalists and news photographers who took some pictures. There were also a lot of police at the airport. One of them said to Banks: 'So you're going to Kinshasa?' And when he said 'Yes', he said: 'We've been waiting for you here.'

Banks went to talk to the chief of the airport security, because of the journalists. He asked them to go away, or else to put the men in a reserved room, so as to avoid problems. We went back to the departure lounge and Banks made a call which I think was to London. Meanwhile the second group of mercenaries had arrived from London ...

We reached Kinshasa at about 1 o'clock in the morning on 29 January. We left the airport without going through any kind of control ...

'Can we conclude,' asked the presiding judge, 'that there was some sort of understanding between the Brussels and London police?' – a question to which Fortuin and the others to whom it was put could hardly answer otherwise than 'Yes'! John Lawlor, a twenty-three-year-old night watchman at the time he was recruited, also had been given a rendezvous at Paddington station.

I met a man who was an ex-marine, according to what he told me, who told me to go to a bus and wait. He gave me a little white cardboard disc and told me to fix it to my jacket ... When we got to the hotel someone gave us entry forms with false names ...

The next day, 28 January 1976, we left for London airport in a bus. With us was the ex-marine who was at Paddington station the day before, who gave us pieces of paper on which to write our next-of-kin and later he gave each of us an envelope containing £150 telling us to address it to the person we wanted the money to be sent to.

After putting in all the money I had on me, I addressed it to my parents. We got to London airport. Two airport officials came in the bus and gave us tickets on which the original names had been crossed out, and over them, we wrote our names. After that we got out of the bus and went into the airport.

When we went through passport control, where our passports were not really checked, the men who didn't have passports were put in a group on one side and filled in a form. We all went to the departure lounge. At about 12.30 we left for Brussels. We met Banks and the men who had left on the first flight, in Brussels. After eating and waiting a bit, we left for Kinshasa. It was about 3.30 p.m.

Obviously there were no formalities on leaving Zaire and crossing the frontier into Angola, which means that by the time the mercenaries had reached San Salvador, their first destination in Angola, they had traversed four frontiers without any normal form of passport, security or customs formalities.

It is true that British subjects do not need passports to travel abroad. But they do need identification documents and proof that they are British subjects. Otherwise they would be subject to the strict controls to which non-British (including British Commonwealth) subjects are submitted on leaving and entering England. An intriguing aspect is that, according to a former partner of the SAS, Nick Hall, the American Embassy in London had a hand in ensuring this formality-free passage through passport and customs controls. Journalists Linda Melvern and Stephen Clackson quoted Hall as claiming that:

When he returned to Britain [from Angola] to recruit a mercenary force, he was given a contact name at the American Embassy. He asked this contact for more money and was refused. He also claims to have asked for assistance in getting men without passports out of Heathrow ... Hall claims he provided his Embassy contact with their Brussels-bound flight number and time, was told to approach a specific immigration point at Heathrow's Terminal Two. The men passed through as a group without any formal restrictions.[2]

The policy of 'non-intervention' by the British authorities reached its high point with the departure of the third batch, which left London on 8 February. That they were allowed to leave, the police actively preventing them from being interviewed by journalists, after news of the execution of fourteen of their predecessors, implies some very special dispensations, almost certainly taken at no less than ministerial level.

John Nammock, the youngest of the accused, recalled that at Heathrow airport a journalist tried to contact him and failed, because the police were turning journalists away, but he did succeed in showing his friend Andy Holland – later killed in action – a telex reporting the executions. Holland shrugged it off as a journalistic

2. *Evening Standard*, 29 July 1976. As an experiment, one of the authors left Heathrow recently without showing his British passport. The formalities were simple: the completion of a form indemnifying the airline from the expense of carrying him back if turned away by the French immigration authorities and the production of satisfactory proof of identification, in his case an International Driving Licence, with a photograph. Though the formalities took only a few minutes they were taken seriously by all concerned.

stunt – a pretext to get an airport interview which they had been instructed to avoid – and they both went on their way.

That the authorities knew exactly what was going on, and who was leaving, is clear from the following paragraph in the *Daily Telegraph* of 29 January, reporting the departure of the second group:

Special Branch detectives kept watch on the men as they left the departure lounge. They are understood to have been checking on passengers in the hope of finding a man wanted for the shooting of a British soldier in Ulster . . .

That Special Branch men were at the airport is not surprising in view of the fact that not only did they know exactly what was going on but, according to subsequent revelations by John Banks, they had arranged – with Banks's complicity – to have British intelligence men planted within the group. These were agents from MI6, the British foreign espionage service. In an interview with the *News of the World* of 4 July 1976, Banks said:

Before my main force men left for Angola, I was approached by the Special Branch in a pub at Camberley, Surrey. Ever since I'd started operations I'd been under their surveillance and I told them everything they wanted to know.

Once they were sure I wasn't raising some ridiculous domestic revolutionary force – and that it was going where I said it was and to do what I said it was going to do – we got along fine. I think they were personally interested and sympathetic. However – and this is important in view of the inaccurate blather in Parliament about us – the Special Branch asked me if I could include two of their agents in my force.

I agreed subject to them being up to soldier standards. What the hell, two James Bonds would be a welcome addition to my force, I thought. I was duly introduced to these characters – one Smith and one Brown. 'Ha, ha,' I thought, 'pull the other one.'

They were probably men from MI6. After all, how can the foreign intelligence service tell the Prime Minister anything if they don't go and find out? But their documents were in order and out they went with us from London airport. Naturally we had a Special Branch send-off. And you don't need to ask why the Special Branch were there to meet us when we came back . . . One of the two agents was killed. The other was wounded when his jeep got blown up. He is back in Britain and I know his name, but Special Branch has asked me to keep it secret, though both men made no secret of why they were in Angola . . .

In the same article one of the mercenary survivors, Keith Henderson, named one of the men as John Lockyer, who had told him that he had been sent out by MI6 and that the other, whose name he did not know, was 'middle-aged and overweight and died of a heart attack in his first patrol'. The only mercenary whom the authors know to have died of a heart attack was Vic Gawthrop. In his diary, 'Canada', or Doug Newby (named as 'chief intelligence officer' of the whole mercenary unit by Major Roden), mentions the case of 'one of my men', an unnamed mercenary, who had a heart attack because of the heat and died on patrol. He mentions also that the man's younger brother, 'who is also with us, took it well'. There were only three cases of two mercenaries with the same name, Saunders, McAleese and Gawthrop. Both the Saunders and McAleeses returned. Of the Gawthrops, only Brian came back. Interviewed by journalist Frank Branston, he confirmed that his brother had died of a heart attack on 9 February. 'I think the heat got him,' he said.

One day the truth will be told, said Henderson. There have been official efforts to shut me up. The truth is embarrassing not only for Britain but for many other nations.

A reporter who checked with Scotland Yard whether a member of Special Branch had been killed – as the *News of the World* had reported – with the mercenaries in Angola was told that it was not true. In fact Special Branch is concerned with internal security and would hardly be likely to send their own men to Angola, but it works hand-in-glove with MI6, which specializes in external intelligence-gathering. The reporter rang the Ministry of Defence and was told that his editor should know that there was a 'D' notice on the story, which means that it was censored for security reasons. This explains why there was no further press coverage of this fascinating story.

Another mercenary, Tom Chambers, named two other men, Lou Elford and Barry Thorpe, as MI6 agents. Obviously these are difficult matters to confirm, but the Banks–Henderson account seems authentic. It also seems a more logical reason for the presence – and inactivity – of Special Branch agents at Heathrow on 28 January than that given in the *Daily Telegraph*.

The laxity – if that is the correct word – of the authorities in allowing the departure of men with criminal records was rapidly changed when the survivors started to return. Thus *The Times* reported the arrest of one of the first of the returners, Terence White, for the unlawful possession of a pistol and ammunition, and reports of two others:

Sent to prison after appearing in court on charges for offences *committed before they left*. Mr Norman Trevor Hollanby, aged 22, an ex-Guardsman of Earl's Court, was sentenced to 9 months at Maidstone Crown Court for theft and breaking the conditions of a suspended sentence. Mr Dennis Andrew O'Brien, aged 27, of Sandhurst, Berkshire, was sentenced to 12 months' imprisonment for burglary.[3]

One would have thought – to be logical – that some passport control officers or Special Branch police should have been prosecuted for connivance in the 'breaking of conditions of a suspended sentence' in the case of Hollanby, and the bail-jumping of Barker, to mention only two of over a dozen known cases of illegal departures, and leaving aside the known illegal intentions of the departers and the illegal manner of their departure.

That there was also an official 'blind eye to the telescope' in the United States was clear from the testimony of Gary Martin Acker. After the TV interview which Frank Mariano of ABC television had made with Acker, Bufkin and Lobo del Sol had been broadcast on 27 December 1975, Acker got a call from an FBI agent, named Swenson, asking him to present himself to FBI headquarters regarding the TV interview:

I went to the FBI building, Acker told the investigating officer, and was interviewed by Mr Swenson and Mr Teeran, both FBI agents They told me they had been investigating a possible violation of the Neutrality Act, according to which recruiting anyone to fight against another country, with which the United States is not at war, is against the law. They asked about David Bufkin and Lobo. They asked me if I had paid Bufkin 35 dollars to go to Angola. I said that I had not.

3. *The Times*, 12 February 1976. Authors' italics.

Anyone who contacted Bufkin was asked to send 35 dollars, in exchange for a bulletin to be published every two months listing the sort of global mercenary jobs available. The FBI agents asked what sort of work Acker would be doing in Angola and he told them he would be a mercenary. From Acker's written and oral statements, the impression is that the FBI were more interested in checking on what the CIA was up to than in preventing any transgression of the Neutrality Act! When asked by the People's Prosecutor whether the FBI could have stopped him from going to Angola, he replied:

I don't think they could have. I had not then been recruited. So I did not violate the Neutrality Act. The FBI was not going to act because there were no more funds to finance the sending of mercenaries.

Do you know any action of the FBI to stop people going to Angola?

I know of no such action.

Acker gave the impression of being a very loyal American citizen, one to whom a strong hint from the FBI that he was on the wrong track and should get off it smartly would have rung out like a presidential command. But there was no such hint. Nor was there to Grillo, Gearhart, Lobo del Sol or Bufkin or anyone else who ended up – even temporarily – in Angola. The only incident in which US officialdom did act underlined the other cases in which it did not. One mercenary volunteer, Eugene Scaley, who flew out to Kinshasa with Acker and the others, had second thoughts when he heard of the desperate military situation and Callan's executions. From Holden Roberto's headquarters, where the American mercenaries were lodged, he set off for the US Embassy. When he returned, he demanded of Bufkin his return fare, got it and flew back home. Thus the US Embassy, even if it did not know from other sources, knew from Scaley exactly what was going on, but it never lifted a finger to intervene. Scaley went to the Embassy on 8 or 9 February – which was only some six weeks after US Congressional action to halt all overt and covert UN involvement in Angola. The minimum one would expect from a responsible embassy would have been to send at least a second secretary to explain to these US citizens that they were about to commit a

breach of the Neutrality Act or of the Foreign Enlistment Act –
even more specific in forbidding military service under a foreign
flag – and liable to lose their US citizenship. But nothing of the
kind was done.

4 Mercenaries: British Export Model

Only someone made of stone could have sat unmoved through the nine days of the Luanda trial. It was a tense human drama, charged with complexities of human character and emotions – nuances and contradictions of behaviour which would have been difficult to imagine beforehand. What was specially interesting was the evidence showing what kind of person becomes a mercenary.

The thirteen accused were not swashbuckling ex-Legionnaires or SS types, the veteran killers who swarmed through the Congo in the 1960s. Apart from Callan the cold-blooded and Barker the hot-blooded killers, and Gearhart eager for hot or cold killing, they were rather ordinary examples of the underprivileged of Western society. Even allowing for hard-luck stories exaggerated to excuse their actions, there was a reasonable chance that some of them had been tricked into believing they were going to well-paid non-combatant jobs behind the lines. To be mercenaries – yes; killers – no. But even if compassion could be felt for these victims of the society which formed them, there could be nothing but contempt for those who sped them on their way at a 'body count' fee of two or three hundred pounds a head.

It is frightening to take the backgrounds of each of the accused and to consider the mercenary potential in Britain and the United States, indeed in the Western world in general. The reasons most of the thirteen gave for enlisting – unemployment, financial difficulties, boredom of colourless lives, insoluble family problems, yearning to be back in uniform – show that the number could be multiplied by millions. Over 300 replies to that first tiny advertisement in one British newspaper alone! The same sort of response to one small publicity effort by Bufkin. The neat hand-written statement of Acker revealed that while he was waiting to leave for Angola he had stayed for a few days at Bufkin's house in California:

While at Dave's house he had Lobo and myself set up a file system of all the people who had written to Dave concerning Angola. We listed their names, qualifications and experience, address etc. These were only people who would be useful. Those who would not be useful were discarded. At this time we had approximately 120–150 names. Letters were coming from as far as Israel, Hongkong, Belgium, Germany and England. This doesn't include the telephone calls of people interested. Dave also had us start a newsletter to those people who had sent letters and qualified. This letter explained about mercenary jobs in Rhodesia and possible jobs in South America. The letter explained that there was no more money funded for Angola and there would not be for some time . . .

This newsletter, a copy of which was found on Grillo, was undated, but a reference in it to a contact made on 6 January 1976 shows that it was sent out between that date and departure of the American group on 6 February – after the Congressional ban on further funds for Angola.

It is clear that people like Banks and Bufkin realized they were on to a major racket, on a par with drugs, white-slaving and Mafia operations – trading in human flesh on a lucrative per capita basis, with an unlimited market as the liberation struggles in southern Africa and elsewhere got into full stride. Their raw material came from society's rejects and victims of social systems that condemned humans by the millions to unemployment and drab existences on the borderline of hunger and despair.

All thirteen were case studies, as star witnesses not only against mercenarism but against the societies which educated and conditioned them, including in all cases but one, McIntyre, military systems that threw them back into civvy street alienated from the world in which they were supposed to make their living.

McIntyre had left school at fifteen and his first job was as cook's apprentice in a hotel. Later he studied at night to become a nurse, graduating after a three-year course at the Edinburgh Royal Hospital. This is what he told the court.

Between 1970 and 1972 I worked at the Perth Royal Infirmary. In 1972, I left to go to the Orsett Hospital, Essex, and after I had been there six months I began to be ill with my nerves and depression. I went into Warley Hospital, that is Warley Mental Hospital, Brentwood,

Essex. I went in and out of this hospital until December 1975. While I was at Orsett Hospital, a friend ... came to see me to help him to end his drug addiction. I said yes. I helped him and nine months later he was cured.

To do this is forbidden in England because treatment must be done in specialized hospitals and by authorized personnel. However, as his girl-friend was also an addict ... she came and threatened me, saying she would denounce me if I did not supply her with drugs. As my work meant a great deal to me I had to help her, giving her drugs. Every week she asked for larger quantities. I did not want to give them to her, but it was the only way out I had. My wife finally got to know what was going on, abandoned me, and I stayed with the two children – later they went to my parents. I left the hospital and changed my original name of Wright to McIntyre, which means exactly the same thing, except that one is English and the other Scottish. By doing this I wanted to prevent the girl-friend ... locating me. I found work in a hotel, the Queen's Hotel, Southend, but a few months later I had to go into hospital again for mental illness. I was discharged on 23 December 1975. Meanwhile I knew that my wife had died, in September. I spent Christmas with my family, and I continued to have difficulty in concentrating and continuing the treatment ...

As we have seen, Wright–McIntyre was contacted on about 20 January by another 'very close friend', John Cook, who put him in touch with the mercenary recruiters. He was a victim of his own weakness of character and exceptional circumstances. For Banks, he meant another £200 or £300.

At the opposite end of the scale was thirty-five-year-old Derek John Barker, one of several old soldiers contacted directly by John Banks. The following, in Barker's printed handwriting with spelling uncorrected, is his account of what happened:

I was drinking in a public house in Aldershot with friends when I was asked by a man named John Banks if I would like to go to Angola as an Special Avice Service, SAS! He said we get 600 dollars every two weeks. With this he gave us ten English pounds each and said he would meet us in London hotel named the Tower Hotel, London, next day. I then traveled to London with my friends, McKenzie, Mc Farson, Saunders and Aves. When we got there, there was ex-army men from some parts of England. We was told we were to stay in the hotel till 8 o'clock that same day when we was to have a talk.

Then at 8 o'clock that evening we was told we was to go to Angola,

West Africa, to help train an army of natives whose moral was very low. This army was named FNLA. This talk was given by a man named John Banks. We was told we would not leave the hotel so me and my friends had a talk and we agreed it was a very expensive hotel. 22 English pounds per person for one night only and lots of drinks. We thought this job we was going to do, if it was like this, was OK seeing I was out of work and things was expensive in England . . .

A private coach came at six o'clock Sunday night and we got on to go to Heathrow airport London. On the coach we was given an envelope containing 500 dollars American. We was told we was to get another 100 dollars when we arrive at the other end which was Kinshasa. It was a six month contract . . .

When he was asked why he had come to fight in Angola against the legitimate government of that country, Barker replied:

I was wanted by the police for assault in December 1975, and I was on £200 sterling bail. I was released just before Christmas . . .

Asked if he had been in prison before, he replied:

Yes. I had a prison record before I joined the British army. This was when I was about seventeen year old and was in Borstal for stealing cars, house-breaking – in fact I was a juvenile delinquent. In 1968, I served a nine months' prison sentence for stealing, and a six months' sentence in 1969–70 for assault over a woman I had been living with.

One of the trial's surprises was the playing of the sound track of a BBC *Panorama* programme on mercenaries, broadcast on 26 April 1976. It produced varied reactions among the accused. Wiseman, who was in tears when he heard the voices of his wife and children, burst into hysterical laughter when he heard the description of the incident which led to the assault charge against Barker in December 1975. The interviewer, Michael Cockerell, was speaking to Douglas Saunders:

COCKERELL: In Angola both Saunders and Barker were immediately promoted to majors. He now works as a hod-carrier – the job 'Brummy' Barker once had. In their time in Aldershot the two men made many enemies. Last November they gate-crashed a party given by their local rivals, the Long family.

SAUNDERS: This man came, picked on 'Brummy' and 'Brummy' had no option but to defend himself.

BENNY LONG: Barker came up to me. We had a few words and then he lunged at me and before I could realize it he was biting off the end of my nose . . .

It was at this point that Wiseman almost went into hysterics, which only a glowering look from Callan halted.

Michael Cockerell then produced Mary Slattery, a landlady in whose lodging-house Barker had lived for a while and who put up the £200 bail when he was charged with biting off the tip of Benny Long's nose. Mary Slattery expressed the opinion that if Barker 'had a bit of mother's love, he would have been a different boy altogether'.

COCKERELL: How disappointed were you when you put up bail for him and suddenly he skipped off to Angola?

MARY SLATTERY: I was hurt, I was really hurt, because I never dreamed that 'Brummy' would do that on me, never.

MICHAEL COCKERELL TO SAUNDERS: Did Banks promise you anything apart from £150 per week?

SAUNDERS: He said something about the President, you know, you would be stopping at the Palace, and you wouldn't go short of girls, you know, if you were destitute.

MARY SLATTERY'S SON, MIKE SLATTERY: I think they just thought they were going to fight a lot of backward niggers, you know, fire a few shots and out they would come. But . . . £150 is like the moon, isn't it? And a six months' tour, I mean they had all spent £5,000 before they even left Aldershot, you know, in a month.

COCKERELL: What do you think was the specific attraction for Barker himself?

MIKE SLATTERY: Well, Barker to me – he just likes fighting. And it's a sort of fight, isn't it, being a mercenary? I mean, if he stands behind a tree and shoots you, that's lovely isn't it? There's no rules, is there, as a mercenary?

COCKERELL TO JOHN BANKS, also on the programme: John Banks and his associates maintain the main reason why men become mercenaries is not for money, nor to escape the shambles of their personal lives, and they are now writing a book about it.

BANKS: Why shouldn't they fight against Communism, whether it be for money or for a cause they believe in? Sure – how many English people want to be a bloody Communist state? I don't – he doesn't! I don't want to be a bloody Communist. People should listen to people a bit more before it's too late . . .

COCKERELL: How responsible, John, do you feel for the fact that ten of them are now facing trial, perhaps trial for their lives?

BANKS: Every man that left UK for Africa must be extremely naïve. He knew he was going to war. Every African war is very, very dirty – very ill-equipped, very dirty wars. They were going to a war, they were not going to play games. They took their chances of being killed, maimed, wounded or captured, the same as any other man.

The ten British in the Luanda court-room listened to this with suppressed, bitter rage clearly expressed on their faces as Banks spoke his 'serve the bastards right' line. This was the ultimate betrayal. They believed by then that apart from having pocketed his 'head' money – for their heads – Banks had also pocketed the pay which was supposed to be sent to their families. Cockerell's ironic last words were:

Banks received thousands of letters from would-be mercenaries. He believes that whatever happens to the ten men in Angola, if you are buying mercenaries these days, you are buying British.

Michael Douglas Wiseman, a short man with a round head and a self-assured look, was another who featured *in absentia* in the *Panorama* programme.

COCKERELL TO MICHAEL GIFFIN [an old school-friend with whom Wiseman went to live after he left his parents]: Why do you think he did want to go to Angola?

GIFFIN: He said on more than one occasion that it was for the money, so that he could get back and give to his children what he wanted, believe me, he did think the world of those kids. And he told me that he was hoping to get back with his wife . . .

LYNN WISEMAN: He phoned me on the Saturday before he went, to see the children. And I knew next day about his volunteering – it was the way he was looking at the children. On the next day he popped in from work again, in the afternoon, he said: 'I'm off now. He said that's where I'm going.' He had a pamphlet with Angola on it.

COCKERELL: Did he ever explain why?

LYNN WISEMAN: No, well – presumably for the money. He can't stand black people. I don't know . . .

The other family investigated in the *Panorama* programme was that of Cecil Martin (Satch) Fortuin. Born in South Africa,

Fortuin – a well-built, powerful man – has slightly negroid lips and crinkly hair. He had been a bosom friend of Banks and, with two more of Banks's friends in the 2nd Parachute Regiment, they had each other's names tattooed on their arms.

COCKERELL TO JOHN BANKS: And all four of you had that tattoo? Did you keep in touch with Satch Fortuin?

BANKS: Yes. Satch was a remarkable guy, always happy. Down in Aden, we used to drive around and say: 'look at those black bastards!' And we used to turn round to Satch and say: 'the pot calling the kettle black', you know?

COCKERELL: Fortuin, who was born in South Africa, was himself coloured, but his parents were classified as white.

His parents and a Catholic priest (Father Matthews) spoke of Fortuin's early youth and his regular church attendance, 'a very devout boy' according to Father Matthews.

COCKERELL TO FATHER MATTHEWS: There seems to be some contrast between the devout young altar boy and the chap who now ends up as a mercenary on trial for his life in Angola.

FATHER MATTHEWS: I don't really think so. Myself, I would disagree with that. I think that Christians have always been adventurous people, and there does not seem to be any conflict between devotion to God and an adventurous life.

Michael Cockerell described how Fortuin had served in various parts of the world during five years as a paratrooper; how his first marriage broke up soon after he left the army and that, in 1974, he had married again.

COCKERELL: ... With his second marriage ended after only eighteen months, Satch went on to live with Hilary Roberts who served behind the bar of the New Inn, in Kettering. Can you remember at all what your first thoughts were when you met him?

HILARY ROBERTS: Well ... he was a very smart fella, unusual, had this flair about him that attracted me.

In his written statement to the investigators, Fortuin said: 'I am now living with another woman who has four children and with whom I am very happy.'

COCKERELL TO HILARY ROBERTS: What did you feel when he actually went?

HILARY ROBERTS: I don't really know. A bit numb, I suppose, apprehensive. From the reports out there, the FNLA were losing anyway. I asked him to come home. It wasn't worth staying out there any more. Told him that I missed him. They went with the warning of what would happen to them if they were caught. And now he's been caught so I don't think he should expect the government or the people of this country to fall out and help him.

COCKERELL: Do you feel any sympathy for him?

HILARY ROBERTS: No.

Fortuin's face was a study in incredulity as he heard that dry, crisp 'No', from the only person he still thought he had to fall back on. If he ever had faith in old loyalties, and men on trial for their lives have to have something to support them, it cannot have survived this rejection, added to the betrayal by his old comrade-in-arms Banks, whose name was tattooed on his arm and who had recruited him by assuring him that he would only be a bodyguard. But under the first pressure from Callan, Banks had tricked him into the front line and abandoned him.

Callan had maintained a swaggering, arrogant posture throughout the trial, nudging and glaring at 'his men', still obviously in command. But his body sagged and his face went livid as he listened first in anger then shock to Cockerell:

In Angola it was the psychopathic exploits of the mercenary leader, the self-styled Colonel Callan, that caused public outrage. Callan, a dishonourably discharged paratrooper, ordered the execution of twelve mercenaries sent out by John Banks when they refused to fight. One of Banks' associates, the mercenary Chris Dempster, witnessed what Callan and his henchman Copeland did . . .

At this point, Callan started to wilt and never regained his composure. He had believed he was some kind of hero to the British public. To hear this from the BBC forced him to give up his self-deception. From then on his determination to say nothing faltered. His impersonation of a disciplined army officer carried no conviction. Not only did he lose control of himself: the leadership of the group passed at that moment to Grillo.

5 As Told by the Survivors

To what extent did the versions given by the British mercenaries at the Luanda trial – and under interrogation after capture – tally with the real facts? It was to check this that the authors secured the co-operation of a responsible British journalist, Frank Branston, to interview a cross-section of those who returned to England. Their accounts not only confirmed the veracity of the evidence given in Luanda but revealed many aspects and facts which the accused either did not know about or preferred not to disclose.

For instance, the account by ex-Lieutenant Frank Roden of the Parachutists of the follow-up of the tiny advertisement in the 2 June 1975 issue of the *Daily Express*. Thirteen of the 300 men said to have answered the advertisement gathered in the Skyline Hotel, Heathrow, on 25 and 26 July. They had obviously been carefully selected. The rooms were booked in the name of the International Security Organization, headed by John Banks, who also presided over the meeting. Roden was present, with the future 'RSM', Sammy Copeland, and three men later killed in Angola: Jamie McCandlers, former Special Air Services, Major Mike Johnson, who ran a private investigation service, and Tony Boddy, ex-RAF Regiment; also Vic Kerry, ex-British army, wounded in Angola; 'Pinky' Terry Wilson, who claimed to be an assassin; Brian Butcher, ex-paratrooper; Ken Aitken, ex-SAS; an unnamed Scot who claimed to have been a strong-arm man for the Ulster Loyalists and a member of the 'Royal Black Precipitators of the Orange Order'; André Blavier, a Belgian who boasted of mercenary service in the Congo; and Andover Jones, who said his real name was Van der Schwartz and that he had worked for Israeli intelligence. All except Blavier, who was arrested by Belgian police at Brussels airport, later saw service in Angola.

Of the thirteen, three were ex-SAS; one ex-French Foreign

Legion; one ex-Belgian army; three ex-Parachute Brigade; one ex-RAF Regiment; one ex-Royal Army Ordnance Corps; one unspecified. Three were unemployed, three had marriage problems; eleven had money problems; five were seeking escape, three more were out for adventure.

Banks, according to Roden, opened proceedings by introducing an insurance broker, apparently as a guarantee of the respectability of the enterprise. Those present were to be the advance party of a force of 500 British mercenaries to be based in Zambia to overthrow the Smith régime in Rhodesia. Banks did his best to make it seem a serious proposition and jocularly threatened to 'knee-cap' (a bullet through the knee-cap is an IRA first warning for informers) anyone who took his money and then absconded. Financial matters would be handled via Barclay's Bank. In charge of the advance party would be a South African, Colonel Andy Dennison, who had served in Indochina, Algeria and Chad, and was a former SAS officer and member of the Duke of York's Regiment. The group would be supported by another under Major 'Mad Mike' Hoare of Congo notoriety, and a French contingent headed by a Major le Roche. One part of the advance group would contact the Rhodesian Security Forces, Banks said, in order to act as 'double agents'.

The absurdity of all this – 'Mad Mike' Hoare siding with Zimbabwe blacks to overthrow the racist whites in Rhodesia, the talk about 'double agents' and so on – confirms that the whole venture was a pretext to get a nucleus of professionals together to build up a mercenary force, in all probability originally intended to help the Smith régime. By the second day the would-be mercenaries started to get restive. They had to be mollified by being allowed to order anything they wanted at ISO expense – according to Roden, they ordered bottles of spirits which they packed into their cases, the most expensive food and anything else they could think of. A waiter who told one man that he was not allowed into the restaurant without a tie was assaulted. The bill which Banks paid for that two days was £2,330.

On the second day, Banks pretended that the Rhodesian Security Forces had 'attacked the base camp and virtually wiped it out'. The group broke up, but agreed to keep in touch. In

January 1976, Jamie McCandlers phoned Roden to say he was leaving for Angola. He wanted Roden to go with him, but Roden could not settle his affairs in time. McCandlers went out with the first group on 18 January. 'By the time I went out twelve days later,' said Roden, 'he was already dead.'

Roden's account of recruitment for Angola – rendezvous under a clock at Paddington station with 'Frank' and the briefing by Banks at the Park Court Hotel – was a replica of the accounts given at the trial but he said that Aspin told them that they would have 'an immense amount of American air support from warships', that 'the FNLA equipment included ground-to-air missiles' and that the wounded would be treated at the 'American Hospital' at Kinshasa which was supposed to be manned by 6,000 Americans! Of the approximately 200 would-be recruits gathered in the hotel, Roden – as a professional – was given the task of weeding out the obviously unsuitable, who, together with those who had second thoughts when they realized what they were in for, cut the original 200 down to less than ninety. 'Banks grew angry,' Roden said. 'He had transport laid on for many more and was determined to take at least 100 with him.' So they lowered the standards; the misfits were put back on the roster and some Londoners were allowed to leave the church to see if they could round up any of their friends. One of those thus recruited was a David Wileman, 'recruited Wednesday – dead by Sunday', killed by Callan personally.

During that evening Roden demanded an advance of £500 in cash and, as he was obviously a valued and competent professional, Aspin gave it to him. He then left for the all-night post office in Trafalgar Square, escorted by bodyguard 'Ginger' Best. 'Ginger' was there to ensure that Roden returned to the hotel. The following day, the ninety-seven whom Banks had been able to retain set out for London's Heathrow airport in two coaches. Roden was in the first coach and his party managed to evade the press. But those in the second coach caught the full brunt of the attentions of press and security: 'They were photographed leaving the coach and publicly searched in the airport on the pretext that two men wanted for shooting a British soldier in Ulster were being sought.' But no attempt was made to persuade them not to go, nor was there any real control of identity. Waiting in the departure lounge at Brussels was Colin Taylor, 'small, sandy, seedy and sinister,' said Roden. 'He was wearing dark glasses and a James Cagney raincoat and was treated with caution because of his role as head of FNLA security. He claimed to have worked for Holden Roberto for fifteen years. It was more like eighteen months. When the flight was called, each man was thoroughly searched before being allowed through the barrier. André Blavier, edgy ever since the party arrived, was detained by men in plain clothes. Taylor was the last to board the Boeing 707, accompanied by a "coffee-coloured Angolan introduced as Mr Joseph, a nephew of the President . . ." The flight to Kinshasa was uneventful, the plane touching down at 11 p.m. on Wednesday, 28 January.'

Roden found the atmosphere at the FNLA Kinshasa head-quarters anything but reassuring. The compound was dominated by two machine-gun posts, grim-faced African troops wandering around with FN rifles at the ready. He and another friend, Vic Kerry, found Holden Roberto 'sorting through mounds of jungle camouflage combat suits' in a storeroom. A quick professional glance at the equipment uncovered the fact that the excellent-quality 'Belgian calf-length boots were all size ten'. The weapons were Belgian FN rifles and American M1 carbines.

Roden and Banks were rather dismayed that there was no one from the first batch of mercenaries to deliver 'an up-to-date intelligence report', and they wanted to discuss the military situation with Holden Roberto, but all he was interested in was getting them off to the front as soon as possible.

The mercenaries were tired, hungry, ill-at-ease and queuing for the one tap and one lavatory. They knew that some of the lads being ordered to the front had hardly seen a rifle before. It was all in sad contrast to Leslie Aspin's briefing, when they were told: 'You will have time to acclimatize yourself and there will be at least two weeks of training. You will be paid £150 on arrival and cigarettes will be on open issue. Women too, if you feel like that. Food will be compo rations, but plenty of it. Travel from Zaire to the front will be by armoured personnel carriers. There is a radio link from the front to the Kinshasa headquarters and you will have full air and armoured support.' Now ninety-seven weary men were being asked to climb into two rickety, native buses for a destination which a week before the Western press had reported to be in enemy hands ... Two of the hard-core mercenaries, with experience from Chad to the Congo, changed back into civilian clothes.

When one of them, John O'Connor, suffered a heart attack, Roden suggested to Taylor that they get the man down to the American hospital – fast. Taylor looked puzzled. 'What American hospital? There is no American hospital.' O'Connors went with McIntyre to a Zairean hospital.

Roden asked about the equipment they had been led to expect. Taylor replied: 'We are buying two helicopters and two Chinese anti-tank weapons. Everything else you need is at San Salvador. Now will you order the men into the buses?' Roden countered with a proposal for a volunteer reconnaissance patrol to San Salvador, providing Holden Roberto accompany them. 'Roberto looked put out, but nodded his head.' Banks then asked for fifteen volunteers, claiming that the advance party was in difficulties at San Salvador and needed a fighting patrol to get them out. Before they agreed, according to Roden, Roberto ordered a regiment of Zairean troops to surround the compound. Shortly after the group left, McIntyre turned up and said to Roden:

Christ, Sir. You've got to get O'Connor out of that hospital. I've never seen such a place. There were bloody swabs all over the floor and there was a dead man propped up in a corner of the casualty room. I've never seen anything like it. He looked as though he had been there a long time, too.

McIntyre then went looking for medical supplies and returned to report that there was not as much as a field dressing or an aspirin and that he had trampled on some unrefrigerated, out-of-date serum.

The SAS prospectus referred to earlier, under the heading MEDICS, stated:

Fully trained medics accompany every team and are capable of field surgery (minor) under active conditions. It is obvious that a seriously injured soldier would have to receive advanced treatment. We feel that primary medical attention is of paramount importance as it helps morale within the unit.

One of the questions asked of McIntyre by the People's Prosecutor was how he expected the court to believe that he came as a medic when he had no medical supplies or equipment with him! Morale obviously sank still further at McIntyre's report on the medical situation. Discussing among themselves, the men came to the conclusion that either the operation was genuine but badly organized or they were to be victims in a massacre aimed at bringing in the Western powers on the side of the FNLA. In case the second thesis was correct, they discussed plans of seizing the compound and holding Roberto and his family hostage until outside pressure got them released, or making off for the airport with Roberto as hostage. A major worry was whether the money would ever reach their families. At the trial, several accused testified that Roden volunteered to return to England and act as their agent to ensure that their wages were regularly paid to their families and to forward mail. His own version is that the mercenaries chose him to go back, something which he reluctantly accepted because he would have neither job nor salary: 'I'd come a long way to make a profit,' he said, 'and an empty-handed return held no attraction. But the men had made up their minds and said if I didn't return they would take Kinshasa airport.' After receiving Roden's promise to return and protect their interests, a consensus was reached that the operation was genuine but badly organized, and they unanimously agreed to go to the front.

At 8 p.m. that night, Banks and one of the mercenaries he had taken with him, Barry Madison, returned from San Salvador:

Banks was almost incoherent with rage while Madison, stripped to the waist, was high with excitement. Banks strode up waving a Uzi [Israeli-made sub-machine gun]. 'My best mate has had his fucking arse blown off because of you [Roden],' he spluttered. 'There's a bastard up front, a Greek called Colonel Callan. He had me and Barry Madison up against a wall with an automatic in my neck, all because you stopped the squadron going forward. He's bloody crazy.'

Callan had apparently been assured by Holden Roberto that at least 200 reinforcements were on the way, experienced veterans who would reverse the desperate military situation. He reacted characteristically when fifteen very suspicious mercenaries turned up to sound out the situation. Banks said he was told that McCandlers was out on patrol, Johnson was doing intelligence work and Peter McAleese was in Santo Antonio do Zaire training troops. 'He executed twelve blacks while I was there,' Banks told Roden. 'Blew the head off one, put a shotgun in his mouth.'

When Roden told Banks that he was going to return to look after the mercenaries' interests in England, he claimed that Banks shoved his Uzi in his stomach, but that he pushed it away. Other mercenaries, guns in hands, had them both covered 'in case Banks turned nasty'. An ex-Marine sergeant, Ray Bayliss, told Banks that until Roden had reported back from London that the money was arriving where it should, nobody was moving from Kinshasa. At that, Banks left to see Holden Roberto. Meanwhile the 'hat was passed round' to raise the fare for Roden's return flight, and names of next-of-kin and numbers of bank accounts were scribbled on scraps of paper and cigarette packets. 'Of two factors we had not been aware,' said Roden. 'One was the existence of a Colonel Callan and the other was the fact that the aim of the whole operation was the recovery of diamonds.'[1]

Next morning Banks contacted Roden and said it was agreed that he could leave for London that night. Later the group were taken to a meal of horse steaks at Kinshasa's Palace Hotel. When they returned to the compound, Roden said the atmosphere had changed for the worse. 'FNLA followed every move we made, guns in hands.'

By the time he was ready to leave for the airport, another mercenary, Tom Chambers, had gone sick, and two more – including Barry Madison – had decided to return home. At the airport, tickets were issued by a 'Dutch liaison officer' for the four men – including O'Connor – but not for Roden. Ten minutes before the plane was due to leave, Banks, 'pale and drawn', and Taylor, 'furious', turned up with four Zairean armed guards. According to Roden the following dialogue took place.

TAYLOR: The President wants to know why a good soldier is leaving.

RODEN: You know why.

1. Of the subject of the diamonds, of which Angola is a major producer, and related subjects, more later.

TAYLOR: These four can go, but you are not leaving Zaire ever, you fucking bastard.

BANKS: Give him the tickets.

TAYLOR (shaking O'Connor by the hand and turning to the others): Call yourselves mercenaries! You yellow bastards.

The six men – including Banks – boarded the plane. None returned to Kinshasa.

John Chownes ('Ginger' Best) had some interesting details to add. He had been recruited by Leslie Aspin to find some 'minders' at £50 a day to look after money matters: 'So I took some boys along,' he said, 'paid them fifteen pounds each and kept the change.' One of his men became a chauffeur for the recruiters:

One day, when the recruiters were gathered at the Park Court Hotel, Banks and Aspin were running short of money. My boy was told to take Nick Hall to the US Embassy. Hall disappeared inside and came back a few minutes later carrying a briefcase. It had £36,000 in it. There was one American who was pointed out as a CIA agent. I think his name was Katz. He was always whispering in Aspin's ear. There was another fellow whose picture I saw in *Soldier of Fortune* magazine. He was receiving a medal or something from the CIA. It was something to do with stopping the opium traffic from the Golden Triangle.[2] Well, he was around as well. It was commonly said that the money behind the whole operation was American money – supposed to have been paid over before the US Congress put a block on it.

There were enormous amounts of money being spent. We spent £129,000 with Sabena alone . . .

2. The 'other fellow' was indeed a CIA agent, an important one at that. It was George Bacon, former CIA case officer – the CIA professional term for agent – in Laos, recipient of the CIA Intelligence Star decoration, one-time medico attached to US Special Forces in Vietnam. He was killed in action in Angola. The citation for the Intelligence Star mentioned his 'outstanding services . . . while serving as an adviser to a large indigenous force in Southeast Asia . . .' Bacon was, in fact, adviser to the notorious 'General' Vang Pao, leader of the CIA-run 'Meo Mercenaries' in Laos. His association with Vang Pao and Colonel Lon Non – brother of the Cambodian dictator Lon Nol – in heroin smuggling in the 'Golden Triangle' of Laos, Burma and Thailand almost ended his career in the CIA. But as in many other areas drug-smuggling and CIA activities continued to run hand-in-hand.

Chownes, who showed a keen sense for business and financial affairs, added regretfully:

We didn't even bother to get any block booking concessions. I could have got 12½ per cent if they'd let me. Or at least Sabena would have given them 10 per cent and me two and a half. Colin Taylor went over to Kinshasa and came back with a shoeful of money and McDonald Belford had it under the floorboards of his council house in Leeds. I don't think Taylor made much out of it. He really believed in Holden Roberto and the FNLA ... Anyway, he's now selling stuff from a suitcase in Oxford Street, so he can't have made a lot of money ...

On one occasion when money was getting short – it must have been after the US Embassy said the till was empty – Chownes said:

We knew Taylor was still carrying a lot of FNLA money so I got him drunk – champagne's his tipple – and took £14,000 off him to pay the men.

The second flight of mercenaries – the one described by Roden – was a shambles, according to Chownes.

We hadn't got enough to start with and even then they kept disappearing. We'd booked 200 seats on a Sabena flight to Kinshasa and we hadn't got half that number. We was getting desperate. We were losing £200 for every bloke dropped out. I went looking for men and booked in a couple of road-sweepers. I just went out of the hotel and found these two blokes and said: 'Hey! You want to earn £150 a week?' They said 'yes' so I took them in and signed them up. They went, too. I don't know what happened to them.

If the second group was a shambles, the third group – which left on 4 February – was a disaster. By then news of the Callan executions had got back to England. Banks split with Aspin and Chownes. Chownes summed Banks up as follows:

He was such a bleeding idiot. Aspin's not much better. Anyway Banks was carting these blokes [the third-group recruits] around the country, ending up at Gatwick. The bill at the Post House for two hundred men for one night alone was £1,000. But the news was coming through about what was happening in Angola and they went off, most of them. There was only thirty left and Aspin and me pinched them off

Banks. We just went up to them and said: 'Do you want to go to Angola?' They said they did, so we sent them out by scheduled airline. The FNLA paid a heavy price for those thirty men. Banks had paid the original two hundred £150 each and most of them run away. He had also paid a £24,000 deposit for a chartered Dan Air Flight. The FNLA paid us again for the thirty that we sent.

Perhaps there are exaggerations and inaccuracies in this story but John Nammock, who was part of the third group, testified at the trial that the group in the church crypt numbered about 200 men. The indictment said:

This group was made up of about twenty-five mercenaries. They met in the Post House Hotel, London, on 4 February 1976, left London on 8 February, arrived in Kinshasa 9 February, via Brussels and Athens. Approximately 175 had changed their minds between 4 and 8 February.

Chownes revealed that when the party of six, including Banks and Roden, returned from Kinshasa, Banks was carrying the equivalent of £186,000, presumably to recruit the third British group. He adds this detail:

Taylor used to get money from a US bank. Once he gave me some to change so I took it to the Midland Bank. They asked where I got it from so I told them. They refused to change it. Said it was tainted money.

Remarkably frank about his own involvement, Chownes said that he made over £20,000 out of the Angolan mercenary enterprise, mostly out of the last group of forty South Africans and Americans who never got beyond Brussels because the FNLA had already 'folded up'. 'I was given £40,000 to charter an aircraft,' he said, 'but found I could get one for half the price so I kept the difference.' Alas, he now says his solicitors have tricked him out of it!

6 Mercenaries: US Export Model

I come from a good and cultured family. My grandfather was a very rich man and my parents gave me the best of everything: Catholic private school, private tutors, a governess, piano teacher, German school, finishing school. We also had servants. They gave me the best of everything and look how I turned out – a bandit!

This was how Gustavo Marcelo Grillo described himself to his captors. An Argentinian by birth, whose family got mixed up in Peronist politics – some for, some against – his mother brought him and his sister Sylvia to the USA when he was eleven. At seventeen he enlisted in the US Marine Corps; the following year he was in Vietnam.

A big man, with bunched powerful shoulders and a blue jaw by late afternoon, it was not only his name that conjured up a 'gorilla' image. Yet his liveliness of mind and pungent expression considerably enlivened the court proceedings; at least he appeared sensitive to the situation. To what extent he was sincere in his reactions, to what extent he was using his considerable native wit to gain the sympathy of the court and save his life, is impossible to determine. To his great surprise, he had been treated humanely and with respect for his human dignity from the moment of capture. None of the accused had been humiliated. They all attested to having been well-treated, and receiving medical treatment that had saved the lives of several. Their relaxed relationship with the guards in the court-room was a testimonial in itself. For some of them it was possibly the first time in their lives that they had been treated with normal human consideration and as equals. The irony that it was the blacks – whom they had been conditioned to regard as inferiors and savages – who were treating them thus would have passed over the head of Barker or Gearhart. Not Grillo. Gearhart and

Grillo represented opposite poles of behaviour. The introvert Gearhart, crafty, calculating, trying to outwit the court by concealing as much as he could, conceding facts only when certain that they were already in the dossier, was completely out of touch with the aim of the trial. It was not to convict Gearhart as an individual but to convict mercenarism as a system. Grillo had obviously accepted that the aim of the court was to get at the truth about what forces were behind the use of mercenaries and what motives pushed human beings along such an inglorious path. Extrovert Grillo had no inhibitions, and nothing to lose, in helping the court to do this.

It was clear that Gearhart was protecting a system with which Grillo did not identify himself. As an immigrant from Latin America, Grillo could not but have suffered from both class and racist discrimination. How had he come to be in Vietnam? He told the presiding judge:

Things were going bad in Vietnam in 1967–8. I thought it was the right thing to do. They cut my training period in half and sent me. I began as a rifleman, that is rifle infantryman, later as team leader – head of five soldiers. Squad leader – over fifteen soldiers. Then platoon sergeant – over thirty-five soldiers. We were always at the front. It was our job to chase the enemy, to try to get information to destroy the enemy – patrols by day, ambushes at night. We never stayed in the same place – always on the move. A dirty, painful war with many lives lost on both sides. I began in 1967 and was there through 1968 and 1969. Malaria twice and a small wound in the left knee.

After Vietnam, what did you do in civilian life?

Getting a job was pretty hard. I had no trade. I started working in restaurants and learned culinary arts. But I was pretty rotten by then.

In his written statement – hand-written in Spanish, the language he still knows best – Grillo spelt things out a little more clearly.

In 1970, I returned home [from Vietnam] with letters of recommendation, but with no training for normal civilian life. I managed, with great difficulty, to get a job as a mechanic etc. I began to work in construction, but I didn't make enough money to live. Then I began to get involved with gangsters I knew, to get more money – always some dirty business. One day, someone under police pressure squealed – and I did eighteen months in prison for armed robbery. Well, prison was another kind of school – for crime ... When I came out in 1972, everything was the same as before. I found work but it was even harder than before. I began to work in an Italian restaurant called the 'Esposito', washing dishes and saucepans ...

All the restaurants in which he worked were connected with gangsters.

One gangster I knew sent me to work with another gangster who specialized in gambling and sports. He was called Roberto and was very good – a heart of gold. The work I did for him was as bodyguard, chauffeur and debt collector. I also paid 'payoff' money to other gangsters and paid his debts. I got him up in the morning and I put him to bed at night. He gave me a flat that cost 325 dollars a month, a new car, expenses paid, lawyers paid – and not only this ...

Among the documents found on Grillo were various passes, such as 'The Honour Legion', Police Departments, State of New Jersey, the 'New Jersey State Association of Chiefs of Police' and half a dozen cards of detectives and lawyers, presumably at the disposal of the various racketeers with whom he had contacts.

Grillo then came to the point at which a friend drew his attention to the TV programme about mercenaries and the perspectives this opened up. He sent the thirty-five dollars to Bufkin for more detailed information.

Three or four days later he phoned me from another state, Missouri, saying that he had just come back from South America, that he was short of money to return to California and if I could help him with money. I told him that I didn't know him well enough to lend money and that in money-lending I didn't have confidence in anyone and that crooks shouldn't do the dirty on each other. I also told him that if he did the dirty on me, I would spend all the money I had to find him and break him into small pieces – so that we should understand each other from the start.

One of the British lawyers, Warburton-Jones, to emphasize a point he was trying to make in defence of his client, ironically referred to 'philosopher Grillo' and there was more than a grain of truth in this. He at least drew conclusions from his experiences:

If one has to rob, one shouldn't rob from the poor, from the people who work for their living, or people without money. One should rather steal from the gangsters and functionaries, corrupt authorities. These are the scoundrels who grow fat, who have the money and don't let the others eat. Take it from them and give it to those who have nothing.

This Grillo brand of philosophy appeared again in the following exchanges he had with the presiding judge, Texeiro da Silva, the latter probing as always to find the motives of mercenaries:

How do you see the society in which you live?

US society, of which I am a product, is a monster. As I said before, it's a society of power-seekers, status-seekers, waste-makers, where the weak get weaker and the strong get stronger. It's a country that moves at a very fast pace – the weak can't keep up. People seek methods of escape, drugs, alcohol and so on. People are very selfish. They have no thought for others. It's a rat race.

Institutions like the FBI and CIA – what role do they play in the whole set-up?

I don't know about the CIA, but the FBI gets involved in federal crime throughout the country. The CIA is an institution of mercenaries which uses other men, buys other mercenaries. They try to put their hands on everything as far as I know . . .

Do you have any ideas about those who say they have innocently been fooled and came here to do some humanitarian sort of work? That it was only Callan who was a 'monster', a 'bandit' etcetera? Is it possible that one man could have done all that? Controlled all that?

I have a saying: 'Between two bits of soap without water you can't make bubbles.' I'm sure that they all came here consciously to fight. Sure, they all know what a mercenary is, why he is sent, what work he does. They've seen films, read newspapers on World War II, World War I. They know what war is – what they came for. They want to tell you they came as cooks or mechanics. I don't go for this. I came here myself for the money, for adventure . . .

At this point, the People's Prosecutor, Manuel Rui Alves Monteiro, took over the cross-examination.

. . . Don't you think that the real reason that you and the others are unfortunate enough to be here is the fault of your society, the fault of your government?

No. I'd say it's half and half. The government and society is half responsible and I am half responsible . . .

I'm not a political man, but I'm beginning to understand some things. [Our] systems are as different as day from night. When I was in bed in the military hospital, there was a guard – an older man. Perhaps 45–50 years, with a good, noble face, I can see it still – burned by the sun. He was a peasant, worked in the sugar-cane fields – that's all he knows, he told me. But he volunteered to come and fight here, without money, for the People's Republic. He left his family, his friends, his little home where he was very happy, to come to fight – for nothing. He really put me to shame. I felt very small – didn't know where to hide. The difference between him and me, is night and day. I came here for greed, for money. That's the US system. There if you have two shirts, you want twenty more. Here, if you've two you're happy and to hell with everybody. Here everybody's equal and that's the big difference . . .

I never heard much about the idea of mercenaries as 'heroes'. They are usually not well regarded. A mercenary is like a prostitute – sells himself to other countries for money. I can never say I'm proud to have been a mercenary. It's one of the lowest things.

At the end of Grillo's testimony, the People's Prosecutor pointed to his 'high political consciousness' and said that his 'conduct in Court will be taken into consideration'. There is also no question but that Gearhart's conduct was also 'taken into consideration' and the difference was expressed in the firing squad for Gearhart and thirty years' imprisonment for Grillo, although there was a strong probability that Grillo – on his own testimony – had killed FAPLA personnel and Gearhart – on his own and Grillo's testimony – had not. Grillo succeeded in convincing the Tribunal that he sincerely regretted what he had done and recognized the enormity of the use of mercenaries. Gearhart's demeanour, if not his actual words, betrayed regret that his efforts had not succeeded. He never displayed any regret for his own activities. The following is a typical crossing of swords with the People's Prosecutor, who started by reading the advertisement Gearhart had placed in the *Soldier of Fortune* magazine. In that issue there was a long article about the activities of mercenaries in Angola.

So did you know what the war in Angola was about?

I don't understand.

You never read about Angola in that magazine?

I never read *Soldier of Fortune*.

How did you know it existed in order to place an advertisement?

I found out from another publication dealing with hunting and fishing: *Shotgun News*.

There must have been a link between those who recruited you and that magazine?

Not to my knowledge.

Did you send advertisements to others?

Yes. For security work. But I can't remember whether I mailed them.

You said in your original statement in explaining how David Bufkin contacted you, 'Perhaps he had seen some advertisement that I had sent to various publications . . .' Do you confirm that?

No.

So you knew when you left the USA that you were going to a war?

Nobody ever said that.

In the advertisement you offered yourself as a full-time mercenary?

Yes.

Aren't you used to war?

We had a cook in San Salvador who didn't fight.

But you weren't a cook. Didn't you come to fight? You said so yourself. A person who goes into another country to fight – is he there to attack or defend himself?

Probably both.

And so it went on, with Gearhart doing his best to evade the most obvious truths. It gradually became clear that, unlike Grillo, who almost cheerfully admitted that he was a money-motivated mercenary, Gearhart was a political mercenary. After a long session in which his American lawyer, Robert Cesner, made much of Gearhart's financial difficulties as the compulsive reason for him offering himself as a mercenary, presiding judge Ernesto Texeiro

da Silva took the unusual step – the only time during the trial – of
re-examining Gearhart:

I can understand about your economic situation, but how did this lead
to you becoming a member of the 'Wild Geese Club'?

At that time I was looking for information – not necessarily employment.

What sort of information?

Political information. What people were fighting – who they were
fighting. Things not usually available in books. On all of Africa.

And you wrote to the mercenary organization for that?

Yes . . .

For this Court, it's a little strange that someone who wants to study the
political situation in a country comes as a mercenary.

It's the only way I could come. I came to study people. I am interested
in all peoples. Not that I am interested in their political views as such.
You ask whether my coming as a mercenary was a cover for something
else? No, I came as a mercenary to stop, as I thought, a Russian Communist takeover of Angola. I came to help the people of Angola.

That is clearly why you wanted to become a member of the Wild Geese
Club?

Among the documents found in Gearhart's possession was one
showing he belonged to an American parachutist club.

You were a civilian or a military paratrooper?

Yes, sir. I was a civilian parachutist.

It was perhaps unfortunate for him that on page 4 of the SAS
prospectus, under the heading of Personnel Background, it is
stated that:

We also have a small contingent of foreign nationals who have seen
active service with the unit in the past. We have men trained in tactical
assault parachuting and basic military parachuting; they train at
regular intervals with civilian parachute clubs.

At the end of his second cross-questioning of Gearhart, presiding
judge Texeiro da Silva turned to lawyer Cesner and said: 'Given

the gravity of the issues raised, do you want to address the Court, Mr Cesner?'

Cesner, a sophisticated and politically minded lawyer, rose and did his best, but towards the end seemed to have slipped on to the wrong track. His last three questions to Gearhart were:

Do you have any connection with subversive organizations?

Gearhart (straighter than ever) shouted: No, sir!

Have you ever collected any information for any subversive organization for your own or any other government?

No, sir!

You have told the truth?

Yes, sir!

The audience at least, and presumably the court, was left wondering whether Cesner was implying that he considered the CIA a 'subversive organization'! While it was not established that Gearhart was an agent, the CIA employed ex-servicemen in a number of capacities, both as para-military and as contract officers. Gearhart admitted to having served with the Special Forces in South Vietnam and also as a security guard to the commander of the US 1st Division there. He denied in court rumours that he had also served as a security guard for General Westmoreland, when the latter was the US Commander in South Vietnam. He admitted to having entered Angola in uniform and carrying a weapon, as a mercenary, with the aim of helping to crush the MPLA and overthrow the internationally recognized government of the People's Republic of Angola.

The third American to stand trial, twenty-one-year-old Gary Martin Acker, was the image of the clean-living, God-fearing American lad. Tall, slim, erect, pink-faced and almost angelic-looking, his experience belied the innocence of his appearance. At seventeen, he had tried to enter the toughest of all branches of the American armed forces, the 'Green Berets', or Special Forces. Rejected, he joined the next toughest – the Marines. At eighteen, Lance-Corporal Acker was a Marine guard looking after the nuclear weapons arsenal aboard the aircraft carrier *USS Ranger*.

It carried A-6, A-7 and F-4 planes and its mission was to bomb
Vietnam.

Acker remained with the *USS Ranger* from February 1972
until August 1973, when it returned to the USA. He then shifted
to a preparatory course for entrance to the US Naval Academy,
failed to adapt, and was transferred to the 2nd Marine Division.
After a two weeks' course, he was appointed by the Alcohol–Drug
Abuse Centre as an adviser on such matters for rank-and-filers in
his Marine Company, with the rank of corporal. After a quarrel
with his platoon commander, Acker went over his head and protested to the company commander. The platoon commander was
reprimanded and, as is standard practice under such circumstances,
made life unbearable for Acker. He went absent without leave for
four months, then presented himself again to his unit. A Special
Court-Martial demoted him from corporal to lance-corporal.
Eventually he was passed on to the 2nd Marine Division's
psychiatrist who, in Acker's words:

decided that I was a 'passive-aggressive moderate' and that I should
undergo group therapy treatment, which I did for a certain time. Later
I decided to consult a psychologist and a psychiatrist who had a joint
practice. They were of the opinion that I was a severe schizophrenic
passive aggressive. Apart from this I was also seen by a military
psychiatrist who decided to demobilize me. I left military service on 25
April 1975 . . .

In other words, if the MPLA had instructed some special
commando unit to sally forth and capture specimens representing
three different facets of a sick American society, they could not
have done better than bagging Grillo, Gearhart and Acker. The
only thing they had in common was that they had all seen service in
Vietnam! Each revealed in depth some of the chronic ills of a
system in decline. After demobilization Acker drifted from job to
job, unfit for anything but unskilled work, living mainly on the
meagre income of his parents and what was left from his Army pay.

'Up to the time I met Bufkin, I never had a permanent job . . .'
And what of Bufkin? His name, like Banks's, was as frequently
mentioned in the court as those of the accused.

My entire association with David Bufkin was one of lies and deceit on his part. It was not until we arrived in Kinshasa that I fully became aware of the extent of his lies.

David Bufkin began his series of lies when I first met him at the airport in Fresno, California. There he told of the vast numbers of mercenary troops in Angola. He stated that there were approximately 250 British troops in Angola. He said there were groups of Belgian, French and German troops in Angola. He said there was a special commando group there also. He said that I would be his personal assistant and that we, the Americans, would primarily be in charge of training the Angolan troops. Basically we would be functioning as military advisers.

Acker related how the various recruits exchanged experiences in their Kinshasa hotel and came to the conclusion that Bufkin was just a big crook. It was decided to have a show-down.

Everything Dave told me from beginning to end was a lie. We got all the Americans together and found that all had been lied to. We got together and held Dave and Nick at gun-point in one of the rooms, I with a P.38 [pistol] and Danny [Gearhart] with a Uzi [sub-machine gun], both of which were in Dave's duffle bag. Lobo and Captain Tom[1] exposed Dave's plan to be the only recruiter and skim money from the FNLA. How Dave told Nick and the President that he had 100 men in New York waiting to come to Angola, when there were none and about all the lies that were told to all. The outcome was that Dave should go to San Salvador and not back to the United States . . . The second day there he had a court-martial. The outcome – 200 dollars' fine and a reduction from colonel to regular soldier . . .

Grillo's version of the same incident was to the same effect.

In San Salvador we held a small trial of Mr Bufkin, because he took arms out of Holden Roberto's place, because he had photos and documents of diamond mines, information and plans to rob diamonds, and because of the way he had swindled the men. Mr Bufkin was found guilty of taking arms out of Holden Roberto's place without permission, but nothing else. He was given a 200 dollar fine.

The main thing that emerged from the 'trial' was the rivalry

1. Almost invariably referred to as 'Captain Tom', his full name was Tom Oates, an American who had already been for several months in Angola before the mercenaries arrived. British mercenaries believed he was from the CIA.

between Bufkin and Lobo del Sol as to who should have the monopoly of the mercenary racket in the USA. When, in San Salvador, it was clear that the military situation was desperate, Bufkin saved his skin by pretending he would go to Kinshasa and return with an aircraft on which a machine-gun would be mounted to strafe the advancing FAPLA troops. Obviously he never came back. Lobo del Sol also managed to persuade the others that it was essential for him to fly back to the USA and return with reinforcements. Instead he made off with the money the mercenaries trusted him with, behaving to the end like a true mercenary.

7   What Mercenaries Do

The final report of the Angolan officers charged with investigating the activities of the thirteen accused mercenaries concludes:

From a military viewpoint, the mercenaries constituted a structurally organized force, charged with the task of organizing and training FNLA troops. In combat they acted autonomously as shock troops. They were organized into attack groups of about twelve men (Killer Group) and reconnaissance groups (Exploration Group).

At that time, the greatest problem of the mercenaries was to try to halt the advance of the liberating FAPLA column which from Damba was on its way to Maquela do Zombo. To this end, the mercenary Callan set up an advance post between Quibocolo and Maquela, and mined the road to the south of Quibocolo. He organized an attack on Damba, in which he used all the troops and military means at his disposal in Maquela [about sixty men, and in which all the captured mercenaries of the second group took part, as well as Andrew McKenzie]. This attack was driven off by the FAPLA [1 February 1976].

The mercenary troops regrouped again in Maquela and from the next day tried a new tactic, the disorganization of the liberating FAPLA column by means of successive ambushes. They set up an ambush on 3 February of two FAPLA reconnaissance vehicles, causing the death of three combatants. On the same day Callan mistook a truck loaded with explosives for a tank and caused an explosion as a result of which he himself was wounded and his group was completely destroyed. Thus began the period of the flight of the survivors and their later capture by the people – who handed them over to the FAPLA [Marchant, McIntyre, Wiseman, Evans].

McAleese substituted for Callan as commander of the mercenary soldiers. Maquela do Zombo, Santo Antonio do Zaire and Tomboco were liberated by the FAPLA, and on 9 and 10 February, the third and fourth group of mercenaries, constituted respectively of Americans and British, arrived in San Salvador. The military activity of the mercenaries centred on an attempt to defend San Salvador and, in particular, an attempt to stop the advance of the liberating column along the Maquela–Cuimba–San Salvador road. To do this they tried to blow up a bridge across the Luvo river and sent successive reconnaissance patrols out. On 14 February, the FAPLA captured the mercenaries Gustavo Marcelo Grillo, Daniel Gearhart and John Nammock, and the next day caught Gary Martin Acker. It was the fast and forceful liberation activity of the FAPLA which prevented the mercenary forces recruited by imperialism, under the cover of the FNLA, in order to recolonize the Angolan people, from achieving their aim of creating chaos and terrorist oppression against the Angolan people as has been seen to happen in other African countries.

In fact, all the characteristics of mercenary activity were demonstrated in the short time these groups spent in Angola. Individual characteristics, resulting from the social environment in which they developed and were recruited, and group characteristics in which they constituted a completely foreign body in the human and geographic environment in which they operated; having considerable military means and not being restricted by any kind of control.

In reality, the mercenaries who came to Angola had as common characteristics that the majority of them were of working-class origin, and/or were from differing/minority (ethnic) groups. They had volunteered for the army as a means of escaping their exploited and segregated situation and had become transformed into repressive agents, serving the exploiters.

They had belonged to specialized troop sections of the British or United States army; or they had done military service in colonial countries or countries militarily invaded by imperialist countries, and had participated in the repression of national independence struggles; or having been demobilized from the armed forces they were unable to adapt to civilian life, because of the resultant drop in their standard of living and social positions; or they had criminal records.

These individual characteristics are present, in whole or in part, in each of the mercenaries captured.

In their group action the mercenaries acted in Angola as a body completely foreign to the country and its people. They made their own rules, were responsible to only one authority – their leader – who had the right of life or death over them. They imposed themselves by force or terror on the civilian population and carried out acts of war to reach the objective for which their services had been bought: to maintain a bridgehead in the extreme north of Angola, which would enable the regular troops of Zaire, and the FNLA in the rearguard, to reorganize for a new attempt against the Angolan patriotic forces.

This report, on which the indictment was based, then set forth the individual and group offences of each of the accused. Apart from the advance group of Callan and four others, who arrived in early December 1975, the final report listed four groups, totalling 185 mercenaries, which arrived in San Salvador between 16 January and 10 February 1976. The group offences are described as follows:

(1) All of them received pay to carry out acts of war against the legitimate government of the People's Republic of Angola. This they did voluntarily and with previous knowledge of the objective of their mission.
(2) They all violated the frontier of the People's Republic of Angola, armed and in uniform.
(3) They all participated in acts of war: ambushes, mining of roads and bridges, mining of tracks leading to villagers' cultivated fields, patrols, training of troops.
(4) They all coerced the civilian population.

If this sober and restrained appraisal is how mercenary activity was seen from the 'receiving end', how was it seen from the 'giving end'? From the trial accounts and from diaries and letters found with bodies on the battlefield, it is clear that 'Operation Mercenary' was a shambles, a text-book example of military bungling and inefficiency which no ruthlessness of method could offset. The fact that the end of 'Colonel' Callan's group came when Callan fired a bazooka shell at short range into an ammunition-laden truck which he had mistaken for a tank symbolizes the whole enterprise. Some may be tempted to remark that it could not be otherwise when privates became captains, majors and colonels at the whim of another private who hired them, with their stripes and pips bought in a London military supplies shop!

In fact being a private is no automatic bar to becoming a first-rate military leader. Vo Nguyen Giap and Fidel Castro – not even privates when they started their military careers – became first-rate military technicians, running rings around the most 'distinguished' products of the world's leading military academies. So it was not just the question that former private Costas Georgiou, or sergeant Peter McAleese, suddenly blossomed into 'Colonel' Callan, and 'Captain', later 'Colonel' McAleese! The problem was not there. It was a question of motivation, fighting for a cause you believe in – not for dollars and booty!

How did Callan perceive his task? He refused to discuss it during the trial and was, in general, uncooperative with his interrogators after capture. At that time he refused to make an oral statement like the others, but he did answer some questions and subsequently penned two short hand-written statements. What emerged from his reply to questions was that, when he assumed command, the FNLA armed forces were down to about a hundred men. (Nicholas Hall had been rebuked for giving the figure of 300!) Callan said he had no idea how much military equipment was available. The military situation he described tersely as that 'The FAPLA was advancing and had already taken Damba and Ambriz.' As for what actions he had undertaken to try to halt the FAPLA advance towards San Salvador, he said 'general defence', and when pressed to define what this meant he said 'digging trenches and gun emplacements'.

Regarding the military structure of the FNLA after he took command, Callan said that he had reorganized them into 'killer groups' of ten plus a commander and second-in-command of each group. There was no general staff or high command. Callan had one adjutant, 'Charlie', referred to by various of the accused as 'Captain' or 'Shotgun' Charlie, whose speciality according to several of the accused was shooting his victims in the stomach with phosphorus shells, leaving others to finish them off. Throughout the trial the identity of 'Charlie' remained a mystery.[1] As for weapons, Callan said: 'We had anti-tank guns, a tank, one scout car – and that was all.' This was not true, as documents and evidence from other mercenaries made clear. Callan listed an 'ambush of two FAPLA Land Rovers on the Quibocolo–Damba road' as his only successful military action.

1. It was later revealed that his full name was Charles Christodoulou, a Greek-Cypriot cousin of Callan and, like the other three members of Callan's advance party, a former member of the 1st British Parachute Regiment. They had served together in Northern Ireland.

The text of these questions and answers was signed by Callan and included the following supplementary information:

Asked why he left the British army in 1972, he answered that he had finished his time.

Asked whether, since that time, he had ever been sentenced by any court, he answered that he was in prison from 1972 to 1975, sentenced by an Irish court to three and a half years for a military offence which he preferred not to explain.[2]

Asked if he knew of any action against the civilian population by FNLA fighters, whether Angolans or not, he answered that he did not.

Asked if he had ordered the execution of fourteen British mercenaries serving in the FNLA forces, he answered that he did. Asked why, he answered it was because of desertion in the face of the enemy and mutiny.

Asked if, before giving the order, he himself shot one of the mercenaries, he answered that he did shoot their leader.

Asked why he had agreed to come to Angola to fight against the legitimately constituted Government of the People's Republic of Angola, he answered that it was for money . . .

In Chapter 5 we mentioned Roden's surprise at discovering the existence of a 'Colonel' Callan in Angola and that the aim of the operation was the 'recovery of diamonds'. Banks also seemed to have received a rude shock to find 'a bastard up front, a Greek called Colonel Callan' in command. No evidence presented at the trial suggested that Callan had been recruited by the SAS, although all the other British accused had been. Barker, who arrived with the first small British group at San Salvador on 20 January, said:

We were met there by Callan, who was introduced as Commandant by Holden Roberto. There was another British bloke called Mike, tall and thin with a little moustache. There was another dark-haired man with a moustache. All three of them were very tanned and it seemed to me that they must have been there for some months. Commandant Callan started shouting orders about our hair, saying that everyone must have a haircut. It seemed to me that he was a Greek and a psychopath. Callan said that we were not mercenaries but FNLA soldiers.

2. Callan had been dishonourably discharged from the British army and sentenced to five years for the armed robbery of a post office in Northern Ireland. He served three and a half years.

Roden's version is that 'Dr' MacDonald Belford, Holden Roberto's man in Leeds, had placed an advertisement in the press requesting ex-military of around twenty-four to twenty-five years fancying 'a job overseas' to ring his Leeds telephone number:

The advertisement was seen by three men, all ex-paratroopers working as jobbing builders in London. They were Costas Georgiou, Charles Christodoulou and Michael Wainhouse . . . When contact was made, they were told that a diamond courier, with a load of rough diamonds worth between ten and twelve million pounds, had been trapped in an Angolan town called Damba. He had secreted the diamonds in a safe place and got out. The FNLA offered the ex-paratroopers ten per cent to get the diamonds out. They left for Angola in November 1975 to make a reconnaissance, apparently believing they could do the job in a James Bond style operation . . .

They failed to find the diamonds, and the vehicle in which Georgiou was travelling – escorted by some FNLA troops – south of Damba was ambushed by an MPLA tank. The FNLA escort fled, but Callan, whom no one has ever reproached for lack of courage, 'stood his ground and knocked out the tank single-handed', according to Roden, who says that this action 'so impressed Holden Roberto' that he made Georgiou commander of the northern front. Thus Costas Georgiou became 'Colonel Callan'. Roden claimed that all of Callan's subsequent actions were aimed at recovering the diamonds, which explains his obsession about capturing Damba. 'Why else would he keep butting his head against Damba?' asked Roden.

There was constant reference to diamonds throughout the Luanda trial. Several of the accused said they were briefed on the necessity of holding the north-east corner of Angola because it was 'rich in diamonds', the production of which would enable the FNLA to continue the war indefinitely. Bufkin was accused by his fellow American mercenaries of being primarily interested in getting out diamonds – among his possessions was an aerial photograph of some diamond diggings and it was suspected that he wanted to organize a commando raid to get his hands on a fistful of sparklers. Diamonds were held out, at least to some of the higher-ranking mercenaries, as that extra bit of loot always associated with mercenary enterprises. Checks made by the authors in Carmona and Negage – just south of Damba – shortly after the FNLA–Zaire troops withdrew, confirmed that bank safes and vaults had all been blown open with explosives – and the looters were not after paper currency. Several witnesses at the trial testified to the mercenaries burning bundles of notes in their cooking fires.

Frustration over his failure to get his hands on the missing diamonds could explain the ferocity of Callan's reactions to every setback to his plans. A detailed account of his moods and activities came from an American-trained Ghanaian electrician, Ako Joseph Nai, who, by a series of misadventures, got drawn into the Angolan drama and escaped with his life only because Callan snatched him from prison to serve as his interpreter. As his evidence concerned Callan and the latter refused any participation in the court proceedings, there was little point in a Nai–Callan confrontation and he was called neither by prosecution nor defence, but his statement went into the court record.

After graduating as an electrician in the United States, Joseph Nai worked on hydroelectric projects in Ghana and the Ivory Coast. Then in March 1975 he took a job in Zaire with Construction Ingashaba. He was recalled to Kinshasa on 14 October 1975 and was asked by the company's chief engineer to accompany Holden Roberto to Ambriz (on the Angolan coast about 250 kilometres south of Matadi) to install an electric generator. The job was to last three days, after which he was to return to Kinshasa. But, after the generator was installed, Holden Roberto insisted that Joseph Nai accompany him to Ambrizete, also on the coast about 100 kilometres north of Ambriz. The electrician refused. Early on the morning of 20 October, he was about to board a plane back to Kinshasa when he was stopped by Holden Roberto's bodyguard, taken to prison and robbed of all his belongings. Two months later he was taken from prison to become Callan's French interpreter.

On 24 January, Callan took most of the detachment 'including heavy weapons' and set up an ambush about twenty kilometres north of Damba. After two hours the only sign of action was the appearance of a group of women coming from the direction of Damba. The women were questioned and said that there were a lot of MPLA troops in Damba.

This discussion was in the local language of the area. The FNLA interpreter translated into French and I into English.

Callan ordered the men to leave their positions and the detachment headed back to Maquela. Nai's statement continues:

When they turned around to return to Maquela an old man was seen coming down the road towards the column of vehicles. The man began to shout: 'MPLA! MPLA!' Callan ordered the column to stop and got out of his jeep. He held the man and asked why he was shouting MPLA. The man replied through the interpreter that he thought Callan's men were MPLA ...

Callan put the man in his jeep and ordered the man to take him to his house which was near the road. The house was searched but in this simple wooden house nothing of importance was found. Callan took the man, leaving his wife and children in tears, into the jeep. He was taken to a two-storey house, seventeen kilometres from Maquela. There Callan questioned the man, who showed Callan the documents he had when he was in hospital in Carmona. He said he was arrested in Carmona by the MPLA and then released.

What he told to Callan was the truth because I was there and saw the documents. Then Callan took from the man his wrist watch and about 2,000 escudos and ordered his brother, Charlie, to take the man outside to the bush, which was about twenty-five to thirty metres from the house. I heard one shot. Charlie returned without the man and he and Callan spoke together in a way I could not understand what they were saying. They were speaking in their dialect.

We got back to Maquela on 25 January. On the way we met Holden Roberto in a Toyota jeep. On seeing me, Holden Roberto asked Callan what I was doing there and Callan explained that he was in need of an interpreter – that was why he had taken me from prison.

Next day they headed for Damba again. On the road they met a man who, on being questioned, said that a messenger on a bicycle had been sent by the FAPLA to say that their forces would be advancing and the messenger should tell the local village chiefs to put up white flags in order 'to avoid mistakes'. The messenger was alerting village after village along the road to Maquela. Callan's column turned back, catching up with the messenger after a few kilometres. He admitted he was on his way to see the FNLA Commissioner of Quibocolo. Callan took him to the Commissioner's headquarters while other mercenaries were sent to round up a village chief whose name had been mentioned by the man encountered on the road.

They brought the chief to the house of the Commissioner where Callan was waiting. The old man was questioned. When told by Callan that he was MPLA, the man replied that he was an old man, not a politician. He put the three in a car and drove to the new camp which was about twelve kilometres from Maquela. He ordered them out of the jeep and told one of his men to put a military knife in the fire. He searched the messenger and took 10,000 escudos away from him. The money was in fifty-escudo notes. He wanted to know where the messenger had got so much money from. The messenger said it was his money.

I told Callan that it could be the truth because it was war and everybody carried all the money they had with them. He told me to shut up, that I am not here to defend the MPLA and that I am still a prisoner.

Callan got one of the men to tie up the messenger with a rope which was tied around his neck and the same rope was used to tie the man's hands behind his back. Then the man's mouth was stuffed with cloth and Callan took the red hot knife and placed the blade on the man's chest, over his heart. The man made a sign for Callan to take the cloth out of his mouth so that he could answer the questions . . .

The man said he was coming from Damba where there were MPLA soldiers with military weapons but he did not know what weapons. He then took the messenger out to the woods behind the house since he said this man is not speaking the truth. There was one shot. He then took the chief of the village to the same spot where he had taken the messenger. There he shot him with one shot. He then ordered one of his men to take away the Commissioner and execute him.

He sent an FNLA soldier to buy a goat which they roasted. I did not eat because I was feeling bad and this I told to Callan when he asked me why I was not eating. The shooting of the three men, the messenger and the chief of the village shot by Callan, and the Commissioner by one of his men, took place in the morning . . .

While the goat was being roasted, Joseph Nai was sent, together with a mercenary, referred to as 'Canada', to fetch water from a nearby river. 'Canada' warned Nai that Holden Roberto had ordered Callan to shoot him and that the reason why Callan had not yet done this was that he still needed Nai as an interpreter. This naturally reinforced Nai's determination to escape at the earliest opportunity. Back at Callan's headquarters, two FNLA soldiers were escorted in by four mercenaries:

> The first one to be brought to Callan was a young, bearded man who handed Callan a letter. After reading the letter, Callan told the soldier to remove his pistol and his Omega watch and undo his shirt. He stripped him of all his clothes, leaving him only in his underpants and his vest. He ordered Charlie to take the stripped FNLA soldier to the same spot where the messenger and chief were shot. When Charlie returned Callan asked him why did he shoot twice. Charlie said the man was trying to escape so he had to shoot two times. Another FNLA soldier arrived from Maquela and this time there was no questioning. All that happened was that he was immediately stripped and taken by a mercenary to the place where the commissioner was killed and was shot with a single bullet.

Ako Joseph Nai eventually escaped and made contact with the FAPLA at Damba. From the viewpoint of keeping track of what was going on from the inside at the top, a keen observer with a retentive memory was withdrawn from circulation. Undoubtedly he thus saved his life and also an invaluable account of what went on in Callan's entourage.

From a military point of view Callan was trying, with the aid of his white 'shock troops', to put enough backbone into the FNLA remnants to defend, in shallow depth, a line running from Santo Antonio do Zaire, at the mouth of the Congo river, 260 kilometres by road east to San Salvador and another 150 kilometres east to Maquela do Zombo, ranging from twenty to seventy kilometres south of the border with Zaire. In addition to the between 100 and 300 of the original FNLA troops left, according to the figures given by Callan and Hall, there were several hundred fresh recruits that had been rounded up by Holden Roberto's press gangs. Why Holden Roberto was so short of troops only a few months after he had boasted of his capacity to put 10,000 troops into Luanda alone became clear when the authors interviewed one of his former top commanders, the redoubtable Comandante Margoso, who commanded the northern front.

Barker gave his impressions of the situation at Santo Antonio do

Zaire – obviously a key position for supplying the rest of what was left of the northern front, with a big airfield and positions north of the town commanding the entrance to the Congo river. At that point, the centre of the river formed the frontier with Zaire. On 21 January, the day after Barker and his group, the first batch of mercenaries, arrived in San Salvador, he and a few others were sent off to Santo Antonio do Zaire by plane. He made it clear for the first time that the British mercenaries were not operating *under* the FNLA – except in the sense that it was Holden Roberto who was formally hiring them – but that they *were* the FNLA and what was left of the FNLA forces were entirely under Callan's command. This was one of the major revelations of the Luanda trial.

Barker noted that there were about 500 soldiers at the airport and barracks, that there was: 'a lot of indiscipline as the soldiers were just wandering about'. His hand-written account continued:

The next day we was given companys to train. These consisted of about sixty natives each which was very hard for none of us spoke a word of native tongue which they spoke to us.

They would not do as they were told. They had complaints about food, weapons, ammunitions, clothes, boots and money, for some had not been paid money for years . . .

How the 'natives' were supposed to know what they had been told Barker does not make clear! 'Captain' McAleese, who was in charge at Santo Antonio do Zaire at that point, put Barker in charge of a company to defend the airport, and McPherson and Saunders in charge of another at the former Portuguese barracks. John Tilsey and 'Mike' were each entrusted with other companies. Mike Johnson was made quartermaster, responsible for feeding both troops and civilians and also for looking after radio communications. On 23 January, according to Barker's oral account:

We were to put the four companies on parade at the Portuguese barracks, where Capt. McAleese gave a boost talk interpreted by Lima. All of us British soldiers were appointed as commanders of companies . . .

He went on to list the various weapons they had – FN rifles Chinese automatic rifles, Sten guns, an anti-aircraft gun at the air-

port, two- and three-inch mortars and, in addition to the 106-milli-
metre cannon brought in by plane, another one 'pointed out to
sea', various types of machine-guns, Chinese 'stick grenades',
American bazookas and carbines and some German pistols. 'We
also had Land Rovers belonging to the Petrangol company which
we stripped and camouflaged for our personal transport.' McAleese
briefed Barker to the effect that the overall task was to defend
Santo Antonio and Barker's specific job was to train the men at the
airfield. He went about it in regulation British military style:

> The following morning we woke up at 5 o'clock and were given
> reports on the day's operations. I put the men on muster parade and
> divided them into groups of twelve men to a section, introducing the
> wearing of green flashes for the Angolan soldiers at the airfield, white
> flashes for the rear defence at the airport. We then started digging
> trenches and sand-bagging them and I taught them camouflage tech-
> niques and all the necessary military–physical training exercises. These
> routine exercises carried on for about three weeks during which there
> was no combat.
>
> We had been at the airfield for about five days when a small, six-
> seater aircraft landed with four Americans aboard, who, we were told,
> were CIA men, by McAleese. McAleese told me afterwards that the
> thin American[3] had been in Vietnam for about ten years. McAleese
> presented a report to the four Americans, who left after about two
> hours in a small yellow and white aircraft with a 'G' on the tailpiece.
> McAleese had asked the Americans for AK ammunition and anti-
> malaria tablets which were in short supply. A week later the small
> aircraft returned with the tablets, escape rations, Yashica binoculars,
> but not ammunition which was promised for later . . .

What is extraordinary from a military viewpoint is that there
seems to have been no attempt to defend Santo Antonio in depth –
at least according to Barker's report. There was no forward patrolling nor any attempt to control the only two access roads – from
Benza in the east and Corta Ferro in the south. About 4 February,
another small aircraft arrived, as mentioned earlier, this time with
Holden Roberto and the American woman journalist – Robin
Wright – aboard. Regarding the latter – who was expelled from
Luanda when she turned up to cover the trial – Barker told the
court:

3. Later identified as 'Captain Tom' Oates.

She had no camera or note-books. She went around with John Tilsey, an ex-marine, visiting the hospital and the defensive positions at the airport.

Barker stated that he was on a small reconnaissance mission along the road to Porto Rico – twenty kilometres east of Santo Antonio – when Holden Roberto arrived and, by the time he got back, Roberto had left for San Salvador taking McAleese and 'Mike' with him, because:

We heard that Callan had been killing FNLA soldiers and British mercenaries there.

It was then that Barker was informed that McAleese had been appointed commander at San Salvador – promoted to 'colonel' to replace Callan as overall commander – and that Barker was to take over at Santo Antonio. The end was fast approaching. On 7 February:

We relaxed to have some breakfast and soon after this we saw tanks advancing and they opened fire on us. As we were not equipped to fight against them, everyone panicked and scattered all round and tried to change into civilian clothing.

There was an exchange of fire and I told the British soldiers and the American girl, Robin Wright, to try and get to the boat that John Tilsey had arranged. The boat was heading towards Zaire with about twenty-one people aboard, including McPherson, Tilsey, Doug Saunders and Robin Wright. Tilsey had panicked and left Johnson and myself on the jetty. I started to panic too and ran towards the beach and a number of people followed. I saw two tanks approaching me and decided to swim to the nearest island. I stripped and started swimming across . . .

I was fired on and decided to hand myself over, heading back towards the shore. I was captured by Commander Nelson and put into an armoured car and taken to the hospital to take a FAPLA soldier to be treated. While I was in the armoured car, I told Commander Nelson that I was not a mercenary, but a newspaper reporter, because I was afraid of being shot immediately . . . but I was later identified as one by a commander who had been in Saunders' company . . .

That was the inglorious end of the western anchor of the front that Callan's mercenaries had been instructed to hold 'at all costs'. The end on the eastern sector was even more dramatic.

8 The End of the Road

On the body of a mortally wounded, fair-haired, thinnish man with a missing finger on his left hand was found a diary, with the last long entry marked: 'Feb 11/76. *Tuesday*'. (Actually, 11 February was a Wednesday, but on the battlefield – as was demonstrated by some of the witnesses at the trial – participants tend to be confused about days and dates.) It is a sombre document full of gloomy forebodings, and reveals that the author was more than just an ordinary, rank-and-file mercenary. It starts:

More English arrived on Sunday, about 24 or so – some good some bad. Also seven Americans on Monday.[1] The fiasco in England and HQ in Kinshasa is escalating and doing us no good at all. They are bleeding the Organisation and further ruining any chances we might have had.

Had a recc. to Madimba today and about 15 km walk in heat unbearable – that route again OK. One of my men, an older man died of a heart attack from heat and exhaustion – it all seems so ridiculously waistful at times. Brought the body back and informed his younger brother who is also with us – he took it well. Had a burial on Wensday morning with a proper send of. Looks very much like we will pull out if no more men or supplies are forthcoming, and that seems highly unlikely.

The problem of retreating troops has become acute with louting etc Linca [name illegible] and Sonny seem unable to inforce the curfew even at treat [threat?] of death – the Angolans are lousy and only come for what they can grab and eat. I have little respect or simpathy left for them.

The refugees are crowding the boarder and slowly the troops are going over the walls and out – but problem with the transport as they

1. Actually the groups arrived on Monday, 9 February, and Tuesday, 10 February, respectively. We have retained 'Canada's' own spelling and grammar.

take what they can and charge civilians taxi service. Made a recce to Tomboco without contact except with the Commander [Angolan] in retreat. He had the fright of his life and bailled out, smashing himself quite badly. Accidents continue. AD's [probably accidental discharges] constant and one boy with tank and barbed wire. Really they are a pathetic bunch at times – all bitch and big talk. Every time a AD happens, the Angolans fly out the gate and down the road. We can expect no support from them. Our cyanide pills become an incredible joke – to think we've been counting on them all the time!

There is nothing to elucidate this last remark, either in the diary or in statements by other mercenaries.

Part of one of the pages which preceded the 11 February diary entry – or was it a draft dispatch? – had been ripped diagonally, the way it would be done if something important had to be swallowed. The undestroyed half was headed: 'ENE', which one could imagine might have been: 'ENEMY POSITIONS', and underneath was written: 'Canada' and under that again: 'Group Two'. The entry in the diary continues:

The last two days I've spent on Recc. Megala-Lubico-Noqui [the area north-west of San Salvador reaching to the banks of the Congo river] – no problems there. But should the enemy appear the same course of events would arise. To many Chiefs and no Indians. Funny to see the River again – was a pleasant night in the Gov. house. Tried to place what arms we had in advantageous positions and organize them to some extent. To see these people one would hardly think there was a war within a thousand miles.

The enemy are advancing from Maquela and are now around Cuimba. [A little more than half-way between Maquela do Zombo and San Salvador – sixty-two kilometres east of the latter] Charley and a group went out today but have not returned. Sent my explosives men out along with an armoured car for FOP [probably Forward Observation Post] for the night.

All is set for a strike tomorrow – could be the last stand. With a little luck all could be quite effective – we shall see tomorrow. I would dearly love to hit the one last time with some success. The plan is feasable and could halt them for some time. Although I can't see us here for many more days . . . It is only a matter of time before we have to close – there strength is such that we could not possibly hold indefinitely. The south seems finished and no further support seems likely here. Talk of guerilla tactics across the boarder is purely speculative – all depends on Zaire's policy once we evacuate. All of us in Command hesitate to risk any more lives. One would appear to be in a lost cause. The lack of support from the free world makes me ashamed and sick not to say frustrated and furious at the very thought.

Many men among us won't forget – the two Mikes, Mac, Charlie and the Portuguese. Also all those who died for nothing and Callan the bastard – may he rot in hell – never could I have imagined one man could be so devastatingly destructive . . .

Meanwhile, what had Callan and his men been doing further south to warrant such criticism from this mystery man, obviously at the very top level of command? By this time, one has to distinguish two separate areas of action. One around San Salvador itself, the other around – and to the south of – Maquela do Zombo. First there is Callan's own account, written in mainly neat handwriting, addressed obviously to the interrogating officer and starting as follows (the spelling is Callan's):

Sir,
From the time I was told to move to Maquela because Damba [100 kilometres to the south] had fallen to the enemy, I had at any time only ten English soldiers manning the front at all times. We had been there for nearly two weeks constantly on patrols to keep us informed where the enemy was at all times, allways on alert. If the enemy knew how weak we was, they would have over-run us overnight, the men were getting weary and tired – not that they moaned, they were professionals. We were told by Holden Roberto that there is more men coming and to hold on, no matter what, so every man at the front was anticipating the arrival of this men, to lift the burden and to be on the offensive for a change.

After two days they came. After a meal, a cup of tea and some rest, they formed up outside our make-shift HQ in Maquela. After a quick glance around, I spotted two elderly gentlemen in their 50's. I asked them their years of service, which was about twenty to twenty-five years each with the famous battalions and a few other details, just routine procedure to give me some idea of the capabilitys. I told them I was glad to have them in charge of stores.[2] They were sergeant-majors, very capable men. I told the rest how glad I was to have them in my

2. These were subsequently identified as Brian Butcher and Ken Aitken. They both survived and will be referred to in a later chapter regarding their subsequent activities in the Lebanon.

company, and straight away I began to lay down rules and regulations and strictest discipline, and to emfasise that point, I told them that from now on I don't want to hear that word Mercenary and that they were part of a discipline unit, and discipline was more important out here because the temptations were higher. I emfasised also that any man found guilty of braking that Code of discipline – same rules as in the British Army – here there is no hanging, any man found breaking these rules – and I emfasised it strongly – they will be shot. I asked if any one does not exept this formed of discipline can leave now. No-one moved.

Next I covered the point of where the enemy was situated, our present strength, what tipe of equipment the enemy had, what little we had, and I explained my intention of going up against the tanks and the tackticks I intended to use, i.e. small killer groups with deep penetration behind enemy lines. As soon as I told my intended plan of action, there was a sudden interest among them.

Next I started asking each man, to find out his capabilities, where, what battalion and [few words illegible]. At that point it started all to come out with some telling me that they did not expect to go up against the enemy so soon, and especially against tanks and that they did not want to have anything to do with it. I asked them what the heck are they doing out here. Then they gave me a blank look and said they thought it would be different. I place all the ones that didn't want to go to the front on Side and the ones that did on the other Side.

At this point a soldier brought a message from the president Holden Roberto. It read that the enemy were breaking through the Tomboco front of my right flank, and that if I would go there straight away to stop them.

I told the men what the message read, and I asked for twenty men and one anti-tank gun 106 mm to get ready to move that minute. The men that did not want to go to the front, I told that they had to wait there and make themselves useful until I came back from Tomboco, before they can go anywhere and to start cleaning the weapons in the armoury. Before I left, I gave the order to my RSM [regimental sergeant-major Sammy Copeland] to go after the tanks with the remainder of the men, who was about twenty men left, because if they came any closer to Maquela and found no resistance they would make a [illegible, but perhaps 'thrust'] towards our position, that what they have been doing . . .

This briefing in general is confirmed by the statements of several of the mercenaries, especially those who arrived in the second group to leave London, arriving in San Salvador in two batches on 29 and 30 January respectively. The first group to leave London, including Barker, Saunders and the others, had been sent to Santo Antonio do Zaire, the others divided up between San Salvador and Maquela. Kevin Marchant described the trip by road to Maquela on the night of 1 and 2 February; a Bedford fuel truck getting stuck in the mud, also another 'over-loaded with combat rations'. They spent the night on the road. Early the following morning another big truck and a Land Rover appeared, coming south from Maquela. In the Land Rover was R S M Copeland

accompanied by a man of middle height, with dark hair and an automatic rifle, like the FAPLA use, and a pistol. It was Colonel Callan. That was the first time I had seen him. He was furious ...

The freshly arrived truck pulled the Bedford out of the mud, after the fuel cans were transferred, and Marchant continued on in the Land Rover with Callan and Copeland:

On the way Colonel Callan was arguing with R S M Sammy Copeland making comments about the 'load of shit' that had been sent to him and out of which he had to make 'a group of killers'. When we got to Maquela, we were lined up in three rows and, one by one, Callan asked us about who had recruited us and why we thought we were there. We answered him. I said that I had come as a PT instructor. That I was there for the money and that John Banks had spoken to me. After speaking to all the men, there were about twenty men lined up in a separate row. These were the ones who did not want to fight. All the others had come to fight and I could see the majority of them were ex-paratroopers or ex-SAS. When we had finished forming up, Callan said that we were 'a load of shit', that we shouldn't be there and that he would send us back to England and that he would talk about us to Banks. Turning to the other men he told them to take off us what ever we had with us. Some took away our trousers, others our equipment. Callan ordered us to stay there until he could manage to send us away and that meanwhile we should get on with cleaning and cooking. This is what we did. A little later Callan took his men and went from Maquela to I don't know where ...

Andrew McKenzie, who arrived in the first group with Barker, but had been sent to Maquela, confirmed that there had been no action at all before Callan got the urgent message from Holden Roberto. His group had spent its time in setting booby traps, planting mines and preparing defensive positions around Maquela and making a few reconnaissance patrols.

Marchant's version of what happened was that on the night of 2 February an armoured car with mercenaries aboard arrived in Maquela. They said they had just come from the front and that FAPLA tanks were on their way to Maquela.

The sergeants [Aitken and Butcher] didn't know what to do. Callan had told them we couldn't have arms, but in any case they had two trucks and a Land Rover loaded and ready to go to San Salvador.

They told us that if the FAPLA tanks arrived, we would get on the trucks and leave. Some of us were given automatic rifles and others M76 rocket-launchers. That night we saw lights approaching and, as the chief sergeant had said, we got into the trucks and waited a little while. From there we could see a series of lights, we heard some shots and there was an explosion. It had been one of us shooting a rocket-launcher, in the direction of the lights, from the top of the truck. Then the truck left . . .

According to another of the mercenaries, Barry Freeman, who managed to get back to England, the Land Rover in which Copeland had been travelling had been deliberately ambushed, after which the mercenaries who did not want to fight fled towards the Zaire border with most of the fuel and rations left at the Maquela base. McKenzie states that at Maquela, when they found the ration truck and men were missing, his group were ordered to try to catch them:

On the way, we bumped into Callan who was on his way back. We explained what had happened. Callan said: 'They're just down the road,' and said that the group who had run away had said that the Cubans and Angolans had advanced into Maquela, wiped out the forward positions, and that they had retreated. We rounded them all up and went back to Maquela. At Maquela they were told to empty their pockets, strip down to their underwear and line up against the wall. Callan then asked who had fired the 66. A man stepped forward and said: 'I did.' Callan then said that there was only one law in this land, and that was the law of the gun. He then shot him . . .

Marchant's version is that Callan shouted: 'You nearly killed

some of my men' and shot three times, waving his pistol and yell-
ing: 'This is the only law here.'

The three shots hit him in the head, the first in the forehead, the
other two in the right temple, when already on the ground. After
the first shot had been fired, he fell against the garden wall of the
house that had served as the general barracks. Immediately after,
Callan called for a driver and I immediately stepped forward. Four
other men who hadn't come to fight did the same thing when Callan
asked for four men to fight. I offered myself as driver because I was
sure that if I didn't, I would be killed one way or the other. After the
five of us had stepped forward, Callan turned to the RSM – Sammy –
and ordered that the rest of the group be put into a truck and he should
'wipe 'em out'. Another mercenary told Callan he had a friend in the
group, and Callan called him out. I didn't have a chance to say the
same for Brooks and Mott because as I came forward, Callan sent me
away . . . [Brooks and Mott were Marchant's closest friends, whom he
had persuaded to enlist].

Callan claims in his hand-written statement that, when he took
off for San Salvador after receiving the alarmist message from
Holden Roberto, he drove through torrential rain for five hours
and on arrival found the situation 'not as bad as anticipated'.
Someone in Tomboco had 'panicked a little and made the situation
worse than it was', so he turned round and headed back to
Maquela. About twenty kilometres from there, he ran into an
advance party of the runaways who told him that Maquela had
been captured and that there was a force of 'twenty tanks and a lot
of infantry there'. It was 2 a.m. on 3 February. Callan decided to
deploy his forces – mainly the runaways – in position for an
ambush in case the 'tanks' started moving on San Salvador. After
daybreak he sent a small patrol into Maquela to find out what the
'enemy' was up to and what had happened to the rest of his
company. In the meantime defensive positions were prepared and
early in the afternoon Copeland turned up and reported on having
been fired on by fellow-mercenaries. Callan gathered everyone
together and headed back for Maquela where he claimed to have
'carried out an investigation as to what had happened'. According
to him:

The two sergeant-majors told me the group [non-fighters] had got together and they were planning to mutiny, go their own way and do what they ... [an illegible word] and carry out the full meaning of the ... [two illegible words]. The one who conspired all this was pointed out for me by the sergeant major.

At this stage I would have hoped they would have realized the seriousness of the situation which they were in, and I hoped for good sense to prevail.

So once more I asked if they would come to the front. Six of them came forward, the rest stayed. I explained that in the British army the sentence for deserting and mutiny was death by hanging, out here they were to be shot.

To them it was just a joke. I could tell by their faces, like the whole trip. One big joke.

I shot the insticator of the group, and the rest were taken away for the same purpose by men of my company.

> 14/3/1976 (Signed)
> C. Georgiou.

In his confused final statement at the trial, answering a few questions by the presiding judge, Callan justified the executions as follows:

Why did I kill the mercenaries? The reason is this – an ambush is an ambush. Men with many years of experience do not exaggerate about an ambush. The men in the vehicle which was the object of the ambush were all my friends. We had been together at the front for a long time ...

In McKenzie's original oral statement about the executions, he simply said that Callan and Copeland ordered the thirteen remaining non-fighters into a truck together with Aves and McKenzie, while Copeland and the other three from the 'ambushed' Land Rover followed the truck. The body of the one shot by Callan – whose name the accused did not seem to know but who was described as an ex-paratrooper – was also placed in the truck. 'They got off the lorry, were told to walk down a hill and they were shot,' said McKenzie. 'The shots were fired by Copeland, Brody, the mechanic and a bloke called Chris. There were a couple more whose names I don't know. Then we went back to the camp.'

When McKenzie appeared in court, the version of the shooting given by Chris Dempster in the BBC *Panorama* Programme[3] was read out and he was asked if this was correct. He replied:

Yes. The executions took place in the valley. We were ordered to fire which we did. I also shot.

Did they die straight away?

I think so.

The evidence was that not a single one of the victims was killed outright. Each had to be finished off individually. Among those who admitted having delivered the *coups de grâce* was Barry Freeman of Manchester, which could explain why he was at some pains to assert that the victims of the massacre were indeed guilty of mutiny. This version however is hotly disputed by many of the others who returned. One of them, Kevin Whirity, an ex-para-trooper, gave the most complete and convincing version – confirmed in its essentials by some of the accused and by the survivors. After describing the scene in which Callan had lined up those who had come with the second British group into three rows and asked each individually who wanted to fight and who did not, Whirity said that he and his friend Dave Payden were among those who did not want 'to soldier'.

When he had finished, Callan turned round to the boys who were going to soldier and said: 'Anything you need, take it off them over there. Kit, cigarettes, watches, rings, anything you want – take it.' The others came over. One might have a short that was too tight. He'd go over to somebody his size and said 'short', and take it. Some had no right-size boots so they'd take them. The only thing I lost was a watch that was given to me by my wife. They took whatever they wanted. There was nothing we could do. We were lined up and Callan turned round and pointed to a line of wogs and said: 'These people are black – they will follow me anywhere.'

He took the men who were going to fight and loaded them on to the wagons and told us we were going to stay, under guard. They disappeared and we were left with a man called 'Butch', Brian Butcher, and Ken Aitken in command. The RSM, Copeland, left them in command. Aitken was company sergeant-major and 'Butch' was

3. See Chapter 4.

company quartermaster. 'Butch' got it into his mind that we'd all got to be kept in one place – a sort of guardroom.

The guys that were there decided that at night we were going to make a break for it because it was clear what Callan was thinking of. Some of us thought even then he was capable of shooting us. Butcher and Aitken herded us into a building which turned out to be the armoury, which suited us fine. After we were left alone, I said to the boys: 'Grab yourselves a weapon and keep it close to you. If anything happens, pick it up and start firing through doors and windows.' The armoury was a wooden building on a low brick wall which would have given some cover. During the day we wandered around, eyeing up the vehicles. A long-haired lad came along and said he could get a compass if we could raise some money. I gave him some money, others gave him cigarettes and he came back with the compass. Later we were in the HQ trying to get some food when Chris Dempster came in. He said he was up at the forward ambush position near Damba and the Cubans were coming that way. He said he would try and get back around nightfall but if anything came down the road after nightfall we would know it was the Cubans. He said this to Butcher and Aitken. As near as I can remember, he said that he was at the forward position with nothing but a group of men: 'I can't hold them,' he said, meaning the Cubans. 'They'll wipe us out and they'll come up here. They'll roll right across Maquela. There's nowhere you can go. You can stay here and wait for the Cubans to come or you can come forward with us and try to stop them.' Nobody wanted to go so he said: 'Okay.' Then he turned to Butcher and Aitken and said: 'If by dark I don't come up that road, there'll be nothing coming but Cuban tanks, troops – they've even got their own bloody aircraft.' And off he went.

At about four p.m., we noticed Aitken and Butcher looking a bit worried. They knew something was going on. You couldn't *not* know. Portuguese and black troops were coming in and at every key point they stationed a Portuguese or a black. There were some chaps on the far side of the compound, watching. Watching us. We were under armed guard. It got dark. We had some grub served up – still in the armoury ready for a break. Butcher came in and ordered us all out into slit trenches. You could see the road winding for miles to some hills. Butcher and Aitken got into a Land Rover – Payden and I rode 'shotgun' for them as we toured the town perimeter. I said: 'Hey, look at that light.' I saw a vehicle coming over the hill with only one light. Then another and another and another – until there were about nine. To me, there was only one thing it could be. Tanks travelling at night use only one light. Somebody wondered if they were Dempster's patrol, but somebody who'd seen a bit of service said wheeled vehicles don't use only one light. 'Them's tanks,' he said. A wind started up and over it everyone imagined they could hear the clatter of tank tracks. That was enough for Aitken and Butcher. 'Get moving,' they said. Before we could move there was a roar of a motor and a vehicle flashed past. It had two lights. So I thought: 'Them's tanks and that's a Cuban scout car.' Me and Dave were having a giggle at the thought that one moment we were under arrest and the next we've got weapons and were going to fight. The vehicle which went past us went up a slight gradient towards Maquela. We heard a bang and Aitken said: 'Move out' ... Away we went. We started. The vehicle after us started. Everybody started moving. We went down the road, smashed through a barrier, others went round it into the bush. One vehicle broke down and its passengers jumped on to others. Then a shell burst behind us. We thought it *must* be the Cubans, so away we went down the road, heading back towards San Salvador. We stopped outside a little village and met a patrol coming up the road. The guy in charge told us to line up by the road. He knew who we were. We were the bad guys who weren't going to fight. We thought: 'This is it.' We had our weapons and were going to have a go at them. Then Ken Aitken came along. It all stems from Aitken, and if ever I see him I'll fucking choke him. You can tell him [speaking to journalist Frank Branston] if you ever see him. Dave Payden will and all. Aitken came along, being the fucking big hero, and said: 'Everybody behind the huts and into the bush.' We all thought the Cubans were coming so everyone dived into the bush.

A few minutes later Aitken came along again, screaming and shouting: 'If everyone isn't out of that bush in three seconds I'm going to start shooting. One, two, three' – and he fires a couple of shots. I thought this was bloody serious, there's something going on. He's set us up. So we came out of the bush and lined up again. Aitken said: 'Throw your weapons on the floor. There's rifles pointing at you, machine-guns pointing at you, heavy weapons pointing at you.' There were all the vehicle lights shining on us. We thought: 'This is it.' Dave Payden and I were holding hands, squeezing, because we were frightened to bloody death. One boy dropped. The tension was too much for him. He just dropped. The tension was there. You knew what was going to happen.

He then referred to another mercenary, 'tall and stocky with a beard', still unidentified, who apparently out-ranked Aitken, and started to give orders.

We got back into the vehicles and went down the road. Callan came up later. The tall, bearded guy told Callan we were deserters, that we'd tried to make a break for it out of Maquela. We went down the road to set up an ambush for the Cubans supposed to be coming into Maquela. This speaks for itself. They gave everybody their weapons back and everybody was willing to fight then. Everybody was in the ambush position – waiting for the Cubans to come up. We were all going to take the Cubans on.

Callan came up shouting: 'Back into your vehicles! Back to Maquela!' So we went back. When we got out of the vehicles, this dirty big calibre gun [an artillery piece manned by Portuguese mercenaries] was pointing at us. We were all lined up against the wall. Callan snapped: 'Strip off!'

People have different ways of stripping. Some take their shirts off first, I take off my boots. I was bending over to undo them when Callan came up with a pistol in his hand. He said: 'Who shot at the truck?' The boy next to me said: 'I did, sir'. I was still bending at this time. Callan shot the boy in the leg ['kneecapped' him, according to other eye-witnesses] and I felt blood and bits of leg splatter into my face. The boy fell against me and said: 'Help me, Kevin,' but I pushed him away. He fell back against the wall and Callan shot him in the body and then in the head, and finished him off. [Other eye-witnesses say that the victim, David Wileman, was finished off by a Portuguese who slit his throat.]

Callan went back to Copeland and said: 'You haven't tried the machine-gun yet?' I saw Copeland looking at me. Callan said: 'You, Para, are you prepared to soldier?' I said, 'Yes, Sir.' He said: 'Out.' I said: 'What about him?', pointing at Dave Payden. 'He's a good soldier.' Callan called him out. Others said they wanted to soldier and Callan pulled them out of the line also, about half-a-dozen, including Dave and me. The rest of them, he told to continue stripping off, and when they were down to their underpants, he told them to get into the truck. He said to Copeland: 'You know what to do.' The truck moved off with a jeep with the machine-gun in it behind, trained on the truck.

In Barry Freeman's account, as published under Stewart Tendler's name in the London *Times* of 14 February – which formed part of the documentation for the trial – Freeman said that after Callan had shot the first man:

Mr Copeland was told: 'take them out of town. You know what to do with them!' Copeland laughed and ordered the recruits to strip, saying: 'You should have said you would fight but in five minutes you're going to die.'

The recruits and the execution party drove a mile out of the town, followed by the Portuguese mercenaries who had a mounted 15 mm gun. Mr Freeman said: The recruits were ordered to the left-hand side of the road and I immediately turned down the gas regulator on my FN rifle which would cause it to jam. As I was getting out of the Land Rover, Mr Copeland opened fire with a burst from his sub-machine-gun, cutting down three or four of them immediately. The others started running. Mr Copeland changed his magazine and fired after them, hitting them in the legs, back and shoulders. None of them died from the fire. We were ordered to fan out and walk along the valley shooting anybody who was alive. The Portuguese at the back of us had cocked their guns so we had no choice but to do the job. We were all forced to shoot at least one of the men in the head but to us it was just a mercy killing. Mr Freeman said: All the men were in agony. The one I shot had his left arm and shoulder hanging off. His right kneecap and the bottom part of his leg were hanging only by tendons. My rifle kept jamming, but Mr Copeland then turned his machine-gun on me. He gave me his pistol and said: 'Shoot that man.' I did so and afterwards I felt sick.

Mr Freeman said two of the other men who delivered the *coup de grâce* had died later in enemy ambushes . . .

Freeman himself, according to several of the mercenaries, later threw himself out of the Land Rover and pretended to have broken his spine – and thus saved his life. Immediately after the executions were over, Callan formed up a task force to move down the Maquela–Damba road. Marchant related what happened after he and the five other survivors were handed back their uniforms:

After we had dressed, the six of us who had escaped saw Callan and he said that I would drive the first truck and go at the head of the column and that: 'if we were men, we would save our lives'. When RSM Sammy returned [from the executions] we got into our trucks and drove out.

I was a driver for the RSM, Sammy. There were five trucks in all. When we passed the gully, the RSM said that if we looked down we would see our mates. 'Don't hold this against me,' he said, 'and don't think of shooting me. Not me, or the Colonel in the back, because if we don't get back you will be killed. So look after us.' Then he began to laugh, which made me feel sick and I could have cried. In fact, we did pass the place. I looked down to the ravine on my left and saw the bodies there, unburied. In all there must have been fourteen dead, whose names I don't know, except Brooks and Mott.

The column proceeded to Quibocolo, where it dropped off some men to reinforce the local garrison under the British mercenary, 'Captain' Spider, picking up two more Land Rovers there. It then continued southwards. Because sections of the road had been mined by McKenzie and his group, an armoured car took the lead after Quibocolo, followed by Callan in a Land Rover, then the truck driven by Marchant, with three more Land Rovers bringing up the rear. Distributed among the vehicles were thirty mercenaries. Marchant continued:

One of the Land Rovers struck a mine. Three inside died and two were wounded. A little later we came into contact with the FAPLA tanks and troops. All I remember was hearing a loud explosion in front of the armoured car and the cannon beginning to fire. We stopped, got out of the cars and hid in the grass. My truck was hit, and two Land Rovers immediately afterwards. The last carried ammunition and took ages exploding. After some time our men got into the vehicles that hadn't been destroyed and we returned to Maquela. Together with me was a mercenary medic, McIntyre, who had come with us from London, and another – seriously wounded – that we took to Maquela.
When Callan returned he sent us to rest a little and said that he had destroyed one of the FAPLA tanks. We had, I think – to be exact – three dead and twelve wounded . . .

The night was spent in Maquela and next morning – 4 February – Callan said they were to go on to a tank-destruction mission. Weapons were distributed, at least three M76s per man as well as hand-grenades, and a column of twenty-four men, with heavier supporting weapons, headed south again. This time the armoured car was missing. Marchant said that it had turned back when the column ran into the ambush the previous afternoon and, although it was not hit, it was not seen again by the survivors of the previous day's column.

We went along the road a certain time [Marchant said] but after Quibocolo we stopped the Land Rovers and continued on foot – formed into two groups. On the right hand side of the road was the group commanded by Callan. On the left was the group RSM Sammy commanded. We went on all the afternoon until at nightfall we came to a village whose name I don't know, without having encountered any FAPLA troops. We slept in this village and the next day continued walking all day. That was 5 February. At dusk we heard the sound of a Land Rover. At that time we were moving in one single group, in single file. When a Land Rover passed us coming from behind us, the shooting began. It was Callan, or a Portuguese with him, who opened fire. I think all the occupants of that Land Rover died. I was the fourth in the column, counting from the back end, with some twenty men in front of me. When the shooting began, I threw myself to the ground, that is practically didn't see anything. I heard someone say that one of the occupants was running away. A hand grenade was thrown at him. I heard Callan shout: 'Don't use hand grenades!'

Someone jumped into the road and shot the man running away with a shot from a grenade-launcher, according to what I was told later. After this incident [in which two FAPLA Land Rovers were destroyed and not one as Marchant's report suggests] we went along the road until we came across what I thought was a tank. Callan's men were at the end of the column when the shooting began. All I heard was Callan shouting – asking for more and more M76s. As fast as they passed them to him, he fired them.

Suddenly there was a big explosion and I was thrown off my feet into the middle of the road. When I recovered everybody was running, retreating and Callan and another man were being carried. We hid in the bush to pass the night and rest. We were Callan, RSM Sammy, Captain Charlie and about twenty men. Callan and another mercenary, Ginger to be precise, who had come with us in the same plane from London, were wounded. The next morning, RSM Sammy made a stretcher to carry Callan on. Later he left with another man, I mean mercenary, according to him to go and look for help in Maquela. We never saw him again.

Very few people ever saw RSM Sammy Copeland again. A description of what happened to him came from Terence White, a British helicopter pilot, also stationed in Maquela. Callan, who was badly wounded in the knees, ordered Copeland to make his way back to Maquela and get White to fly in and pick him up. White refused the rescue mission.

Mr Copeland and the corporal took me to the airport. I had a loaded gun in my pocket and was about to shoot him. But Mr Holden Roberto, the National Front president and Colonel McAleese, were there. They seemed to greet the RSM and corporal as old friends and then Colonel McAleese hit the RSM with the butt of a rifle four or five times . . .[4]

In fact, Terence White was mistaken. It was 'Shotgun' Charlie who was hit by McAleese, not Copeland.

He was wrong on several other counts – typical of a number of mercenaries who were eager to jump into print – for money or vanity – as soon as they returned. What probably happened was this.

Soon after word of the executions reached Holden Roberto's headquarters in Kinshasa, Roberto, Nick Hall, Mike Wainhouse, Peter McAleese, 'Captain Tom' Oates – with a Polaroid camera – and Mick Rennie set out in a Fokker Friendship for Maquela. At the airstrip they were met by a Portuguese mercenary sergeant whose *nom de guerre* was 'Sergeanaro' and who immediately confirmed the executions – and that Callan had been captured by the FAPLA three days earlier. Copeland and 'Shotgun' Charlie were on their way to the airstrip. A few minutes later, a Land Rover arrived. 'Shotgun' Charlie was driving, Copeland – with an AK47 in his hand – was standing up, holding on to a Browning machine-gun mounting in the rear of the vehicle. He jumped out to announce to Roberto that Callan had been captured. 'Shotgun' Charlie stood behind him, an automatic pistol strapped into his holster. Hall and McAleese had decided to greet them normally so as not to arouse suspicion but to disarm them as soon as possible.

Copeland started to describe what had happened near Damba where Callan and the others had been captured. Setting his AK47 on the ground, he knelt down to sketch a map to illustrate his account. McAleese came up behind him and kicked the gun several yards away, telling the dazed Copeland that he was under arrest, ordering him to lie face down in the dirt with his hands behind his head. Then turning on 'Shotgun' Charlie he smashed the butt of his M2 carbine into his mouth several times to stop his protests, and then ordered him to lie down, in the same position, alongside Copeland. Leaving Rennie and Wainhouse to guard the prisoners, Hall, McAleese and 'Captain Tom' set out for the scene of the

4. London *Times*, 12 February 1976.

massacre. Holden Roberto refused an invitation to join them. They dropped in at the Maquela headquarters – the former governor's palace – to pick up a guide, but it seems that the stench from the rotting bodies made the guide superfluous. It was obviously a horrifying sight. They stayed long enough to count eleven bloated bodies scattered among the bushes, in grotesque postures, with arms and legs missing. 'Captain Tom' took eight pictures and they then sped back to the airstrip, where Hall handed over the eight photos to Holden Roberto.

The prisoners were bundled into the back of the Land Rover, their hands still behind their heads and, together with Holden Roberto, they went to the Maquela headquarters. A court was improvised on the veranda. Hall, using a shabby pocket New Testament, from which the first chapters had been removed for cigarette papers, swore himself in as the 'presiding judge', McAleese as 'clerk of court' and 'Captain Tom' as the 'usher'. Hall had to turn his mind back four years to his own court-martial – at which he was sentenced to two years for black-marketing firearms and dishonourably discharged from the British Army – to get the procedure right. Seven mercenary witnesses were called to testify to Copeland's guilt – and all present volunteered to take part in the firing squad once Hall had found him guilty and pronounced the death sentence. 'Shotgun' Charlie was found not guilty – he had been elsewhere when the massacre took place – but he admitted that he had threatened 'to blow the head off' one of the witnesses, if he ever revealed what had happened. Pushing the barrel of his gun into the man's mouth, 'Shotgun' Charlie had told him he was to say the Cubans had carried out the massacre.

Wainhouse selected four from among the volunteers for a firing squad. While he was trying to get them into a kneeling position, Copeland started to run for it. Everyone fired and he was shot down a few yards from the edge of a banana grove, Wainhouse firing three pistol shots into his head to finish him off.

Holden Roberto remained inside the headquarters during the 'trial' and execution. On his instructions, Hall told McAleese that he would now replace Callan and that he had been promoted from 'Captain' to 'Colonel'.

The bazooka shot on the Maquela–Damba road at a wrongly

identified target, which hit an ammunition truck and blew up a 'killer group' instead of a tank, putting 'Commander' Callan out of action, was the end of the road for the Maquela-based operation. From then on it was every man for himself to get back across the frontier into Zaire.

A week after the executions, the American group arrived in San Salvador with a 105 mm Chinese howitzer. Their arrival brought the number of mercenaries up to about seventy-five, including forty-five British and fourteen Portuguese, together with about 500 FNLA troops – mostly raw recruits quartered in the former Portuguese barracks alongside the 'big house'. On arrival they were told by 'Colonel' McAleese that not only had Santo Antonio do Zaire and Maquela do Zombo fallen – which they knew – but also Tomboco, 150 kilometres south-west of San Salvador, which they did not know. According to McAleese, he was awaiting instructions as to which of these places he should counter-attack! One of the drawbacks, he explained, was lack of fuel. He had trucks, Land Rovers and two Chinese T-34 tanks, but only enough fuel to advance – not to retreat. Not a very reassuring situation. The group was also informed about the details of the executions of the reluctant British mercenaries. Gearhart described the situation, following the first briefing:

I had the impression of chaos. Everything seemed to be disorganized. There were arms lying about all over the place, people running from one place to another without knowing exactly what they were doing . . .

On the morning of 11 February, Colonel Mack [McAleese] sent me and Lobo del Sol, two English mercenaries and an African FNLA commander called Lima to a village near to San Salvador where, according to the colonel, there were about 600 FNLA soldiers, whom we should train. When we got there, there was only about 150 men, with arms of all types, in very bad condition, and a further seventy-five unarmed. We were there all day trying to train them . . .

On 11 February, the mercenaries were formed into three sections, each with two Americans in them. One was commanded by Grillo, who was in overall command of the Americans, another by 'Canada' and the third by the 'other' Charlie – not Callan's cousin. It was on the night of the eleventh that Lobo del Sol, having collected as much money as he could from the other American mercenaries, persuaded them that his best contribution would be to return to Kinshasa and the USA to recruit 'reinforcements'.

For the first two days, the Americans were engaged in teaching the FNLA troops:

How to throw grenades, how to use the light 66 mm anti-tank weapon, how to move under fire and other basic military tactics.

With his customary bluntness, Grillo described his disgust at the state of disorganization the Americans found on arrival:

I was given the rank of commander of the American troops and a section of eleven British soldiers. There were also 360 Angolan troops [presumably including the press-ganged raw recruits for the FNLA] to try to organize, equip, teach guerrilla tactics to, for fighting the enemy.

In two days, I did what I could. The third day they asked me if I would like to go to Cuimba [almost exactly half way between Maquela and San Salvador] to explore . . .

We never got to Cuimba because we were caught on the road. The shooting began. I jumped out of the jeep and as I tried to cross the road I realized I was wounded in the left leg. I began to shoot with the rifle but it stopped firing. I had a Uzi machine-gun. I dragged my way into the tall grass to hide. I fired about twenty-five shots and heard no more. I realized that the other soldiers were dead or captured. It wasn't worth dying for the thousand dollars I had in my pocket. [Grillo was the only one to refuse to hand over his money to Lobo del Sol!] So I let the Cuban soldiers take me prisoner. They put me on the road and I told them I would tell all the others not to shoot any more. I shouted three or four times and nobody did anything else, because they were dead or captured. They put me in a truck to go to Cuimba hospital. In Cuimba the doctors treated me and from there we went to Luanda military hospital where we were treated by surgeons . . .

In Gearhart's version:

We left San Salvador in two Land Rovers. We were: me, two English, a Portuguese, Charlie, Gus and six or seven FNLA soldiers. We stopped a few times. Gus was the commander of the group, but never actually told me what we were supposed to be doing. He just said: 'hit and run'. I thought this was some kind of reconnaissance. Every time we stopped Gus tried to see the road with his binoculars. I remember that the FNLA soldiers were the team who manned the Chinese multiple rocket launcher that we had been towing. One of the

Land Rovers broke down. We all continued in the other Land Rover. A little way from Cuimba the Land Rover was hit. We jumped into the grass. I remember that one of the English was wounded in the hand. I asked him after a while where the rest of us were. I heard Gus say that he had been hit and that we should retreat, which I could see no possibility of doing. Later, I got up and saw a soldier. I didn't shoot. I threw my gun down and gave myself up . . .

Cross-questioned at the trial by Cesner in defence of Gearhart, Grillo said:

This particular ambush could be singled out as a very good one. Gearhart never fired a shot. I believe at the very first firing he dropped his weapon and held up his hands.

On the day that Grillo and his group set out for Cuimba, Bufkin left for Kinshasa, ostensibly to bring back a Cessna-172 plane on which he was to mount a machine-gun. Bufkin was to pilot the plane while Acker would strafe the advancing MPLA troops! Bufkin took with him fifty Uzi machine-guns – highly priced on the black market in weapons – ostensibly to 'prevent them falling into FAPLA hands' according to the explanations he gave Acker. This was 14 February and on that evening Acker left with an armoured troop carrier and a Land Rover, with four British mercenaries, to observe the situation at a bridge across the Luvo river, which was being prepared for destruction by a group of sappers. This was forty kilometres north-east of San Salvador on the Cuimba road. The following day, as Acker later recounted:

After Canada's arrival we decided to send a group to Cuimba to look for Charlie and Gus before blowing up the bridge. The group that went to Cuimba was composed of me, Canada, George, a British sapper, two other British mercenaries and a Portuguese. The rest of the group returned to San Salvador because one of the FNLA soldiers had shot himself in the foot. George [Bacon, one of the original American group] and I went in the back of the Land Rover, there were three on the front seat. Some five kilometres after we had passed the turning of the Cuimba road [a junction where another road branched north to Buela, twenty-five kilometres away on the frontier] there suddenly appeared before us a large truck which was in front of the FAPLA column. The FAPLA opened fire immediately. I was wounded in the left leg while I was still in the Land Rover. In fifteen or thirty seconds there were five dead and two wounded . . .

That was virtually the end of the whole inglorious mercenary enterprise. McAleese and some others skipped out to Zaire later that same day. San Salvador was captured the following day with scarcely a shot fired and the whole of the northern front was cleared of mercenary presence – except for those in hospital and prison and a few still wandering around in the bush, plus those who lay on the battlefields and execution ground.

There remains however the cryptic note by 'Canada' of the 'last stand' strike due for the day following his diary entry – either 12 or 13 February. Acker mentions 'Canada' arriving at the bridge over the Luvo with two Englishmen and a Portuguese on the morning of the fifteenth, but he does not mention from what direction 'Canada' was coming. Another cryptic note in the diary of 'Canada' was the following (in his spelling):

C. Moss	– tank – anti-tank
Bacon	– Explosives – Mortar – Recc.
Malloy	– GPMG [probably general-purpose machine-gun]
Farman	– „
Dicken	– Sniper – Explosives – Recc.
Young	– 106 – Stalin organ [multiple rocket-launcher]
Sharpley	– Explosives – Missil
Atkins	– General – recoiless anti-tank
Kavac	– Anti-tank
Patay	–
Simanin	– Medic
Henderson	– Radio-Mortar

The twelve would amount to a fairly high-powered 'killer team' and it is reasonable to assume it was this force on which 'Canada' was counting for his 'last stand' strike. In the interview which the authors had with Comandante Margoso, responsible for the northern front and thus all operations concerned with the mercenaries, he mentioned that just before the capture of Grillo and Gearhart the FAPLA forces had been caught in a rather costly mercenary ambush in which the FAPLA lost fifteen killed and twenty wounded.

Our forces were moving up towards San Salvador when they ran into this ambush. We pulled back and carried out an outflanking manoeuvre, catching them on the San Salvador side of the original ambush. Several of them were killed and Grillo and Gearhart were captured.

The only name of Canada's twelve mentioned in the trial documents is Bacon – who was killed later on the fifteenth in the same ambush in which 'Canada' was mortally wounded and Acker captured. It seems probable that 'Canada' and the other three who turned up at the bridge were the sole survivors of the 'Section 2 – Killer Group' on the 'last stand strike'.

The final passage in 'Canada's' diary – written three or four days before he died – is a fair epitaph.

The waste in general is incalculable. I can't imagine or begin to assess the amount of arms and material already lost and the massive remainder which is sure to go the same way. It seems most men are incapable of discipline or organization – most appear to be devoid of common sense and collectively they disgust me. Most of these men weren't worth tuppence and to see any of them getting a cent for doing fuck-all will disturb me greatly.

9 Overlords and Underdogs

A basic tenet of mercenaries, and above all those that employ them, is that 'white and west are wisest and best'. If 'Canada' could bring himself to admire 'President' Holden Roberto although he is black, it was certainly because Roberto was the person he was professionally engaged to defend. Roberto was the West's man, bought and paid for fifteen years previously. But 'Canada' could not refrain from mixing praise for Roberto with the remark that 'his own people are not better, most even worse' than the white runaways whom he despised. Nor could he refrain from such remarks as that 'the Angolans are lousy and only come for what they can grab and eat', or, most revealing of all, 'We can expect nothing from them . . .' Fascinating questions had 'Canada' survived and been brought to trial would have been exactly who were 'We' and what were 'We' doing in some other people's country, 'expecting' at gun-point that local loyalties should be subordinated to 'Ours'.

What sort of mentality does it require to assume that a semi-illiterate, psychopath-criminal Callan or a lumpen-criminal Barker are superior in the military arts to a doctor-poet, Agostinho Neto, and the innumerable patriots under his command, simply because of the difference in skin pigmentation? Or that a bullet or shell from a white man's weapon speeds faster and straighter to its target than when a black hand is on the trigger? These are the sort of mistaken assumptions that brought the mercenaries to grief in every decisive encounter in Angola.

To present what happened as a white–black confrontation would be very wrong. The mercenaries were white racists to a man, but they were up against combatants with higher political, moral and ideological values – which included belief in racial equality.

The blacks and whites – there were plenty of white Angolans fighting with the MPLA, which led the mercenaries to assume they were often confronted by Cubans when they were not – fought for what they believed in: true independence, an end to colonialist oppression and exploitation, of which racism is but one aspect. Their morale was infinitely higher than that of blacks forced to identify themselves with that oppression and exploitation. If the FNLA recruits were 'going over the wall' as 'Canada' had expressed it, shooting themselves in the feet, or 'flying out the gate and down the road' every time they heard a rifle shot, it was because they instinctively repudiated the things the mercenaries had come to perpetuate and force them to fight for. If they faded away from their barracks at night and went back to their villages, or rallied to the MPLA, it was because their sympathies were with those who really fought to end oppression and exploitation.

The People's Prosecutor at the trial drew blank, uncomprehending stares from Barker, Lawlor, Evans, Wiseman and the others when he asked about their 'ideological beliefs'. The term 'ideological' was beyond them. Had they been asked a few months earlier if they believed blacks could stand up to whites on a battlefield they would have been strong and scornful in their negative responses. Most of the British accused declared themselves Labour Party supporters, but in their racism they identified themselves with the exploiters. Blacks who refused to kill their compatriots were traitors to be shot down like dogs, mongrels at that. An illiterate and chronic criminal like Barker could become an overlord in Santo Antonio do Zaire, simply because of the colour of his skin and some experience in killing fellow-humans. This could happen only because 'President' Holden Roberto, long before he gave foreign mercenaries powers of life and death over his compatriots, had become Angola's No. 1 mercenary. It was because of this that 'Canada' could describe him as 'the only man I have strong feelings for . . .' As for the merits necessary to win the admiration of a 'Canada', there was the testimony of an eighteen-year-old ELNA conscript, Antonio Joaquim Bumba. He had been rounded up with some other youngsters and sent to a training camp at Kienda, thirty-two kilometres south-west of San Salvador.

Officially in charge was ELNA commander Tola, but in fact the camp was run by three mercenaries whose names Bumba did not know. His dictated statement reads:

> During the last period of training only the mercenaries were in charge. During the final marches if anyone got left behind because he was tired, the mercenaries would shoot him dead, saying they wanted soldiers, not women or weaklings . . .

> In early February . . . Holden Roberto, president of the FNLA, came to Kienda with N'Gola Kabango an FNLA leader [Minister of the Interior in the transitional three-movement government], and some mercenaries. We were ordered on parade and Holden Roberto spoke, saying that seeing ELNA troops were retreating from the combat fronts in the face of the women of the FAPLA, he would have to take very tough measures as from that day.

> Discipline was going to change and would be very tough since running away would no longer be tolerated and now there were other commanders who would not run away. He also said that no matter if they were soldiers or commanders, anyone who ran away would be killed by the mercenaries who could do as they liked and were instructed by him to do this.

> In addition, President Holden Roberto said that those who did not want to be soldiers should take off their uniforms, hand over their weapons and go to join their families. I was too afraid to do this having been already beaten several times by the mercenaries using their military belts, as a result of which I have injuries not yet healed.

> Those who handed over their uniforms and weapons went towards the road, and after about five minutes some mercenaries went in the same direction in a car. There was a lot of shooting and we never saw our companions again . . .

Thus it seemed that the technique Callan had used to purge his ranks had quickly been adapted to the ELNA recruits as well. One of the witnesses testified that he had been in Quibocolo when the first mercenaries arrived in January 1976. Garcia Vauma Kenene Gingue said:

> They immediately occupied the former residence of the district officer of Quibocolo. They called together the FNLA garrison and made them stand in formation. They then disarmed them, took away their military equipment including their uniforms, leaving them completely nude, since these men did not have one single article of civilian

clothing. After that they were told they were no longer soldiers and that they should go away and never return to that region or they would be killed immediately. Since two of them were standing in formation in civilian clothes, the chief of the mercenaries asked them if they were FNLA soldiers. When they said they were, he asked why they presented themselves in military formation in civilian clothes. The two replied that this was because they had washed their uniforms which were still drying.

The chief of the mercenaries, speaking in a loud voice, drew his pistol and fired at the two Angolans, killing them. He wore two pistols, one on each hip, and another weapon across his chest . . .

He easily identified Callan as the 'chief of the mercenaries'. He was described by several witnesses as habitually carrying two pistols, plus a sub-machine-gun. Asked how the mercenaries behaved in general, Gingue, a Quibocolo resident, said:

They used to go around in groups. At first they paid for things in money but later they demanded what they wanted and just showed their weapons. When they knew the FAPLA were advancing they got worse, threatening people, shooting people, mining the roads, paths and even the fields.

Two other witnesses described a scene at a club in San Salvador when Callan stalked in, apparently looking for ELNA deserters, firing shots in the air from both his pistols and ordering everyone to stay where they were or be shot. He walked from table to table, pulling up trouser legs, looking for military boots.

As soon as he discovered someone wearing military boots [said Anhibal Palhares Junior], he made them get up and go over to the wall. There were five or six people together there. Looking at them like a madman and roaring with laughter he started beating them up with the help of two African soldiers and two mercenaries. The rest of his group kept their guns pointed at those that were being beaten. After they had beaten them for more than thirty minutes, they made them get into a Land Rover and drove them to the palace . . . [where the mercenaries had their headquarters].

Palhares Junior claimed that no one ever saw or heard of them again, but that he had later seen a Land Rover leave the palace with 'about eight bodies covered with blankets'.

At all levels, it is clear that the mercenaries had nothing but contempt for the ELNA troops they were supposed to be leading into battle. A letter found on the body of Stuart McPherson, apparently to his ex-wife Liz, together with a draft speech to the ELNA troops under his command, speak for themselves:

Dear Liz,
You can see by my address that I am now back fighting with the mercenaries in Angola, you have probably heard it on the television. If I pull out of this alright I will be coming back to England with quite a lot of money so I hope you will allow me to see the kids. I was in no position at Christmas to give the kids anything, but I will make sure they get something when I get back to England. We are fighting against the Russians and Cubans. We are trying to hold the most important town in Angola, but we are vastly outnumbered. These Nig-Nogs have no idea how to be soldiers. If they see a tank they drop their weapons and run. I am working fourteen hours a day trying to get these blokes ready for battle. The big problem is the language barrier. None of them here can speak English and so it is very difficult to get through to them. The whole town is starving and so all the food has to be rationed out. This is a big job on its own as everybody is fighting to get food ...
[Letter unfinished and unsigned]

McPherson's draft pep talk ran as follows:

As from today, I am going to be responsible for making you into soldiers. I want my two companies to be the best in the camp. I want every soldier to be very fit, as a fit soldier is an alert and efficient soldier. His chances for survival is far greater than an unfit soldier. Any soldier who breaches any order given by me or my sergeants will be sent to prison where he will be subject to extreme physical exercise.

I will be giving all drill orders in English and so it is in your interest to learn the sound of them. I will not tolerate slovenliness from any soldier.

You will be known as Four company and Five company and known as Commandant Square. I will get you all the same arms when they arrive. In the meantime I will drill you like soldiers. I do not want any soldiers disappearing after dinner like yesterday. Any soldier who fails to attend muster parade at 2 o'clock will have committed a breach of discipline and will be punished.

If you have any problem such as being sick, report to your section sergeants who in turn will report to me, that way I will know where each soldier is.

One, two and three companies are beginning to look like soldiers, but you have not had any training yet and so we have to catch up with them, then overtake them. I will lead you into battle and I want to be proud of my two companies.

McPherson might as well have been a man from Mars as far as the hapless recruits were concerned. As the penalty of misinterpreting his gibberish drill 'sounds' was prison and very likely a bullet in the head, the total lack of morale of the mercenary-trained ELNA troops was more than understandable. And as Callan's 'law of the gun' applied almost daily to some unfortunate who crossed his path, it could only have confirmed the general impression, among whatever FNLA supporters were still around, that they had been sold out to a bunch of madmen. John Banks repeated to a London press conference what he had told Roden in Kinshasa after his first visit to San Salvador – that he had personally seen Callan shoot twelve people, one of them an ELNA soldier killed by a shot in the mouth because he was accused of rape. Wiseman relates that when his group fell into an ambush on the way to Damba and asked Callan what to do with a wounded mercenary that he had just rescued from an exploding jeep, Callan said 'Shoot him!'

If the mercenaries treated the troops and population under their control, and even their own fellow-mercenaries, in such a way, it is easy to imagine the fate of suspected MPLA supporters. According to the Ghanaian electrician, Nai, Callan told eighty MPLA prisoners in the San Salvador jail that they would all be killed. Anhibal Palhares Junior, quoted earlier, referred to an atrocity which he witnessed on 4 February 1976. There was no mistaking the date because it was the anniversary of the start of the MPLA's national liberation struggle – the day in 1961 when Luanda militants armed with knives and clubs attacked the capital's main prison and other buildings in an effort to free political prisoners. Afraid of reprisals against suspected MPLA supporters – of which he was one – in San Salvador that day, he had left the city on a long walk which brought him to the banks of the Luanda river, south of the city:

At about 4 p.m., I heard the sound of a vehicle approaching. I hid in a field near the river bank. The vehicle stopped and I could hear men speaking in English and the voices of other people saying: 'Please don't kill me.' 'I've not done anything.' 'Please why do you tie my hands?' The only replies were loud laughter. I heard the name 'Charlie' mentioned frequently. After some minutes there was the sound of firing and screams and cries of agony. I ran off further into the bush. I later went home but didn't tell anyone because I was afraid if the mercenaries knew I was present, they would kill me.

On 11 February, I went back. There were still a number of bodies along the river bank and some others caught up in the bridge supports. Again I heard a vehicle approaching and moved back into the field. There were more shots and cries . . .

Nammock told the court that on the day following his arrival in San Salvador he went out on a reconnaissance patrol, with 'Shot-gun' Charlie, his own friend Andy Holland, two other mercenaries and two FNLA soldiers. It was 9 February:

We drove in an armoured personnel carrier. When we were crossing a bridge, we stopped and Charlie, the ex-para, showed us bodies floating in the river. I counted about ten bodies. Later, in San Salvador, I heard some mercenaries saying that the FNLA commander, who I think was an African who spoke English, had taken the people to the bridge and killed them. We saw blood on the bridge . . .

In his hand-written deposition, Nammock stated that the ten bodies he had counted were caught on trees, and as it was a fast-running river he assumed that 'other bodies must have been carried away'. In that same statement, Nammock recounted a conversation with McKenzie:

He told me that Charlie and others I don't know used to go out at night to interrogate and kill people. Charlie didn't kill them but shot them in the stomach. Other mercenaries would shoot them in the head . . . Charlie told me that he himself had killed two people with a Verey pistol that fires phosphorus shells. [Some other witnesses referred to 'Charlie' as having customarily used a sawn-off shot-gun.] 'Charlie' told me that Callan took his shot-gun off him.

He said that he worked for the man at the top, the 'President' Holden Roberto, and did not receive any money, that he would be paid when his work was finished . . .

A question begging an answer was why Holden Roberto had to turn to depraved characters such as Callan, 'Charlie' and other degenerates, especially in the northern frontier area, which was supposed to be his own heartland. If McPherson wrote to 'Liz' about 'trying to hold the most important town in Angola', he had certainly been briefed to that effect. San Salvador was the birthplace of Holden Roberto, the capital of the ancient Kongo kingdom, from the traditional rulers of which Roberto was descended. If there was any place where tribal loyalties were strong, it was there among Holden Roberto's own Bakongo tribal people.

But during almost fifteen years of armed struggle the Angolan people had grown up to a point at which tribal loyalties – although important – were no longer decisive. This is a fact which neither Holden Roberto nor Savimbi, head of UNITA, have ever grasped. An all-Angolan national feeling was born in the armed struggle, as well as a class feeling, both of which cut across tribal boundaries. The most crucial factor was that the people had experienced nothing but oppression at the hands of the FNLA and another was that although Holden Roberto projected himself as an Angolan leader – and for a certain period as the *only* leader – at the time he engaged the mercenaries to fight his war for him, he had spent about five of his fifty-five years in Angola and had never once visited the battle front against the Portuguese. Three of those five years were during his childhood. All the rest of the time he was in Zaire or in other African and Western countries. Holden Roberto was a fabrication of the late President John Kennedy at a time when he was looking around for some compliant potential leaders ready to implement an 'African policy', which Kennedy perceived the United States was going to need. It was at the start of the 'African decade' when many former British, French and Belgian colonies and territories were to get their independence. Holden Roberto was the man chosen for Angola.

When the *New York Times* revealed on 20 December 1975 that Holden Roberto had been on the CIA pay-roll since 1961, this was no surprise to those who had followed the African scene. Some of the details were new and could only come – as they did – from CIA files. The facts that Roberto had an annual retainer of 10,000 dollars to collect and transmit information to the CIA, and that in January 1975, the 'Committee of 40' presided over by Henry Kissinger and CIA chief, William Colby, had given Holden Roberto 300,000 dollars to reactivate his armed struggle against the MPLA, were details that had hitherto not come to light.

It is true that Roberto was helped to a speedy rise in the world by some progressive African leaders who have since bitterly regretted it, among them, President Ahmed Sekou Touré of Guinea. But the murdered Congolese leader, Patrice Lumumba, and the well-known Martinique revolutionary, Franz Fanon, were also taken in by him.

In a very self-critical and frank analysis – made on the eve of a meeting of the Organization of African Unity – at Addis-Ababa in January 1976, Sekou Touré said:

> We discovered that Holden resided permanently in Kinshasa and had never gone to the battle front. Thus we had to change our attitude, confronted with the evidence, and, at the same time, we understood how well-founded were the documents that friends of the peoples of Africa had several times communicated to us and which showed that Holden Roberto had been taken over by imperialist special services from the time when he worked in our diplomatic service ...

Another personality with more intimate details of what had been going on inside the FNLA from the time the first shots were fired in March 1961, by the UPA (Union of Angolan People), the forerunner of the FNLA, is Comandante Margoso, the best Angolan soldier Holden Roberto ever had on his side. He was in charge of the northern front – the only place where the FNLA had any combat troops – from the start of the armed struggle but was later withdrawn by Roberto because he insisted on co-operation with the MPLA in fighting the Portuguese, whereas Holden Roberto's instructions were that he should fight exclusively against the MPLA. For years he was held a virtual prisoner – at times a veritable prisoner – in the FNLA base and training centre at Kinkuzu, south of the Zaire capital. There he found great discontent among officers and men, because of the inaction and total lack of liaison with the FNLA guerrillas inside Angola. This eventually led – in March 1972 – to a mutiny inside the camp and an unsuccessful attempt to assassinate Holden Roberto. The mutiny was suppressed by Zaire tanks and paratroopers; all forty-five staff officers, including the general staff, were executed, only Margoso escaping by crossing the river to Brazzaville. Over a period of almost a year, he organized the gradual escape of many of the FNLA troops at the Kinkuzu base, all of them, with Margoso at their head, placing themselves at the disposal of the MPLA. Holden Roberto's armed forces never recovered from the wiping-out of virtually their entire officer staff and the defection of its best-trained recruits.

It was to repair this damage that he later turned to People's China for instructors and military equipment and had to fill the gap in his armed forces first with Zairean troops, later with mercenaries. As his troops were never engaged in real fighting, there was no graduation of commanders from the ranks, as happened within the FAPLA and in all guerrilla armies constantly engaged in combat. Tribal loyalties were not sufficient to provide a flow of recruits ready to make sacrifices for the sort of régime which the FNLA installed wherever they held temporary power – a régime of plunder, rape and violence, totally lacking anything resembling an administration, capped by the introduction of foreigners with power of life and death over every Angolan citizen.

Small wonder that Callan and his mercenaries, fleeing after Callan's last disastrous bazooka shot, found no support among Holden Roberto's fellow-tribespeople, as they tried to make their way back over the frontier. We left them at the moment when Copeland was dispatched to find a helicopter, with Marchant describing their progress:

After the explosion, Ginger, who had a broken leg, had asked us to leave him where he was and we left him. When Callan heard this, about twenty minutes after the explosion, he sent a group to go and fetch Ginger. There were four or five men. I never heard or saw any more of them.

After Sammy left, we carried Callan for a time, then Captain Charlie, who was Callan's right-hand man, decided to leave, according to him also to go and find a helicopter to get us out of there. He said he would need at least five days. He left with a Portuguese whose name I don't know. The other Portuguese had probably died during the explosion. We were reduced to eight men: me, Callan, McIntyre, McKenzie, Wiseman, Lawlor, Evans and another [Antony Brody] whose name I don't know ... We got to a hut where there was a black man and woman.

It was the cabin of João Antonio, wild animal trapper, and his wife, Sende Isabel. They were two of the most memorable witnesses at the trial not only because of their simple manner and simple truths but also their manner of handling the sophisticated cross-questioning of the British lawyer, Stanbrooke.

João Antonio, tall, straight and lean, with crinkly hair and a face which seemed to have been hewn out of coal, was from the tiny hamlet of Kinsimba, near Quibocolo. He looked somewhat out of place in the solemn atmosphere of the court, with floodlights and two tiers of TV cameras and photographers, not to mention the unaccustomed new sky blue shirt and trousers with which all witnesses from the rural areas were provided. To put him at his ease the People's Prosecutor said:

You may now relax. You are in a People's Court – a true Court of the people. This may all seem like a dream – but we now have our independence. People were badly treated before. Now we all have full and equal rights. Tell us what happened!

João Antonio explained how he had been in his hut one afternoon when he heard a noise. Going to the door he saw some white men approaching with guns. They gestured for him to come and help carry one 'with two pistols' who was wounded. The whole group later installed themselves in the little cabin which he shared with his pregnant wife, Sende Isabel, 'drinking our palm wine and eating our ground-nuts'. As he spoke no Portuguese, an additional court interpreter was required for the rippling, musical Kikongo language which he spoke. After a few days, during which every move was under the guns of one or another of the mercenaries (Callan as usual very quick to draw his pistol), shooting was heard in the distance and the mercenaries made signs that João Antonio must guide them to another place. In the meantime they had eaten up all the meagre food in the couple's kitchen garden, pulling up unripe manioc by the roots or breaking the branches, Callan urinating on the floor and in general making their life intolerable.

After they heard the shooting they thought the FAPLA were very near so they must move to another place. They asked where was the nearest village. I said I don't know. But I was forced to take them. They wanted my wife to stay behind, but she said she would go with her husband. If he died, she would die ... When the way was long they began to threaten me. One grabbed me by the throat. I got down on my knees and said: 'Don't kill me! Don't kill me! We're nearly there!'

When we arrived there, they made me tell the people not to run away. [It transpired that both João Antonio and Callan had enough rudimentary Portuguese to understand each other.] But I tricked them in such a way that the people understood what was going on. The headman told them that the mercenaries were not all they should be.

During that night the people left the village. Next morning the mercenaries questioned me – where have they gone? The headman said they had gone into the surrounding fields because they were afraid of wild animals. Again one of them grabbed me by the neck, but the headman said: 'Better leave him alone. The people will soon come back ...'

Taking advantage of the mercenaries going into a hut where one of them had found some tobacco, João Antonio ran away, explaining it was better for Sende Isabel to stay where she was. (She was about three months pregnant.)

I hid for a while in the grass, then headed towards where I thought the FAPLA were. I ran into two Jeeps with FAPLA in them and explained the situation. They took me straight to a headquarters and then set out to catch them.

One mercenary wrote that it is easier to catch or kill a black man than a lion! Was it not easier for you to hand the mercenaries over to the FAPLA than to catch wild animals?

I've caught leopards and other wild animals – but those mercenaries – really I don't know how I managed it!

Stanbrooke questioned him as follows:

Comrade Antonio: Crops and hunting is a very honourable way to live ... You have also had terrible experiences. Callan had two pistols – yes?

Yes.

Did you understand they were loaded – with bullets?

Someone who goes to hunt with a gun, does he take bullets or not?

Exactly right. Did he wave them at you?

I expected to be killed.

It was he who gave orders to the others?

Yes. He gave the orders.

And to make sure they did what he said, he had the guns?

That's what I understood. He said: 'I am commander' and pointed his gun at me.

In her statement your wife has stated ... that you 'got down on your knees and asked to be forgiven by the mercenaries and one of these, perhaps more humane than the others, began to argue with the others, and put himself between the mercenary and my husband'. Is that right?

My wife has her own mouth and can say what she thinks. She is honourable and always speaks the truth. I am confident she will tell the truth but I don't know what is in my wife's mind.

Did you get on your knees?

Yes.

One mercenary got between you and the man who was threatening and pleaded for you?

I am here before the Court and can't start inventing things. I can't say that happened. I can't tell lies, only say what I know.

Your wife said that happened.

She will come later and you can ask her.

Some behaved better than others?

A hound that hunts an animal is sorry for him? Or just goes after him? If a pack of hounds goes after an animal, are some just going to play with the animal – or are they all out for the kill?

But you weren't killed, were you?

And if I hadn't run away? I didn't offer them ground-nuts, but they took them all ...

So it went on with Stanbrooke unable to extract a single point. Then came the turn of Sende Isabel, by now in an advanced state of pregnancy, a placid beautiful face with a very intent and self-assured gaze. The main questioning was regarding the behaviour of the mercenaries, the threats to herself and João Antonio, and whether one of the accused – Stanbrooke's client – had behaved somewhat better than the others. In her original statement she had conceded this point, but for reasons best known to herself she did not want to concede it in court. There was a dramatic moment, when she was asked to step forward and recognize the one who was 'worse than the others'. She turned round from facing the bench, to gaze at the accused. Her whole body, from swollen stomach to eyes and pursed lips, was a study in concentration, a huntress watching for a rustle of grass or movement of leaves to reveal the prey or a lurking danger. After a long, intense look she pointed with finger, chin and stomach to McKenzie, the only one she recognized because all had had beards and tattered uniforms when she knew them. Now they were clean-shaven and pink, smart in their caramel-coloured overalls. The sort of wild beasts she was used to did not change their appearance from one month to another! So she failed even to identify Callan. Stanbrooke questioned her:

Comrade Isabel, Callan gave orders to the others all the time, didn't he?

I don't know their names.

The one who was injured was the one who gave the orders?

Yes.

Did the mercenaries have arguments among themselves?

We didn't know what they said, they didn't know what we said.

Did you make a statement about what happened?

In my house?

Yes.

When they came about 3 p.m., my husband went outside because of the noise. We thought it was monkeys. He called me. When I came and saw white men with guns, my husband said: 'Put up your hands.' So I did – like that [raising her arms].

You told the investigating officer that one of the mercenaries threatened your husband and another interceded to save his life. That a more 'humane' mercenary saved your husband from being shot. Is that right?

There was not a single good one among them. They were all bad.

Marchant's account was to the effect that after a few days in the hut Callan sent McKenzie and Brody, whom he still referred to as 'another mercenary whose name I do not know', together with João Antonio and Sende Isabel, to see if they could find some people to carry him, but that: 'We didn't see them again either.' McKenzie claimed that he and Brody reached the village, but there were no stretcher-bearers. They headed back towards the cabin, heard shooting in the area, decided the others had been discovered and set out 'to make our way back to our own lines'. They ran into FAPLA at Quibocolo, where Brody was killed and McKenzie captured.

During the four or five days we passed in the hut [continued Marchant] we talked among ourselves and everyone wanted to be rid of Callan because of what he had done. However we were sure that the RSM and Charlie would come back and if they found us without Callan they would kill us.

At last we decided to leave the hut. We took Callan on the stretcher, but it broke and we had to carry him on our backs, taking it in turns. Not very far from the hut, we met FAPLA troops, we saw them and hid. But Callan, who had an M76, began to fire. We only had two automatic rifles and two pistols, one of which was Callan's. The FAPLA's soldiers returned Callan's fire and Callan gave the order to retreat. He called the medic, McIntyre, to have a look at him, and then we started to run. The FAPLA soldiers came after us, continuing to fire. We thought that Callan and the medic had been killed, because according to what Callan had said the FAPLA didn't take prisoners, and he was always saying to his men he didn't want any prisoners and that they didn't take prisoners – that they always killed them. But Callan is a murderer.

I didn't see Callan or McIntyre again. This is when we began our flight which lasted about twenty days. That night we rested and at day we walked northwards, guided by the position of the sun, because we had neither map nor compass.

During those twenty days we had to cross rivers and one of them had such a strong current that we lost the two automatic rifles that went to the bottom of the river. We were left with one pistol and one grenade which we later handed to the peasants that caught us. The group consisted of myself, Lawlor, Evans and Wiseman. We were caught in a village not far from Maquela. Me, Lawlor and Wiseman had gone to try and get some food. Evans had stayed because his feet were hurting. We three were taken prisoners and before the FAPLA arrived next day the people of the village caught Evans. The FAPLA took us to Maquela where they gave us food and medical treatment . . .

In other words, these highly paid soldiers had wandered around in circles for some twenty days, lost their weapons and ended up some thirty-two kilometres from where they started! Fortuin – who had twisted his ankle – had been ordered to hand over his grenade-launcher to Brody in exchange for the latter's automatic rifle, and to make his way back as best he could. After a near encounter with some FAPLA troops, he managed to escape into the woods:

I wandered in the woods for I don't know how many days, passing through several villages where they told me the way to the border, until I arrived at a village where there was a doctor called Antonio, who said he was from the FNLA and told me to rest in his house. In fact the doctor was from the MPLA and, while I was sleeping, he planned my capture with the villagers. After capturing me, they took me to Quibocolo, where they handed me over to FAPLA.

The last to see Callan – until they met in the court – was McIntyre.

We began to run away on Callan's orders. Before that he had held on to my arm and I had the impression he wanted me to stay with him. But later he sent us away. Callan stayed with a pistol and an M66. In the end I found myself alone. Two days later I came to a village where I stayed until the FAPLA came to collect me.

The authors asked Comandante Margoso why the mercenaries had not done better in Angola. After all, across the frontier in the Congo they had been quite effective – even against what were considered the toughest troops of the British army – the famed Gurkhas, serving under the United Nations flag. Margoso, about as tough and experienced a guerrilla fighter as one could find, with fifteen years of military–political struggle behind him, replied:

They were unsuccessful because we had the people, the masses with us. Whenever you have the people on your side you win.

What did this mean in practical terms. Eyes and ears? Information about enemy movements? Protection and food?

More than that. They also participated in the fighting. Even though it was supposed to be FNLA territory, they fought with us against the mercenaries. It was the people who captured most of them and guided us to capture the others.

But, in the Congo, the mercenaries were successful fighting against regular troops under the UN – the Gurkhas for instance who have a high reputation as fighters?

But what were the UN troops fighting for? Were they defending their own country? Was there any reason for the local people to support them? No. And the Gurkhas? They didn't know why they were fighting, except the British paid them to fight. They had no interest in the country – no links with the people. They almost certainly despised the Congolese as the white mercenaries here despised the Angolans. Despite their techniques and weapons, the mercenaries were thrashed here, above all because we had the people with us.

The remarks of Comandante Margoso were like a positive to 'Canada's' negative. The other side of the medal. A lesson for mercenaries and their recruiters – and for their intended victims also!

10 What Next?

When Bufkin had Acker and Lobo del Sol prepare card indexes of the most likely candidates from those who replied to his various advertisements and publicity stunts, Angola figured very small in his schemes. In fact when Acker contacted him, Bufkin had already written off Angola because funds had run out. Once the card indexing was completed, Acker and Lobo del Sol returned home to await possible assignments. A week or so later, Bufkin called Acker to say he had a job for him in Venezuela, 'tracking down some bandits', but the job did not come off. The next offer was 'to break a man out of gaol in Mexico for the Mafia'. According to Grillo, it concerned:

A man of American nationality who was in prison in Mexico for having got involved in some drug traffic deal, and that a California syndicate wanted to have rescued for a million dollars because he had a lot of valuable information about the activities of that California syndicate . . .

This also fell through, but Grillo was asked if he would like a job collecting money for someone in California 'who had a lot of creditors' (presumably debtors). When that was not quite to Grillo's taste – why move to California to perform the same sort of strong-arm 'squeeze' jobs he was doing in New York? – Bufkin, in Grillo's words:

asked me if I would be interested in taking part in an operation which was still being planned which was to blow up a Soviet ship. I didn't show any interest in any of these plans, because I still didn't have much confidence in Bufkin . . .

As related by Gearhart, there was a plan to blow up a Soviet freighter to block the entrance to Luanda harbour to gain time to build up the FNLA–UNITA–mercenary forces. But that Bufkin had much more ambitious, long-range plans was made clear from the circular letter, issued in the name of the MFG (Mercenary Forces Group), found on Grillo at the time of his capture. Although undated, as mentioned earlier, it must have been written between 6 January and the first days of February 1976, that is shortly after Congress cut off funds for Angola. Addressed to 'Bufkin's Mercs.', it ran:

All funds for the Angola contract have run out. However there are hard-core mercs. passing through Kinshasa, Zaire, by way of the FNLA. At the time of this writing, no money is available for transportation, but for those who wish to follow the 'underground railroad' the following steps are necessary:

(1) Make contact with 'Garcia', c/o FNLA headquarters in Kinshasa, Zaire. Phone no. 257-51. He has been meeting personnel at the airport in Kinshasa.
Important: Do not call him unless you will, without a doubt, leave for Kinshasa.

(2) Notify him of the time of your arrival.

(3) Take only civilian clothing that you would be willing to throw away. Take camy [camouflage], jungle fatigues, soft cover boots, back pack, web gear, and normal personal equipment (knife, eating utensils, etc.).

Note: Do not attempt to take a firearm or explosives.

From this part of the circular, one could deduce that, before Congress cut off CIA funds, there was no problem of funds for transportation via the Bufkin network, and the next part also makes it clear that Bufkin was singularly well-informed from what could only have been the CIA's 'dirty tricks department'. Grillo, however, grumbled that when they got to Kinshasa airport: 'General Garcia of the FNLA was supposed to be waiting for us, but he wasn't. So, in order to leave the airport, we had to bribe the customs officials and go by taxi to the barracks of the FNLA...' Bufkin continues:

Most mercs. went up to the UNITA forces in the South by way of South Africa. *Do not* attempt to go this route at this time. You will bomb out. Presently they are not taking American mercs. in the

UNITA forces. There exists, in the near future, a possible change in this area. If so, we will notify you of these changes ...

In fact the UNITA forces seem to have been sufficiently served by the regular units of the South African army and large numbers of Portuguese, either former members of the Portuguese armed forces organized in the Spinolist ELP, referred to earlier, or 'vigilante'-type bands of former Portuguese settlers, integrated into the UNITA command. The extent of Portuguese 'free-booter' participation with both the FNLA and UNITA forces was very great and the fact that large numbers of armed Portuguese were captured after Angola's independence on 11 November 1975 speaks for itself.[1]

The mercenaries to whom Bufkin seems to be referring as having gone via South Africa were probably those who, like Gearhart, had responded to Pierre Walt's 'World Wild Geese Association' advertisements, or had offered their services direct to 'Mad Mike' Hoare through his 'Wild Geese' mercenary centre in South Africa. According to press reports, Hoare was recruiting mercenaries but offering them at higher prices than whoever was footing the bill was prepared – or needed – to pay. South African regulars 'for free' were obviously a more attractive proposition.

The illusions that at least some South Africans had as to the decisive role that the mercenaries could play and the exaggerated reports of their numbers can be judged by a report in the *Daily Telegraph* of 2 February, by that paper's correspondent in Johannesburg, Christopher Munnion. Under the title 'Mercenaries Could Change Course of Civil War' Munnion wrote:

The belated but well-organized arrival of more than 1,000 White mercenaries to oppose the Soviet-backed MPLA movement in Angola

1. The status of captured Portuguese, many of whom were born in Angola, and others who – like the South Africans – were members of regular armed forces, had not been clarified at the time of writing. However they seem to be in a category apart from the imported mercenaries, which is why their activities are not covered here, apart from incidental mention in cases where they were integrated into the forces under Callan's command. *Time* magazine of 23 February 1976 put at 2,500 the number of 'Portuguese–Angolan Volunteers' serving with UNITA, plus 1,000 mercenaries of various nationalities.

might again turn the tide of the civil war, diplomatic observers forecast
yesterday.

Although the mercenaries are assembling in several different groups
in Zaire, South Africa and South West Africa, the organization and
funding behind their emergence on the Angolan scene indicates a large
degree of co-ordination, the sources said. Several hundred mercenaries
from Britain, France, West Germany and Belgium have already joined
the FNLA army of Senhor Holden Roberto in Zaire and have been in
action against the MPLA's Cuban forces in Northern Angola ...

The Zaire-backed FNLA was recently routed from most of its
strongholds in Northern Angola by a steamroller offensive by the
Marxist forces, equipped with advanced Russian weapons and heavy
artillery ...

For the record, the northern campaign was waged almost exclusively by MPLA troops and there were no 'advanced Russian
weapons and heavy artillery', except the multiple rocket-launchers
used to halt the Zaire–FNLA advance on the Bengo river, seventeen kilometres north of Luanda. What heavy weapons were available were used to chase the South African forces south. The
destruction of roads and bridges in the north precluded much
movement of heavy weapons. Examination of the battlefields at
crucial points at Carmona and Negage for example, and the roads
leading to them, showed that the main weapons used by the
FAPLA forces were heavy machine-guns and shoulder-fired
bazookas. This was confirmed by the accused at the Luanda trial.
The Zaire–FNLA forces were essentially put to flight by well-
organized short-range ambushes. Nevertheless the *Daily Telegraph*
report is interesting because of its revelation of the state of mind in
South Africa, its confirmation of certain aspects of the Bufkin circular, and of long-range intentions.

The pro-Western movement, which for years has received the backing
and support of the Central Intelligence Agency, has reverted to guerrilla tactics behind the MPLA lines on the Northern Front and is
preparing for a counter-offensive which will be led by the newly arrived
mercenaries.

Although there is little evidence of large-scale involvement by
American mercenaries, the White soldiers of fortune already in Africa
are prepared to believe they are being funded and equipped indirectly
by the CIA.

In Johannesburg, about 600 mercenaries are assembling, apparently awaiting contracts to fly into Southern Angola to join Dr Jonas Savimbi's hard-pressed UNITA forces.

Many of them are members of the 'Wild Geese' organization of those who fought in the Congo under Col. 'Mad Mike' Hoare in the 1960s. Col. Hoare, in a recent bulletin to members, said he had offered his services to his old friend, President Mobuto of Zaire ... Mercenaries gathering in South Africa believe they will be replacing the South African forces withdrawn from UNITA's frontlines on orders from Pretoria.

One oft-repeated suggestion which is difficult to confirm is that mercenary units and equipment are being flown into Southern Angola in unmarked aircraft from airfields in South West Africa and Rhodesia ...

Munnion's dispatch certainly explains Bufkin's 'hold-down' instructions in his circular letter. Mercenaries were piling up in Johannesburg faster than they could be absorbed – or financed.

American participation in Angola was not limited to those appearing, or named, at the Luanda trial, or to the anonymous CIA agents who flew into Santo Antonio do Zaire. At the Sá da Bandeira (now Lubango) air base, the Portuguese school-teacher who was captured by the South Africans on the first day of their drive north – and who was held prisoner at the air base – told of almost daily landings there by unmarked American C130 cargo planes. Sá da Bandeira was the main logistics base in southern Angola for the South African invasion force, and the C130s were flying in military supplies. These were the sort of air operations performed for the CIA by Air America and Continental Air Service in Laos during the United States' secret war there. The pilots would normally be American. It is also highly probable that the pilots flying the artillery spotter planes directing South African ground fire were also American, as stated in the *Intelligence Report* quoted in Chapter 1. But if continued American participation in the doomed Angolan enterprise seemed limited, Bufkin had other cards up his sleeve:

Presently there exists a long-term contract in Rhodesia. The information on this contract is somewhat sketchy and incomplete. Apparently there are at least four military groups which mercs can get into. These groups are the SAS (Special Air Service), Regular Army and Depot Police. The fourth group is currently unidentified.

The SAS could be likened to the Rhodesian Army as the Special Forces is to our Army.

The Regular Army is their standard service. We understand that you are taken in at the rank that you were discharged from the US Armed Forces. A sgt makes 650 dollars which is not bad since a 16 oz. coke costs 6c, and a movie costs 40c.

The Depot Police has police which go into the bush occasionally on BMW motor-cycles.

We understand that you can only get into the fourth group, currently unidentified, after having served in the SAS. They paint themselves black, speak the language, and actually filter into the terrorist camps.

These contracts will be offered for quite some time. We understand that the length of these contracts can range up to five years. A merc. may only work a part of his contract if he wishes. Rhodesia is becoming continually hotter and there is increased terrorist activity in neighbouring Mozambique and Zambia.

Presently, if you are interested, you can contact Maj. Lamprecht at Army Hqrs, Salisbury, Rhodesia. Much more thorough information will be in the first actual news letter . . .

The sort of prospects implicit in the Munnion dispatch, the Bufkin circular and the continued activities of Banks, Aspin and their like, point to what the Luanda trial was all about. The continuing stockpiling of mercenary raw material for use in South Africa, Namibia and Zimbabwe, the Lebanon, the Persian Gulf states and elsewhere is a constant threat to peace and the legitimate aims of independence and national liberation movements. The belligerency and obstinacy of the racist régimes in South Africa and Rhodesia are bolstered by the reserves of mercenary cannon fodder they are confident are at their disposal. The inaction of the governments of Great Britain on this subject can only reinforce this confidence.

On 16 September 1976, nine months after the Bufkin circular was sent out, a Salisbury-datelined dispatch in the *Washington Post* from Robin Wright – the American woman journalist who had taken such an interest in American mercenaries in Angola – read like a recruiting appeal for red-blooded Americans to rally to the armed forces of gallant Rhodesia. Spotlighting the pro-

régime activities of five prominent naturalized Rhodesians, Robin
Wright reported with evident pride:

All five were born and brought up in the United States and are now
among some 1,200 US residents and 250 US soldiers in the southern
African territory.

Among the five singled out for Miss Wright's approving
attention were 'Dave' and 'Mike', attracted by the appeal of a
former New Jersey resident, Mrs Woram, who distributed circular
letters drawing attention to the 'Communist menace' and to the
fact that 'Rhodesia stands in grave peril of falling a victim of the
USSR's expansionist goals'.

Dave and Mike are among those Americans who have recently
arrived in response to a similar appeal. Both Vietnam veterans and
former Green Berets, they travelled more than 10,000 miles from
Indiana and Washington state to join the Rhodesian Army after seeing
recruiting ads in *Soldier of Fortune* magazine. Mike explained his involvement idealistically . . . 'I consider it my duty to fight in Rhodesia.
After Vietnam and Angola we can't afford to lose any other countries.'
He acknowledged that he was technically breaking US law by serving
in a foreign army, but said that none of the boys who had fought in the
Rhodesian Army and then returned home had been prosecuted . . .
For Dave, politics was not involved: 'I had five contracts to choose
from and this seemed to be the one with the best possibilities . . . If
you're going to be paid to kill you choose employers with the lowest risk
of getting yourself killed.'

After pointing out that the financial conditions in the Rhodesian
army are slightly less advantageous than those in the US army, but
omitting to mention that most US mercenaries are US army
rejects, Miss Wright reports that the various advertisements and
appeals have so far 'lured more than 1,000 "foreign volunteers"
according to "unofficial estimates", mainly Britons, Americans,
Australians, Portuguese and Greeks. New US recruits are coming
in rapidly.' Another of Robin Wright's chosen 'five' has become
'what a South African publication called Rhodesia's leading
"Communist critic" and one of the most outspoken optimists
about the presence of whites in Rhodesia'.

The figures of 250 Americans and over 1,000 'foreign volunteers'

are high by most other accounts of foreigners fighting in Rhodesia.
But the figure for Americans tallies with a report by the *Christian
Science Monitor* of 2 January 1976:

> The CIA is indirectly recruiting American ex-servicemen, training
> them, despatching them to southern Africa, contributing towards their
> pay (via funds for Zaire and the two pro-West factions) and providing
> them and the indigenous forces with light and heavy weaponry ...

Quoting 'senior mercenary officers familiar with the situation
both in Angola and the United States', the *Christian Science
Monitor* claimed that some 300 Americans were already operating
in Angola, with a similar number ready to take off when CIA funds
were available. The latter included:

> American officers and men either on 'indefinite leave' from their
> special forces units in this country and the Panama Canal Zone or
> recently discharged under the RIF (reduction in force) programme as
> well as fifteen South Vietnamese.

In the same report, it was claimed that 150 of the men awaiting
the word to leave for Angola spent the week of Christmas 1975
'undergoing a refresher course at Fort Benning, Georgia', and
that the majority of Americans in Angola were with the UNITA
forces in the south. Three days later, on 6 January, the *Monitor*
claimed that, thanks to its revelations, the 'recruiting and training
in this country of American veterans for mercenary operations in
Angola have come to an abrupt halt'. This was precisely the time
when Bufkin sent his message of dissuasion to any mercenaries
thinking of joining the UNITA forces via the South African
route. Recruiting had been transferred to Europe, according to the
Monitor account, with the United States still footing the bill.

Assuming that only a fraction of the 300 Americans mentioned
by the *Monitor* – mostly for UNITA in the South – ever got to
Angola before the FNLA–UNITA forces collapsed and that,
temporarily blocked in South Africa, they were diverted to become
Robin Wright's 250 Americans in Rhodesia – how had they been
recruited?

The *International Herald Tribune* (Paris) on 23 June 1976 con-
tained a UPI story from Washington on recruiting for Rhodesia,

where it was estimated sixty Americans were already fighting with the Rhodesian security forces. UPI quoted Tapson Mawere, ZANU (Zimbabwe African National Union) representative in the USA, as claiming that more were being 'actively recruited' and that recruits – ostensibly South Africans – were being trained at a Marine Corps base in Quantico, Virginia. Temple Cole, the State Department's Rhodesia 'desk officer', questioned by UPI on Tapson Mawere's charges, said 'there are certainly indications'. Mawere named as the chief recruiter Robert K. Brown, head of an organization known as 'Phoenix Associates', near Denver, Colorado. Contacted by telephone, Brown said that he had been recruiting 'white mercenaries' since September and that 'Phoenix Associates' was in being 'to merchandise information on mercenary opportunities abroad'. Anyone who replied to an advertisement that Brown placed in the February issue of *Shooting Times* magazine received in reply a copy of *Soldier of Fortune* magazine and an application form to join the Rhodesian army. Questioned on the legality of Brown's activities in recruiting on US soil for a foreign army – an illegal one at that according to various UN resolutions – the US Justice Department, according to the UPI story, replied: 'We are aware of his activities but no charges have been placed.' Similarly, in August 1976, the Justice Department admitted that twenty-five specific cases of recruitment of mercenaries in the USA had been brought to the Department's notice but that no legal proceedings had been initiated!

Lt-Col. Robert K. Brown, ex-Special Force 'A' Team leader in Vietnam, editor of *Soldier of Fortune* and political science graduate of the University of Colorado, has a very special brand of philosophy. Richard Woodley, an American writer who wrote a long article on mercenary recruiting and recruiters in the August 1976 issue of *Esquire*, noted a sign when he walked into Brown's editorial office:

> JOIN THE ARMY, TRAVEL TO DISTANT LANDS
> MEET INTERESTING PEOPLE
> AND KILL THEM

Brown himself was wearing a white T-shirt with the inscription

> AIRBORNE – DEATH FROM ABOVE

All this was doubtless intended as a joke, but it requires a very special sense of humour to accept it as such in view of the sort of activities Brown and his magazine promote and the death-inciting weapons and literature they peddle. Brown could afford to be jocular. He had set up business after a visit to Rhodesia, where he collected some of Major Lamprecht's recruiting material and sold it off in packets for five dollars a time. He also sold similar packets on the mercenary potential in Oman until he was informed that Sultan Quaboos ben Said preferred to 'buy British' – it was cheaper. The market for the five-dollar packets was so great that he decided to invest 10,000 dollars of the proceeds into founding the quarterly magazine *Soldier of Fortune* (first edition 4,400 copies; second edition 70,000; third edition 125,000).

Interviewed in a BBC *Panorama* programme,[2] Brown had the following to say to Michael Cockerell:

COCKERELL: The passionately pro-Rhodesian Colonel Robert Brown is back in America after meeting Major Lamprecht in Salisbury.

BROWN: Our attitude towards Rhodesia and the attitude of the United States is probably one of the most blatant acts of political hypocrisy in the twentieth century.

COCKERELL (with images illustrating Brown in action): Brown makes a point of attending regimental reunions to spread the word about military opportunities in Rhodesia. Some eighty Vietnam veterans have reportedly just joined the Rhodesian Army and at the Fort McPherson Officers' Club in Atlanta, Georgia, Bob Brown tries to persuade serving American officers to follow them. He gives each one his card . . .

BROWN: Of course I interviewed Major Lamprecht, who is the recruiting officer for the Rhodesian Army and also Superintendent of Police in the British South African Police, so I gathered up recruiting pamphlets and decided to market packets on the Rhodesian recruiting which was simply reproductions of reprints of Rhodesian recruiting brochures.

COCKERELL: Colonel Brown also has a commercial interest in Rhodesia. He edits a quarterly magazine for mercenaries called *Soldier of Fortune*. He aims to offer a piece of the action wherever possible. On his return from Salisbury, Brown began to sell at five dollars a time the recruiting literature he'd been given free.

BROWN: This caused a great deal of unhappiness for the State Depart-

2. Broadcast on 19 July 1976.

ment and they sent out a representative from the Justice Department and so my attorney advised that I quit marketing, quit selling these things. So what I simply did was in the first issue of my magazine I printed the information, the addresses and I charged no one for the information and there was not a damn thing they could do about it because I am protected under the First Amendment . . .

COCKERELL: What is that?

BROWN: Freedom of speech. So to hell with 'em . . .

A rival of Bufkin and Brown in the mercenary recruiting racket is Pierre Walt,[3] whose real name is Daniel Pierre Waltener, a naturalized American of French origin. He served with French parachutists in Algeria, then joined the fascist OAS underground. According to what he told Richard Woodley of *Esquire*, he had taken part in 'two hundred bank robberies to support the OAS against De Gaulle'. He claims also to have served in the Congo with Six Commando[4] and to have taken part in 'training and advising certain troops in certain places in Indochina . . .' This sounds as if he had served – together with George Washington Bacon – with the Vang Pao mercenaries in Laos. This would make sense as the Meo mercenaries were originally a French creation. To establish his credentials with Woodley, Walt produced an American passport with visas showing he had visited Rhodesia, Oman and Angola. Although he claimed that he had 'the biggest, best and most trustworthy fund of professional soldiers in this country' at his disposal, there is no evidence that he had any at all. When Lobo del Sol returned from Angola with instructions to recruit 300 mercenaries, he went to Walt hoping to raise 100 to 150 but got none. Lobo went back to bar-tending in Los Angeles. The whole incident tended to prove that Bufkin, Brown and Walt were fakes and most probably front men for those who were doing the real recruiting and dispatching. The questions are how such amateur recruiting groups could get training facilities at Fort Benning, Georgia, and Quantico, Virginia, and how American officers and men from

3. See Chapter 3.
4. Six Commando, which fought in the Katangan war of secession in the Congo, was composed of French-speaking mercenaries, originally commanded by the Belgian colonel Lamouline. The French mercenary, former NCO Bob Denard, took over after Mobutu ousted Tshombe and Kasavubu from the Congo leadership in November 1965.

special forces units in the USA could get 'indefinite leave' for service as mercenaries.

To the best of the authors' knowledge, the real recruiting was carried out by the Pentagon, using the following technique. When servicemen are discharged from the US armed forces, their serial number is retained and supplemented by three digits known to GIs as the 'spin-off number', which, when fed through a computer, give some essential information concerning competencies and behaviour, from 'eager beaver' conduct on the battlefield to sexual preferences and drug or alcohol addiction. A certain number of those who had an 'elite' three-digit recommendation, which included high marks for being tight-lipped, were discreetly contacted and asked if they were interested in going to Angola. Those who replied in the affirmative were told to proceed to the Frankfurt Arsenal in Philadelphia. As far as the public is concerned this establishment had been closed down. In fact it is – or at the height of the Angolan crisis was – a secret mercenary recruiting centre. There, if the recruit was willing, he could get a contract of up to 3,000 dollars a month and a phoney Swiss passport. Arrangements for the monthly payments were made through a civilian corporation. The United States government was thus neither officially nor financially involved.

In the BBC TV *Panorama* programme referred to earlier, a British boy soldier, Tom McCarthy, described how he had contacted the South African Embassy in London to make inquiries about joining the Rhodesian army. The reply came in the form of a letter from Rhodesia, with application forms – one of the requirements being that he was 'of pure European descent'. He filled them in and returned them to Rhodesian army headquarters at Salisbury, and was then offered a three-year contract with the rank of trooper:

COCKERELL: Trooper McCarthy was to receive £40 per week. His letter of acceptance from Salisbury was signed by Major Lamprecht. Lamprecht's name recurs throughout the story of Rhodesia's undercover foreign recruitment campaign.

MCCARTHY: They sent a telegram and said they would advise myself personally to take an unorthodox route out of the country and wished me the best of luck and looking forward to seeing you and I can remember the gentleman who signed it you know, the actual name at the bottom ... Major Lamprecht ... And then he said at times they had people ... outside Rhodesia to try and recruit and he mentioned somebody, a Captain, that was actually caught somewhere in Europe.

COCKERELL: Captain Edgar Teilan is Lamprecht's man in Germany. The son of a Nazi officer, Teilan began recruiting after serving in the Rhodesian army. He advertised for well-paid 'safari guides' with military experience for Rhodesia. Major Lamprecht, who initiated the campaign, received 1,300 replies and vetted seventy likely German lads. Teilan went to gaol. Major Lamprecht says over half the new applicants to the Rhodesian army now come from abroad. McCarthy's training confirms this.

MCCARTHY (describing a camp on the TV screen): This is a training camp. These guys (pointing at members of a group) are a mixture of Rhodesian, Italian, Rhodesian, South African, South African, an alien, two Australians, myself, a German, British and South African. He was actually an RSM of the British Coldstream Guards and he used to write out all the training manuals for the Rhodesian Light Infantry ...

McCarthy, who deserted after six months with the Rhodesian forces, had at least taken the initiative in seeking recruitment. Three others interviewed by Cockerell testified that, unsought and unexpected, they had received from Rhodesia, direct and via France and Spain respectively, enlistment application forms for the Rhodesian army. In each case the replies were to be sent to an address in South Africa. Cockerell interviewed an American, Frank Sweeney, who, having served out his contract with the Rhodesian army, went back to the United States to start his own one-man recruitment campaign. He ran into the same difficulties as Colonel Brown when he tried to market his recruitment packets.

COCKERELL: Frank Sweeney is also up against the law. He's now on the run from the authorities and living out of a suitcase in motel bedrooms with his South African Luger. His problem began when he placed a recruiting advertisement in *Shotgun News*.

SWEENEY: When I first came back from Rhodesia I didn't have any problems at all. But when I started to recruit I got a call from the FBI saying they were going to come over to my house to interview me on this matter. Well they came ... They asked me for names and

job assignments of Americans I knew operating now or active with
the Rhodesian army, plus they had a copy of my ad from *Shotgun
News* . . . I've gotten 300 responses to that ad.

COCKERELL: What did the ad say?

SWEENEY: It said: 'Americans of European ancestry, the Rhodesian
Army offers excitement and adventure. I know, I've been there.
Contact me for free details pertaining to recruitment.'

COCKERELL: Who was it in Rhodesia who asked you . . .?

SWEENEY: Oh, Major Lamprecht when I was discharged asked me if I
would contact as many potential applicants as I could . . .

Sweeney gave as one of the reasons why he had joined the
Rhodesian army and had not volunteered for service in the USA
that the idea of serving in an army with blacks in it did not appeal
to him at all. 'I have a strong affinity with European culture.'
Asked about other nationalities he had met and their backgrounds,
Sweeney said there were many West Germans, whose fathers had
served in the Wehrmacht in the Second World War, 'lots of
Australians, New Zealanders, a couple of Scandinavians'.

COCKERELL: Did you ask them how they came to the Rhodesian
army?

SWEENEY: Most of them joined for the same reason I did. Because
their own countries had degenerated to such a point that they just
couldn't live there any more. Most of them, like myself, are racialists.
One doesn't join the Rhodesian army because he wants to make a lot
of money.

An interesting point in Sweeney's account is that the FBI did
intervene – as with Brown – when recruiting became too blatant.
This may have been done more as a protective device against probes
by Congressmen worried about violations of the Neutrality Act, or
UN members pressing for respect of sanctions imposed on
Rhodesia, than out of any real desire to prevent either recruitment
or enlistment of mercenaries for Rhodesia.

Apologists for the Smith régime object to the use of the term
'mercenary' for foreigners serving in their armed forces because
they receive the same rates of pay as Rhodesians. But if one accepts
the definition of mercenary as one who fights in a foreign force for
financial gain, the term is valid. Frank Sweeney may be correct in

implying that others like him did not join up 'to make a lot of money', but the overwhelming majority enlist because they are unemployed or have been declared redundant from their own armed forces.

If there are any grounds to quibble about the status of those who enlist in Rhodesia's regular armed forces, there can be none about those hired as armed guards on white settlers' farms at even higher rates of pay than those of the armed forces. Leslie Aspin had diversified his recruiting activities to include this new activity. In fact he had set up a new firm, BAB (Bishop, Aspin and Best), to handle this – and other sidelines. The following exchange with Cockerell makes this clear:

COCKERELL (the TV screen shows BAB offices in Norwich): It's to Britain that Rhodesian farmers are now turning in their search for armed guards. These are the Norwich offices of men who earlier this year were recruiting mercenaries for Angola.

ASPIN: This morning again we received another fifty letters from potential recruits who specifically say they would like to go to Rhodesia to fight and help the Rhodesians and South Africans, and very few of them even mention money as long as somebody can actually get them there.

COCKERELL: Les Aspin says he is sending out armed guards for farms – not he claims to Rhodesia – but to neighbouring South West Africa (Namibia).

ASPIN: It's my intention to send men out there in twos and threes to make small patrols up of five and six men who will patrol large farmland districts on the South African border. They are there at the invitation of the farmers themselves who feel that some added protection would be very welcome . . .

COCKERELL: It has been said that you are supplying them for Rhodesia, what would you say to that?

ASPIN: That's absolutely incorrect. After all it's against the law to send anybody to Rhodesia . . . But if at the end of their tour of duty they decide to go to Iceland, Timbuktoo or Rhodesia – that's entirely up to them. It's got nothing to do with me whatsoever.

COCKERELL: What about those who might wonder whether your operation is strictly legal, what would you say to that?

ASPIN: Is anything strictly legal? The successful businessman is the man that makes money. In fact if he doesn't make money and he is caught out he then becomes an unsuccessful businessman ... I try not to break the rules. I most certainly bend them and I don't dispute that for a second.

What happens next on the mercenary front is crucially important for tens of millions of people in southern Africa and for hundreds of millions of people elsewhere in non-independent countries, and those living under repressive régimes. Is their fate to be decided by the Bufkins and Browns, the Bankses and Aspins of our age? The question may seem absurd. Morally such people are on the bottom rung of the human ladder, as even their public utterances prove. Traders in human flesh have been despised throughout history. If the authors have adopted the title of *Whores of War* for this book this is not for any lack of understanding for the economic and social realities behind prostitution. But the analogy is apt because mercenaries hire themselves out indiscriminately for money, outside the law, to clients who want the advantage of the services offered without the responsibility of close, permanent, or open association.

It is the forces behind the Bufkins, Browns, Bankses and Aspins that count. Mercenaries skilled in the techniques of modern warfare have tipped the scales before; they may well do so again. In Angola the myth of their invincibility, however, was shattered. Just as the Americans were 'unfortunate' to have made their first experiment in 'special war' against the Vietnamese, who for 2,000 years had been used to dealing with invaders infinitely more powerful than themselves, so were those teleguiding the use of mercenaries in Angola 'unfortunate' in being confronted with combatants united behind a superior ideology, forged and tempered in thirteen years of armed struggle against the Portuguese and two more years of political–military struggle against internal enemies.

It must be assumed that there will be a more intelligent choice and employment of mercenaries in future. Commanders like Callan will be avoided as well as untrained soldiers. More professionals and professionalism will be sought. Reserve forces are being assembled and trained to be thrown into action like fire brigades in emergency situations. Israeli-type commando operations were being launched against Angola and Mozambique from

Namibia and Rhodesia within months of the collapse of Callan's mercenaries in Angola. Multinational units, that can be easily repudiated, can be expected. Units grouped according to their specialities in killing: paratroopers in unmarked planes and helicopters; sea-borne commandos; units wearing the other side's uniforms and bearing forged leaflets; everything that money, guile and anonymity can provide. Methods and techniques far superior to those of the Callans and Barkers.

There was a preview of things to come in the image of gun-powder-sniffing old warhorses pawing at the ground at Heathrow airport, snorting with indignation at the 'rag-bag army' of second-raters being shipped off to Angola that day. Gerard Kemp of the *Daily Telegraph*, at Heathrow to watch the departure of the two batches of 128 mercenaries on 28 January, ran into some 'professional mercenaries' waiting to take off to South Africa. He reported as follows:

A second anti-Marxist force is also being organized. This second group, financed by the CIA, will work with the South Africans and will fly directly to Johannesburg to spearhead an anti-Marxist offensive next month.

Among those involved in the planning is Col. 'Mad Mike' Hoare, a veteran of the Congo mercenary brigade . . .

One of the second force told me . . .

'I was under Mike Hoare in Number Five Commando in the Congo. He's first class. It's a great pity that we are going to be on the same side as this rabble. I wish to God the MPLA had employed the lot of them.'

One of the second force is an ex-British Army major who said they would be working for the South African government as a 'special commando unit'.

There was a year's contract to be signed at £200 a week. Swiss bank accounts would be used.

There can be little doubt that the professionals are being mobilized and already constitute a force in being. The Luanda trial and the resultant sentences are a deterrent, but cannot be decisive. The fact speaks for itself that at least one who had survived Angola promptly came back to Banks and Aspin for more and was dispatched to Lebanon, to get himself killed on the side of the Christian Falangists exterminating Palestinian refugees at the

Tal-Zaatar camp.[5] The international conspiracy of mercenaries is a new factor on the world stage which, like CIA 'destabilization' activities, pollution, plane hijacking and the multinational take-over of countries' economies, requires mobilization of public opinion and national as well as international action.

5. The *Daily Express* of 12 August 1976 reported from Beirut that twenty-eight-year-old Robert Thacker was shot dead leading a squad of Christians into battle. Thacker had served with the Australians in Vietnam and with the Special Air Services in Rhodesia, as well as in Angola!

11 Mercenaries International

When the French police were set the task of discovering the where-
abouts of Louis Hazan, chairman of the board of directors of
Phonogram, one of France's leading gramophone-record manufacturers, it seemed a straightforward assignment. Hazan had
been kidnapped with several of his colleagues at a directors'
meeting at their Paris headquarters on 31 December 1975. The
others had been released. Police instructions were to secure his
release without payment of the fifteen million franc ransom and
arrest the kidnappers. It seemed simple at first. Two of the kidnappers were arrested just seven days later when they turned up at
a rendezvous at Place de la Bastille to collect the ransom. (The
'staff members' of Phonogram who were to turn over the cash
were police officers in disguise!) Louis Hazan was found the
following day – a tribute to the effectiveness of French interrogation techniques – gagged and bound. Otherwise he was little the
worse for his experiences, which included the indignity of being
trussed up in a wicker basket and transported by station wagon
from Phonogram's Paris headquarters to the house in which he
was found in Tremblay-les-Villages in the Eure et Loir district,
about eighty kilometres south-west of Paris. Then things began to
get complicated.

Apart from the fact that the financial director of Phonogram,
Daniel Vergnes, admitted his complicity with the kidnappers from
the start, the house in which Hazan was found had been rented two
months previously by a certain Jacques Prévost and occupied by a
certain Jacques Boisset. Prévost had been a prominent member of
the underground OAS in Algeria, one of those so infuriated by
de Gaulle's 'treachery' in bowing to the inevitable and acknowledging the independence of Algeria that he had taken part in an
almost successful assassination attempt against the French presi-

dent in the Paris suburb of Le Petit Clamart on 22 August 1962.[1]
Prévost, Boisset and a third man, Michel Gobbet – all three
members of a French extreme right-wing group 'Forces Nouvelles'
– fled from the house where Hazan was being held just before the
police arrived on 7 January.

Marcel Pech, the father of the brothers Daniel and Dominique
Pech, arrested in trying to collect the ransom, had been treasurer of
the fascist 'Ordre Nouveau' movement which had been banned in
1973. Among others of the kidnapping gang they named was
Daniel Moschini (Danny the Mercenary), an Italian linked with
rightist terrorist movements in Italy and Spain, also a former member
of the O A S and a mercenary who had served in Angola. Two
days after Hazan was released a boobytrapped delivery-van blew
up in a Paris car-park, killing the sole inmate – Michel Gobbet.
The van's owner, Patrice Combe of Aurillac, asked to explain the
remains of frogmen's diving suits and sophisticated navigation
equipment in the van, pleaded ignorance and said he had lent it a
few days previously to Jacques Prévost to transport some equipment
to Paris. Diligently pursuing their inquiries the police visited
an old farm, l'Étable, of which Patrice Combe was part owner and
which bordered the Saint-Étienne-Cantalès reservoir about
twenty kilometres from Aurillac, in southern France, almost
equidistant from the Atlantic and Mediterranean.

The farm, it transpired, was among other things a sort of staging
post for Prévost's comings and goings between his home in Basle,
on the Swiss side of the French–Swiss border, and France and
Spain. The police were intrigued to find military staff maps of
places like Uganda and elsewhere in Africa, Venezuela and other
Latin American countries, and even more so by powerful sea-going
inflatable boats and more diving equipment. A dozen or so men
had decamped just before the police arrived. Local villagers said
that off and on there had been fifteen to thirty men – not always the
same ones – there for months. They were very busy diving and
boating on the reservoir and, when asked what they were doing,

1. A constant factor during the research into the activities of mercenaries
was the frequency with which the names of old-time fascists and war
criminals turned up, as well as names of the same mercenaries serving on
widely separated battlefields.

replied that they were employed by a company investigating pollution in the reservoir and the river which flowed into it. The police quickly found that there was no such company, and that they had stumbled on a secret training camp for mercenary commandos. The existence of such camps in France had long been suspected but none till then had been pin-pointed. Local people said they had been intrigued by the fact that the 'anti-pollution research' had continued right through the winter. There were very strong rumours that the inflatable boats had been used in training exercises at Fécamp, between Dieppe and Le Havre on the English Channel, at a point near the home of Jacques Bosset, one of the kidnappers.

Daniel Vergnes told the police that Ugo Brunini was the 'brain' of the kidnapping operation, working directly under Prévost, and that Brunini had also forged a cheque in Louis Hazan's name for 3.65 million francs two months before the kidnapping. The money was never recovered. Brunini's brother was reported to run a tourist agency in South Africa which specialized at the height of the Angolan war in transporting European mercenaries to Angola. *Le Monde* commented, with typical French journalistic prudence:

Such a combination prompts us to ask if the team which the police has just dismantled has not been acting for political motives. Was it partly linked with certain groups of mercenaries, the recruitment of whom has suddenly become very active – notably with Angola as their destination?[2]

Paul Tombini, another member of the kidnapping-commando gang who managed to escape arrest, had served as a mercenary in Angola and was said to have close links with Prévost and some of the others. But their interest was not only Angola.

A few weeks after the frogmen commandos fled from their training camp a number of ships carrying arms to the left-wing forces in the Lebanon were wrecked by underwater explosions. Just the sort of work for which the Prévost commandos were trained! They represented the sort of professional specialization which one can expect from the post-Angola crop of mercenaries.

Six months after the Phonogram affair there was another
2. *Le Monde*, 24 January 1976.

astonishing high-level betrayal of trust involving this time the theft of eight million francs by one of the chief accountants of the aircraft manufacturing empire of Marcel Dassault. Implicated up to the eyebrows was Jean Kay, who got clean away to the Lebanon and his old friends, the then President Suleiman Frangié and Falangist leader Pierre Gemayel, with the loot. Among his other activities Kay had been an instructor for Gemayel's Christian militia.

Exploiting the human weaknesses of the Dassault accountant, Hervé de Vathaire – especially the fact that the latter was having a tempestuous affair with a Parisian nightclub 'hostess' – Jean Kay wormed his way into de Vathaire's confidence, apparently by discovering that his 'girl friend' was the dearest friend of the accountant's secret mistress. Kay knew – or he soon found out – that de Vathaire had a dossier on Dassault of blackmail proportions. It soon changed hands and, despite de Vathaire's insistence, Kay refused to return it. But nothing so crude as blackmail! Kay persuaded de Vathaire to use his right to draw cheques in Dassault's name to withdraw eight million francs (one million pounds) in 500-franc notes from the company's bank. This was done, the money being paid out in sixteen 'bricks' of ten packets each of ten wads of 500-franc notes. If the eighty-four-year-old Dassault, ill at the time, took action then the threat of the dossier could be used.

By the time the bank manager got around to checking with one of Dassault's chief aides and found that de Vathaire had no authorization to withdraw such a huge amount, the two couples were speeding, in separate cars, to a hotel rendezvous at Divonne-les-Bains, conveniently close to the Swiss border near Lake Geneva, in case of an emergency. In fact there was none. Dassault lodged an official complaint against Vathaire but withdrew it a week later. Jean Kay left France for the Lebanon at the end of July and Vathaire was left apparently with neither the famous 'dossier' nor the eight million francs. The opinion in 'well-informed circles' in France was that the eight million francs of Dassault and the 3.65 million of Phonogram went to help finance the Falangist attempt to exterminate the PLO forces and the Lebanese left.

Prévost and Kay are the cold, professional, Congo-type mercenaries. Kay deserted the French army in Algeria after six months' service, to join the OAS. Later he turned up with mercenaries in the Yemen, then in Biafra – where there was a heavy French commitment on the side of the secessionists. He even went to Jordan in an attempt to infiltrate the PLO, but as it was known that he had previously offered his services to the Israeli secret service he was turned down. He promptly revealed his true colours again by turning up in the Lebanon as an instructor for Gemayel's Falangist militia. He attracted public attention for a moment – in December 1971 – when he seized a Pakistan Airlines plane at Paris-Orly airport, demanding, in exchange for passengers and plane, twenty tons of medical supplies for Bangladesh. Arrested, he was given a nominal suspended sentence, because of the intervention of personalities like the late André Malraux, who pleaded for his idealism and 'defence of Christian values'! In November 1974, Kay was arrested by the Portuguese in Angola, fighting on the side of the Cabinda secessionists, backed by certain French interests avid to get their hands on such Western 'Christian values' as Cabinda oil.[3]

The name of Jean Kay became more and more associated with the cross-fertilization between ultra-sophisticated crime and ultra-reactionary international politics; more specifically extortion and bank robberies and the financing of mercenary operations. On the night of 17–18 July 1976, in what is known as the 'sewer-rat robbery', thieves broke into the vaults of the Société Générale bank at Nice, and got away with some fifty million francs (over ten million dollars) in one of the world's biggest bank robberies. Later the police found a well-lit and ventilated tunnel had been built from the city's sewer system – it was even carpeted to deaden the noise – and that the loot had been taken away in a small truck and inflatable rafts. On 26 October, police arrested Albert Spaggiari, head of the band of some twenty 'sewer rats', all specialists in bank robberies, who had carried out the coup. Spaggiari admitted that he had planned the operation for some two years, and that the tunnelling had taken two months to complete. Known for his extreme right-wing views and described as the founder of a 'militant underground anti-Communist movement', the police

3. The above summary of the life and activities of Jean Kay is based on an article in the French weekly *Le Point* of 13 September 1976, by journalists Jean-Marie Pontaut, Jacques Duquesne and Maria-Thérèse Guichard.

stated that Spaggiari told them he had given his share of the loot 'to an international group of rightist militants identified as "La Catena" (the chain) ... based in Turin ... devoted to helping rightist extremists in trouble, notably in Italy and Yugoslavia ...'[4]

The Italian police denied any knowledge of this group, as did Italian left-wing journalists contacted by the authors, who were normally well informed about the activities of right-wing Italian terrorist organizations. Like Prévost, Spaggiari had taken part in one of the assassination attempts against de Gaulle, and claimed actually to have had the President in the telescopic sight of his rifle, but had not received the order to fire. Reuter sent a tantalizing report from Nice on 31 October indicating what the French investigators really believed the 'sewer rat' gang was up to.

Police believe that a former paratrooper was trying to put them on a false trail by claiming he gave his share of the fifty-million-franc haul from the 'sewer rat' bank raid here to an Italian right-wing organization.

The suspect M. Albert Spaggiari, aged forty, who says he masterminded the robbery last July, may have had his share passed on to rightist forces in the Lebanese civil war through M. Jean Kay, a former mercenary ...

Police sources said M. Spaggiari was suspected of meeting M. Kay in August and that the former mercenary might have given some of the haul to the Falangist party in Lebanon ... Police sources said yesterday that both M. Kay and M. Spaggiari were known to have links with an international organization with members in right-wing circles in Italy, Lebanon, Britain and elsewhere.

Police said M. Spaggiari hired former members of the Secret Army Organization (OAS) which fought against Algerian independence, for the raid. Among his accomplices was M. Gaby Anglade, a former OAS member involved in an abortive attempt to assassinate General de Gaulle in 1962.

By the second half of 1976, the Lebanon and Rhodesia had become the main focal points for mercenary recruiting and operations. It was symptomatic that one French mercenary, Stéphane Zanettaci, of the neo-fascist 'Action Jeunesse', and one British mercenary, Gerald Thacker, both lost their lives taking part in the Falangist attacks on the Palestine refugee camp at Tel al-Zaatar. Peter Niesewand, reporting from the Christian-held

4. *International Herald Tribune* (Paris) 30–31 October 1976.

port of Jounieh for the London *Guardian* on 21 August 1976, covered the arrival of a small group of mercenaries from Cyprus:

Eleven foreigners were aboard the small boat from Cyprus when it arrived in this Christian-held port, and there was no doubt that they had come to fight.

All were athletically built, with close-cropped hair. They carried army surplus knapsacks and wore camouflage jackets and jeans.

Waiting to meet them were members of the right-wing Falangist militia, who escorted them through entry controls. The men spoke French, and four presented French passports, although two of them looked Japanese . . .

Niesewand spoke to an Australian named Kelly, who preferred to be known as 'Blue' and who had been fighting with what are known as 'Dany Chamoun's Tigers', whereas the French from the newly arrived boat were going to join the Falangists:

Although they're on the same right-wing side, there's not much love lost between the Falangists and the Chamounists, and occasionally they kill each other instead of Leftists and Palestinians . . . Blue said: 'I reckon there are about forty Frenchmen fighting with the Falangists. Mostly they're students who belong to the French Falangist Party. They come over here for three months, get trained, do some fighting. Then they go back and wait to go into action in France. I suppose they'll be fighting there in about two years. On the Chamoun side, there's just me. There was a Brit. but he got killed at the beginning of Tel al-Zaatar.'

That a steady infiltration of French mercenaries to the Falangist forces continued was confirmed by a brief item in the French press on 5 October 1976 to the effect that three Frenchmen had been arrested in Cyprus 'with arms and equipment' while awaiting transport to Jounieh. What worries many French progressives – and not only progressives – is that some of the French fighting and training in the Lebanon belong to President Giscard d'Estaing's 'Service d'Ordre', a type of personal security force. 'Blue's' reference to right-wing student militants who expect to go into action 'in about two years' obviously comes from gossip within their ranks as to probable strong-arm measures to be taken in case of a Socialist–Communist victory in the 1978 French parliamentary elections. As noted above, broad sections of French public opinion are worried at the trend. Thus, a correspondent in *Le Monde* of

5 November 1976, summing up the merger of 'extreme right and gangsterism' in crime from the kidnapping of Louis Hazan to the Nice bank robbery, commented that apart from the fact that there were always mercenaries involved who had participated in 'counter-revolutionary activities in Asia or Africa, or who were declared sympathizers of some neo-fascist international . . .', and continued,

> One sees that all these operations have in common is that they are not just some settling of political accounts or measures of intimidation, but are aimed at procuring for their authors large sums of money – through ransom, pillage of bank vaults, hold-ups or blackmail – quickly leading to the conclusion that there is a connection between them which in turn leads one to think that the extreme right in France, or even in Europe, is preparing a 'major coup' . . .[5]

The author recalls the existence in France before the Second World War of the Cagoulard (Hooded Men) fascist terrorist organization, and warns of the existence and organized activities of former OAS, SS and Nazi collaborators and other 'un-employed' fascist activists, looking for some cause 'worthy of their skills'. Despite their differences and internal rivalries, the author notes that the tendency is 'co-ordination and international-ization' – with Madrid as a chief centre of their operations.

Investigations into how French mercenaries were recruited and dispatched – especially in the case of Angola – led to the Paladin terrorist organization in Spain. This was headed by none other than Otto 'Scarface' Skorzeny, until his death in Madrid on 6 July 1975 an inveterate and unrepentant ex-SS Nazi.[6]

5. Bernard Brigouleix, under the title 'Extrême droite et gangsterism'.
6. Skorzeny was one of Hitler's most trusted – and most efficient – muscle-men. His most famous exploit was a glider-borne raid against a hotel on the tip of the Gran Sasso mountain on 12 September 1943 to free Mussolini, after the latter had been overthrown and arrested by his top soldier, Marshal Pietro Badoglio, six weeks earlier, in an abortive attempt to take Italy out of the war. Tried by an American military tribunal for having shot 300 unarmed American prisoners of war, Skorzeny was acquitted and went to work in the 'Historical Department' of the US occupation army, a favourite American formula for recruiting top Nazis into their intelligence organiza-tion, or at least of extracting the maximum amount of information from them. From 1949 he headed an import–export business in Madrid, con-sidered as a cover for the counter-revolutionary Paladin organization.

Another recruiter-dispatcher agency for mercenaries was in Lisbon, camouflaged as the Aginter Press agency, headed by a French agent of the Gestapo-trained PIDE, Dominique de Roux. He also worked with a French–Portuguese bank and Sonap, the Portuguese state petrol company. De Roux specialized in forwarding mercenaries to Cabinda for the local secessionist movement.

For a more complete example of the cross-fertilization of what one is tempted to call the fascist internationale one only has to scratch the surface of the ELP, the Spinolist 'Portuguese Liberation Army', and its political counterpart, the MDLP, the 'Democratic Movement for the Liberation of Portugal' (from the 'Communist' Armed Forces Movement)! The ELP was formed essentially by right-wing Portuguese officers implicated in Spinola's abortive coup attempt on 11 March 1975. The Spring 1976 issue of *CounterSpy*, a remarkably well-informed exposer of CIA activities, reported as follows:

The strength of the ELP–MDLP has fluctuated with the evolution of political events in Portugal and Angola. After 11 March 1975, ELP directed approximately 800 armed men. In the autumn of 1975, the estimate was just under 2,000. This past winter, ELP was able to field two battalions with FNLA and UNITA in the siege of Sá da Bandeira in Angola. No doubt a number of these troops have returned to Portugal or to the ELP–MDLP bases in Spain. A recent estimate put their strength at between 10,000 and 15,000 armed men. The source of ELP weapons is not yet entirely clear. There is one reliable source, however, who claims Portuguese fishing ships, docked in San Diego and other California ports, are loaded up with newly manufactured M-16s and plastic explosives. Fishermen there claimed the arms were for 'our brothers in Angola'. It is speculated that arms were obtained in the Marine Corps Recruiting Depot (MCRD) in San Diego in the same way that the right-wing Secret Army Organization (SAO) in that city, as well as right-wing groups across the Mexican border, obtained arms from sources at that depot . . .

As it is known that *CounterSpy* sources include a number of disillusioned former CIA operatives, one is inclined to attach special weight to what the editors cite as a 'reliable source'. Another example of the way in which old names keep popping up in the

mercenaries' internationale is the listing by *CounterSpy* of the
Belgian mercenary, Jean Schramme, as 'technical adviser' to the
first commander of ELP, a former lieutenant of the Portuguese
army, Canto Cabuce. Schramme, one of the most bloodthirsty of
the Congo mercenaries, at one time had a private army to defend
his own plantation. He had played a key role in the massacre of
3,000 Katangese troops, after he had switched his loyalty from
Tshombe to Mobuto. He also admitted to a Belgian court to having
murdered a Belgian planter who had proposed that Schramme
should lead a pro-Tshombe revolt against Mobuto. Schramme was
plotting this anyway, but did not want it revealed prematurely.
Treated with extraordinary leniency by the Belgian authorities –
and idolized by rightists who saw in him a 'hero' fighting to restore
Belgian interests – he was allowed to leave the country while the
investigation on murder charges was still continuing. That was in
the spring of 1969. He was next heard of in Spain working for a
publishing house 'with US connections', as *CounterSpy* has it, and
then in his role as 'technical adviser' to ELP. His advice was not
very effective, at least as far as the ELP performance in Angola
was concerned. After some initial successes against poorly armed
MPLA guerrillas in the central-southern regions – and as support
troops following along behind the South Africans – the ELP forces
were badly beaten later, taking heavy losses in killed and captured.

The existence of the ELP was first revealed by Brig. General
Enrico Corvacho, a left-wing member of the Armed Forces
Movement and commander of the northern military region. At a
press conference after the 11 March 1975 rightist coup attempt,
Corvacho announced the arrest of thirteen ELP members who
had infiltrated from Spain and the discovery of documents giving
the code names of 'Castor' and 'Morgan' for two of the main
ELP leaders. Such anonymity was obviously a challenge to the
team which works for *CounterSpy*, and they unearthed the
following:

'Morgan', one of the ELP–MDLP leaders mentioned by Col.
Corvacho in his press conference, is none other than Yves Guillou
(alias Guerin Seyrac), a former OAS officer, a former director of
Aginter Press, and a former adjunct to Pierre La Gaillarde who was the
liaison agent between Caetano's PIDE and the French secret police,

SDECE. The other agent, 'Castor', is Hugues Castor Franklin who travels with a Guatemalan passport, but is an American citizen named Jay S. Sablonsky, also known as Joe Vincente Pepper . . .

Castor is employed by the Madrid company, Tecno-Motor: Tecno-Motor, along with the Mariano S.A., are companies owned by Mariano Sanchez Covisa, the head of the 'Christ the King guerrillas' in Spain, a fanatical Catholic right-wing group with connections to SEIS (the Spanish secret police). The two Covisa companies are tied financially to Banco d'Avila, where such well-known fascists as Prince Borghese and former Nazis, Otto Skorzeny and Herzog van Valencia, hold important interests. Skorzeny is head of the terrorist organzation, Paladin, which acted as intermediary between the ELP–MDLP, and the American company, Worldarmco, noted for its CIA connections . . .

Compared with organizations so powerful and threatening, motivated by political considerations, the most recent efforts by British elements in the mercenary internationale, inspired by reluctance to do an honest day's work and appetites for loot which seem doomed never to be satisfied, have an almost comic look. It would be a mistake, though, to overlook the evil intentions of these would-be professional assassins just because they are less efficient in organizing murder than their European counterparts. Performance in their case fell well short of intentions. In a British TV programme on 28 June 1976, Scotland Yard was quoted as stating that 130 British mercenaries went to Angola and that they had committed 220 murders, including those of 'innocent civilians and friendly African soldiers'. Of the mercenaries, thirty-seven were dead, twenty unaccounted for and ten on trial. All these figures – except for the ten on trial – were in fact understatements, a point that John Banks immediately took up on the same programme: 'Our guys killed more than a thousand Angolans. We had a kill ratio of more than twenty to one.'

As for the morality and technique which secures such a 'kill ratio', there was a revealing passage in the interview that Peter Niesewand made with 'Blue' Kelly, quoted earlier. Having opined that one of the next tasks – after the liquidation of the Tel al-Zaatar Palestine refugee camp – would be to wipe out the Palestinian-held Sabra area of Beirut, Niesewand asked if this would not be a costly operation. 'Blue' replied:

Not if you do it methodically, building by building, going down both sides of a street. Just dynamite them, and then move on to the next. Shoot everyone – men, women and children: no problem.

No problem! And that is how it was done in Tel al-Zaatar, at least as far as shooting everyone – men, women and children – was concerned.

It was logical that the recruiters for Angola in Britain swiftly moved into the Lebanon 'market'. An examination of the Companies Registry in London shows that the company of Jifglen Ltd changed hands on 20 February 1976 and the new company with a nominal capital of £100 had as directors Leslie Aspin, owning fifty-two shares of one pound each, and Peter Bishop, with forty-eight shares. (Bishop had been a bodyguard for Aspin and Banks during the recruitment for Angola.) On 25 March, the name of the firm was changed to B A B, which according to John Chownes ('Ginger' Best) meant Best–Aspin–Bishop, Chownes claiming he had also put up some money in the meantime. The Memorandum of Association recorded in the registry states: 'The company to carry on business as guards, watchmen, messengers, security and detective agents.' Aspin let it be known that the real purpose of the company was to recruit for the Lebanon and that he was in the market for a boat, which would act as his floating headquarters there. He also let it be known that an important part of the operation would be to get at the contents of bank vaults in the battle-ridden or deserted banking sector of Beirut. As one of the great banking centres of the world, the pickings would make Callan's intended diamond loot in Angola look like small stuff.

When Peter Niesewand asked 'Blue' Kelly about Aspin's claim to be recruiting British mercenaries for the Lebanon, the reply was:

Aspin talks shit. He's just trying to give the impression that he's the centre of recruitment and that if anyone wants a job they'd better go to him.

Nevertheless, Aspin was determined to get into the act. What subsequently happened was related to Frank Branston by Ken Aitken, who, together with Brian Butcher, had been charged with keeping guard over the reluctant British mercenaries until the moment of their execution. Were it not for their murderous intentions, this couple would emerge as some sort of Laurel and Hardy comic relief. The following is Aitken's account of Aspin's Lebanon debacle:

I had been back in England a few months, keeping in touch with Brian Butcher. One day he called me and asked if I was interested in doing another job, this time in the Lebanon . . .

We went first to Gorleston to look at the boat and then to Rose Lane – Aspin's office. From then on we worked on the boat all day and slept at Rose Lane. We weren't paid at all, apart from our expenses up to Gorleston, but I got thirty-eight pounds out of Aspin to pay a motoring fine. On the boat was . . . an American who had fought in Vietnam and Rhodesia – and Butcher, apart from Aspin and Bishop. Conditions were lousy. We made the boat habitable but there was no food. One of us pinched a sack of potatoes and we lived on those for several days. I know Aspin later claimed to have spent so much money on the boat, but I can tell you how we got our cordage. We stole it from another boat. Aspin had a book of 'expenses' and he noted down £510 for rope! I spent weeks on that boat for nothing – I must have been crazy.

Aitken went on to relate how various visitors were brought along to inspect the boat, one of them the 'money man', two more who were introduced as *News of the World* reporters and an ex-Guards officer. Before they were due to sail Aspin came down to brief the crew members.

He came out with all sorts of stories about what we were going to do. One was we were going to attack the banks in Beirut and lift the money from the vaults. I told Aspin he was crazy, that you'd need a hundred men to do it. Then it came down to this plan to ferry out refugees at a hundred pounds a time and ferry back petrol – which sounded feasible . . .

We set sail on 5 September. Butcher had dropped out by this time. We had neither life rafts nor emergency lights. Later, I heard . . . that we weren't even insured. Aspin and Bishop came with us as far as Brighton, where we were supposed to pick up another man. He didn't turn up so we went on.

On 10 or 11 September, we ran into a force 9 gale and afterwards the boat was handling very badly. We had no charts for the Bay of Biscay – we had for everywhere else but that didn't help. We also had food for fifteen days only although the journey to Cyprus would have taken at least twenty-one days. We got through the gale and decided to drop anchor at Corunna. We all slept. There was nobody on watch and we had put out no lights. We must have dragged anchor in the night because suddenly we were woken up by a bang as we hit the rocks. We didn't know what the hell had happened and were running around trying to find out what to do . . .

Eventually some Spaniards turned up and they showed us how we could walk ashore. We were put up at a sailors' hostel and given some pocket money. We were there for a week or two before Aspin came out for us . . . All we had to eat was a tin of pilchards and a tin of ham salvaged off the boat. At Boulogne we got a ferry and Aspin got a meal for us by telling the crew we were shipwrecked sailors and had no money . . . We were supposed to get £150 a week from the time we got to the Lebanon . . .

It is difficult to imagine a more appropriate end to this typically piratical enterprise of mercenary recruiter Aspin and his gullible henchmen. But not all Britain's mercenaries are so hopelessly inefficient. Since the Angola disaster, the big mouths like Banks and Aspin have hogged the television appearances and have become in the minds of many people the typical mercenary recruiters and organizers. Nothing could better suit the purposes of the most dangerous mercenary leaders, whose activities are approved by the army, if not also by the government. These are the high-ranking officers, often recently retired, who make their money by acting as advisers and recruiters for foreign governments friendly to Britain, like the client states of what used to be called the Persian Gulf.

These men are eminently respectable, well connected, with not only the 'old-boy network' of their army colleagues to help them with information about available men, but also friends in Parliament who share their political aims. In the British context, these are not outcasts like the Prévosts or Skorzenys. They move from the clubs of Westminster to the palaces of the sheiks and sultans and back, without the need for clandestine methods. They are an integral, if not too visible, part of Britain's military and political establishment. They certainly despise the bunglers and headline-grabbers like Banks and Aspin and are delighted that public attention is diverted from their own activities to those of the mountebanks.

Britain's officially and semi-officially backed mercenaries in the Gulf region are of roughly three categories. The first is usually ex-regular army employed in undercover or irregular operations. During the civil war in North Yemen (1962–70) a few British and French military personnel – supported by Britain, in power in Aden until 1967 – fought on the side of the Yemeni feudal royalists against the Egyptian-backed republic. Britain was in cahoots with Saudi Arabia, which provided bases, Britain helping in training, communications personnel and some combatants.

David Stirling, the founder of the original SAS (Special Air Service) – the name was later perpetuated in the British Army's Special Air Force Regiment – helped to provide recruits for this operation and similar ones. He also conceived the idea of a commando force in Britain in case the trade unions got too uppish there. Readers who take an 'It can't happen here' view of the scary article in *Le Monde* quoted earlier might ponder on the implications of some of the services offered by Colonel David Stirling to Middle East potentates and his 'GB75' plan for Great Britain. Special Air Service, which he invented and led, was a daring commando group of the Second World War. Successful operationally, it was also, by its name, a psychological warfare device, designed to fool the Nazi Middle East Command into believing that British parachutists were active in the area. In fact, Stirling's hit-and-run group, which destroyed over 250 German and Italian aircraft on the ground in fourteen months, operated from motor vehicles or on foot. No one can detract from Stirling's wartime courage, ingenuity and spectacular successes. Nor could anyone do likewise for those of Colonel Otto Skorzeny for *his* side. After the Second World War, Colonel Stirling, having acquired some 4,000 acres of cattle-raising land in Tanganyika, was a leading figure in the Capricorn Africa Society, formed of elitist whites and blacks, intended to persuade nationalist blacks in Tanganyika, Kenya, Rhodesia and Nyasaland to reject what has since become the nationalist 'one man one vote' concept of majority rule, in favour of something similar to what Rhodesia's Ian Smith calls 'responsible' – or elitist, white-weighted – majority rule. Capricorn collapsed.

Stirling then formed Watchguard, which for suitable fees would provide, according to a catalogue listing, as did Banks's other SAS,

the services available: '(a) Military Surveys and Advice ...
(b) Head of State Security. This includes the training of Close
Escort Units of bodyguard teams for Heads of State and other key
officers of government ... (c) Special Forces: The training of
forces to combat insurgency and guerrilla warfare.' A concrete
estimate presented to the Kingdom of Saudi Arabia – for the training of 151 men who would have at their disposal three helicopters,
two light aircraft, mortars and anti-tank weapons – according to a
secret document published in the *Sunday Times* of 18 January
1970, would cost a mere £499,512 sterling. Training would
include 'guerrilla warfare and counter-guerrilla methods' and 'all
forms of counter-revolutionary action'. As an extra inducement,
Colonel Stirling gave an assurance that Watchguard would have
special access to 'the Special Air Force Regiment of the British
Army'. In the end Saudi Arabia declined these services but other
Middle Eastern and East African rulers – including President
Kenneth Kaunda of Zambia – did accept them. The modern non-
Banks SAS, as the *Sunday Times* article stresses, 'is, of course, an
arm of the British Army, and, as Colonel Stirling told us repeatedly,
Watchguard (International) is a profit-making, private commercial
enterprise which moreover works for foreign governments'.

This represented the foreign side of Stirling's activities. But the
British public was astounded to learn – precisely on 22 August 1974
via the *Daily Express* – of the existence of a 'gentle giant who wants
to save Britain from chaos', as the *Daily Express* told its readers,
through its commando organization GB75 which 'offers its
services to whatever Prime Minister is in power if a general strike
or series of strikes threaten to cripple the nation'. Why 'GB75'?
Because there were to be general elections in October 1974 which
could – and did – lead to a Labour Party victory, based on their
'Social Contract' alliance with the Trade Union Congress. In case
the trade unions became too militant and threatened a general
strike or any other measures to paralyse industry, Colonel
Stirling offered a heliborne force to take over such vital services as
power stations and others. Commented the London *Guardian* of
23 August:

Although GB75 may remain a cloud no bigger than a man's pipe-
smoke, however, its very title reflects, if rather perversely, some of the

reasoning behind the organization. It might have been more proper to call it UK75, since Colonel Stirling has clearly been influenced by the inability of the army in Northern Ireland to run the power stations during the Ulster Workers' Council strike . . .

GB75 was not the only force in the strike-breaking field. A rival organization, strongly supported by General Sir Walter Walker, a former Commander-in-Chief, Allied Forces Northern Europe, called Unison Committee for Action – Unison for short – was set up in early 1973. The London *Times* of 29 July 1974 quoted General Sir Walter as saying that: 'Unison is an entirely non-militant organization. Its members would act only if there was a collapse of law and order and they were needed to provide back-up service . . .'

Another, more official type of foreign mercenaries than those offered by Colonel David Stirling are those who come from redundant army personnel to serve, with British government approval, in the armies or defence ministries of independent Gulf states and elsewhere. The most flagrant case of this is in the Sultanate of Oman, where British mercenary personnel under 'contract' to the sultan have been staffing his air force and helping to officer his army. It is generally estimated that about 200 British mercenaries have been constantly in action against the guerrillas in Dhofar since the revolutionary movement started there in 1965. The reply given by the Secretary of State for Defence, Mr Roy Mason, on 25 November 1975, to a question by the Labour member for Barking, Miss Jo Richardson, is revealing in this respect:

MISS RICHARDSON: How many British Servicemen are currently serving in Oman, how many have their salaries paid by the Omani Government, and how many have their salaries paid by the British Government?

MR ROY MASON: 206 members of her Majesty's Armed Forces are currently serving on loan with the Sultan of Oman's armed forces. In addition, a limited number of HM forces was given leave from their regiments in Dhofar in support of the Sultan's forces. It is not the practice to give details of operational deployments. 523 members of HM forces are serving on the Royal Air Force staging post on Masirah Island and four are serving on the permanent staff of HM Embassy Muscat.

The salaries of the personnel on loan are met by the Sultanate and the basic salaries of the other British Service personnel in Oman are paid by the British Government.

A report by Christopher Lee in the *Daily Express* of 31 December 1975 puts some flesh on the bones of Roy Mason's reply.

Here in the hot, dusty deserts and wicked mountains of Oman, 'mercenary' is a dirty word. To the cynic it is difficult to distinguish between a contract officer and a so-called mercenary.

Since the Congo, and stories of white mercenaries hiring their guns and skills to the highest bidder, the term has taken on a sour meaning.

But in Oman there is one difference: the Sultan's war is supported by Whitehall even to the extent of sending out British troops to fight alongside the hired troops and regular forces.

Today there are more than 200 British officers seconded from their regiments to lead the Sultan's mixture of Omani and Baluchistan tribesmen.

A further eighty men of the SAS are up in the *jebel* (mountains) leading the *firquat* – the irregular troops. They fight alongside the contract officers who mainly arrive from the United Kingdom after leaving the Services. The Sultan's armed forces are commanded by a British major-general and the frontline Dhofar Regiment by an English brigadier. Defence Secretary Roy Mason flies out to see how things are going and shakes the hands of a contract officer with as much vigour as he does the general's . . .

The 'seconded' soldier is the third type of overtly official British mercenaries – mainly officers and pilots – supplied on a government-to-government basis, payments made directly to the British government by the state concerned. This is something like the arrangement the Americans had in Vietnam when they paid the South Korean government on a per-head basis for South Korean troops fighting under the US Command. Many of the Gulf states have such arrangements with the British government and altogether some thirty-three governments around the world have such contractual arrangements with Britain. Mercenary troops are thus an accepted form of export and earners of foreign exchange for the British government. Needless to say they are used almost exclusively to maintain in power unpopular régimes which could not otherwise stand on their own feet. Obviously there is a close relationship between military hardware supplied to such countries and the military 'advisers' sent to explain how to use it. The best demonstrations are against live targets under battlefield conditions! This is particularly true in the Gulf states. The *Sunday Times* of 4 July 1976 thus reported:

In Oman, until recently, about 360 officers and NCOs were serving the sultan, of whom about one-third were under contract. No distinction is made between contract and seconded soldiers in fighting the left-wing rebels. Over the past two and a half years, allied (Omani, Iranian and British) casualties have included five hundred dead. During the past five years, eleven members of the Special Air Service regiment have been killed in action. Last year the sultan was offering ex-RAF or Royal Navy Strikemaster pilots £8,250 tax-free plus other perks.

The *Sunday Times* correspondent Tony Geraghty was unable to state just how many British 'contract' soldiers were working for the sultan, but he referred to a British government-owned company, Millbank Technical Services, which 'provide about four hundred military specialists for general support operations'. These contracts do not preclude the possibility of combat. Geraghty quoted the reply of Roy Mason to a question in the House of Commons asking whether the government had circulated invitations to ex-servicemen to enlist as 'mercenaries in the armed forces of foreign countries'. Mason's reply:

In certain cases, assistance is given to friendly foreign governments in the recruitment of retired Service personnel on a contract basis.

A reply which helps to explain why the British government is reluctant to enact legislation to outlaw once and for all the recruitment and enlistment of mercenaries!

Part Two

Mercenaries and the Law

12 A Vast Private Army

The British Government's Attitude

We deplore, and we would seek to do everything in our power to stop, mercenary incursion from this country or any other country into Angola ... we are looking at the applicability of the Foreign Enlistment Act with urgency to see how it can be applied to the Angolan situation.

So said Lord Goronwy Roberts, Minister of State, in the House of Lords on 5 February 1976.[1]

Whatever the efficiency of its intelligence and police forces, the *Daily Mail* advertisements towards the end of May 1975 and the accounts in the *Daily Telegraph* on 2 June 1975 put the government on notice that mercenaries were being recruited in England for service in Angola. By the end of the year there had been questions in Parliament. Yet for eight or nine months the government did nothing. It was suggested in the House of Commons on 2 February 1976 that if the present legislation were of doubtful effect it should be replaced by legislation that worked. The Home Secretary, Roy Jenkins, said that he was not persuaded that it would be appropriate to have legislation making it illegal to recruit mercenaries or para-military forces in Britain. But the news of the murder of the mercenaries in Angola by Callan and his accomplices broke on 8 February and Prime Minister Wilson was forced to make a state-

1. The House of Commons debates on the mercenaries in Angola are in *Hansard*, 24 November 1975, column 22; 19 December 1975, c. 819; 28 January 1976, c. 411; 2 February 1976, c. 428; 9 February 1976, cc. 28, 29; 10 February 1976, cc. 236–47; 19 February 1976, c. 814; 20 February 1976, c. 836; 24 February 1976, cc. 154, 187; 26 February 1976, c. 285; 1 March 1976, c. 456; 10 March 1976, cc. 409, 410; 24 March 1976, c. 205; 21 May 1976, c. 753; and thereafter concerning the trial and not relevant to this chapter. The debates in the House of Lords of special interest are 5 February 1976, cc. 1413, 1414; 10 February 1976, cc. 22–30; 17 February 1976, cc. 423–6 and 437, 438; 9 March 1976, cc. 1201–4.

ment to the House on 10 February in response to growing demands for the Act[2] to be enforced. He was evasive:

There is some doubt about the interpretation of that Act . . . It was last invoked, I think, in the case of the Jameson raid in the last century. Whether or not it is applicable here is a legal matter into which it would not be appropriate for me to enter. I have had advice on this matter . . . We must face the fact that within a few days a small group of people – whatever their background – have been able to raise a vast private army. That this is possible could be a threat to democracy in this country. They have raised a vast private army because they have access to money to enable them to do so. [Interruption] Hon. Gentlemen may sneer at that, but there could be a threat to democracy in this country.

Against such a peril, one might be forgiven for thinking, only the most immediate and effective defences would be enough. Why not then invoke the Act and put a stop to recruiting by punishing the recruiters?

It is extremely difficult to answer that. From the advice one gets from those most highly competent in the matter of the application of the Foreign Enlistment Act 1870 to a situation such as this, it is very difficult to get a clear view. The Act itself is now, I think, very much outdated in some of its particulars. One has only to read what it says about principalities, Powers, peshwas and all the rest of it. It is a little outdated in its language. I find it very difficult to advise the House whether, on the advice given to me, the Act can be invoked in this particular case.

If the threat to democracy were considered important, would it not be best to try a prosecution and see whether it worked? Would not that at least have the merits of showing the government's earnestness and of giving the recruiters something to think about? What alternative was there? The Prime Minister had one. He set up a committee.

We need clarification, and if the Committee recommends that changes in the Act or in other legislation are needed it is for the Committee to say so and for the House to act on its advice . . . All I can say is that,

2. The Foreign Enlistment Act 1870, 33 & 34 Vict. c. 90, was partially repealed in unimportant detail in 1893 and 1953.

within whatever powers are available to the Government under the law as it stands, we shall do everything in our power to prevent the further recruitment and establishment of mercenaries from this country to Angola or to any troubled areas.

The Prime Minister resigned his office in February and no prosecutions were instituted. The Diplock Committee did not report until August. The Angolan people had by that time won their battle against the mercenaries and their masters. The captured British and United States mercenaries had been tried, convicted and punished. The British government's only attempt to restrain their activities had been to confiscate the passports of some of the returning mercenaries for a few weeks. Well within two months, unrestricted passports had been unconditionally restored. They were free to seek similar employment elsewhere, and many have taken full advantage of that freedom, not only in Africa but in the Lebanon and elsewhere.[3]

What a pity then that the government which so strongly deplored the recruitment and enlistment of mercenaries within its jurisdiction should have been hampered by its legislation! But how good an excuse for inactivity is the inadequacy of the Act? Is it true that the language is so outdated as to make it difficult to apply? Is it true that the Act has not been applied in English courts? Is the law generally believed by experts to be complex and uncertain? Is the provenance of the Act obscure and are the present conditions so different from those which prevailed when it was passed that it would be easy to show that its application would be inappropriate or irrelevant? If on examination we find that it is straightforward and that it and the legislation it replaced have been applied before in sufficiently similar circumstances, and that moreover it envisaged just the sort of activity that the government characterized as deplorable, whatever could have been the explanation of the government's inactivity?

3. A mercenary called Robert Thacker, who had fought in Angola, was killed in action in Beirut in August 1976 (*The Times*, 10 August 1976; *Daily Express*, 12 August 1976). Our own inquiries reveal that the recruiters who sent the mercenaries to Angola have recruited some of them on their return for Lebanon and Namibia. Others have gone to Zimbabwe.

The Provisions of the Act

The legislation which prohibits British subjects from becoming mercenaries or recruiting others to be mercenaries is the Foreign Enlistment Act, passed in 1870. The sections which deal with mercenaries are section 4, which makes it an offence to enlist for a foreign state or induce another to do so, section 5, which extends the offence to those who leave Britain, or any other of Her Majesty's dominions, with the intention of enlisting for a foreign state, and section 30, which gives a special meaning to the phrase 'a foreign state'. The rest of the Act is concerned with formal matters, with penalties (for the offences we are concerned with they are an unlimited fine and imprisonment of up to two years' duration) and with the separate offences of fitting out expeditions and building ships for countries involved in wars in which Britain is neutral.

Section 4 reads:

If any person, without the licence of Her Majesty, being a British subject, within or without Her Majesty's dominions, accepts or agrees to accept any commission or engagement in the military or naval service of any foreign state at war with any foreign state at peace with Her Majesty, and in this Act referred to as a friendly state, or whether a British subject or not within Her Majesty's dominions, induces any other person to accept or agree to accept any commission or engagement in the military or naval service of any such foreign state as aforesaid, –

He shall be guilty of an offence against this Act, and shall be punishable by fine and imprisonment . . .

Section 5 reads:

If any person, without the licence of Her Majesty, being a British subject, quits or goes on board any ship with a view of quitting Her Majesty's dominions, with intent to accept any commission or engagement in the military or naval service of any foreign state at war with a friendly state, or, whether a British subject or not, within Her Majesty's dominions, induces any other person to quit or to go on board any ship with a view of quitting Her Majesty's dominions with the like intent, –

He shall be guilty of an offence against this Act, and shall be punishable by fine and imprisonment . . .

If these two sections are shorn of unnecessary words, they are readily understood: 'If any person, being a British subject, agrees to accept any engagement in the military service of any foreign state at war with any friendly foreign state or induces any other person to accept any engagement, he shall be guilty of an offence.' He does not need to be a British subject if he recruits in Britain. Moreover, 'If any British subject quits Her Majesty's dominions, with intent to accept any engagement in the military service of a foreign state at war with a friendly foreign state, or induces any other person to quit, he shall be guilty of an offence.' Again, it does not matter whether he is a British subject if the recruiting is done in Britain.

The reader must judge for himself whether that is too difficult for a judge to fathom. In doing so the reader may like to compare it with sections of Acts relating to taxation or town planning which are applied by the courts every day.

An immediate objection might seem to be that the British government had not recognized the government of Angola, though the government had been in power since 11 November 1975 and had been recognized by more than forty states at the time the offences were committed. This would be an argument were it not for section 30, which gives to the expression 'foreign state', wherever it is used in the Act, a meaning much wider than that which it would have in ordinary usage.

Section 30 reads:

In this Act, if not inconsistent with the context, the following terms have the meanings hereinafter respectively assigned to them; that is to say,

'Foreign state' includes any foreign prince, colony, province or part of any province or people, or any persons exercising or assuming to exercise the powers of government in or over any foreign country, colony, province, or part of any province or people.

In sections 4 and 5 then, the words 'foreign state' must be read so widely that they include any part of any people, and any person or persons assuming to exercise the powers of government in or over any part of any people.

These are certainly very wide and all-embracing words. They catch military service of all kinds abroad (other than in Her

Majesty's forces) against a force which is friendly, that is, not at war with the Crown. The MPLA, and the government of the People's Republic of Angola, have never been at war with the Crown and Parliament would never have tried to foist such a war on the British people.

Whatever happened to the 'principalities, Powers and peshwas' that perplexed Mr Wilson? The most scrupulous reading of the Act shows that there is no mention of them at all. Could the mixture of former Indian potentates and the upper echelons of the heavenly host be the conjuration of the illusionist?

The meaning of the Act is not hard to find and its effect is obvious. In passing the Act, Parliament intended to stop the recruitment and enlistment of mercenaries in England to fight in hostilities in which Britain is neutral, and passed legislation drafted so widely that it catches every kind of military and naval service, combatant and non-combatant, in any foreign country, whether the enlistment is legally accomplished within Britain or the recruit goes abroad to enlist. When we look at the history of the law we see that this is not a bit surprising.

The Early History of the Law[4]

The prohibition of enlistment for a foreign prince is four centuries

4. There is no adequate history of this part of the law. The general legal histories treat it lightly: Sir W. S. Holdsworth, *History of English Law*, Methuen, 16 vols., various dates, IV, 298, 507; V, 49; VI, 308; X, 376; XIII, 216, 217; XIV, 32 and especially 74–81; and Sir J. F. Stephen, *A History of the Criminal Law of England*, Macmillan, 1883, III, 257–62. There is a strange monograph: G. J. Wheeler, *The Act under which Dr Jameson will be Tried &c.*, Eyre and Spottiswode, 1896. It is no more than a print of the Act with a short introduction and an epilogue listing a few cases (price one penny). A fuller treatment (2nd edn of Part I, 1st of Part II) was published later in the year, under the title *The British & American Foreign Enlistment Acts &c.*, by the same publishers. There are one or two articles: E. W. Cox, 'The Case of the "Alexandra"' (1863), 39 *Law Times* 14, 15; E. W. Cox, 'The Case of "The Iron-Clads"' (1863), 39 *Law Times* 25, 26; W. W. Kerr, 'The Principles and Rules of Neutrality – The Foreign Enlistment Act – "The Alabama"' (1858–63), 2 *Papers Read before the Juridical Society* 629–67 (Paper XXXI); F. S. Reilly, 'The Provisions of the Foreign Enlistment Act relating to Ships', 2 *Papers Read before the Juridical Society* 668–80 (Paper XXXII); anonymous editorial in (1871) 6 *Law Journal* 206, 207.

old. Since the time of Elizabeth I, there have been proclamations restricting the freedom of British subjects to fight in foreign armies.[5] In 1561, a Royal Proclamation forbade English sailors to accompany Scotch expeditions against the Portuguese. In 1572, 1573 and 1577 Elizabeth I prohibited any levy of troops for service in countries with which England was at peace. In 1605-6 it was enacted that if any person left the realm to serve a foreign prince without first taking an oath of allegiance to the Crown or, if he had held a commission in the army, without entering into a bond not to be reconciled to the Pope, he would commit a felony. Many proclamations in Tudor and Stuart times repeated the prohibitions in one form or another.

All the early legislation was concerned with protecting the Crown directly, against those who might want to fight for its political opponents, against the diminution of the potential fighting force it could summon, or to avoid reprisals. The legislation of George II in 1735-6 and 1755-6, which was passed by Walpole, dealt only with enlistment and recruitment, making them felonies without benefit of clergy, that is effectively punishable by death for all convicted. The preamble categorized such offences as 'prejudicial to the safety and welfare of this kingdom'.

But by the beginning of the nineteenth century the political significance of neutrality had been recognized.[6] It was the French Revolution and the wars which followed it that brought home first to American and then to British politicians the advantage of having legislation which would make it easy to control the military activities of citizens who wished to fight abroad for causes which were considered by conservative governments to be dangerously revolutionary.

When war broke out in 1793, France called upon the United States to allow the French, under their treaty of 1778, to fit out privateers in American ports, to capture prizes in American waters, to take their prizes back to American ports and to have

5. The proclamations and their sources are listed in Sir W. S. Holdsworth, *History of English Law*, vi, 308.
6. The best historical account is in the memorandum of C. S. Abbott printed as an appendix to the *Report of the Neutrality Laws Commissioners*, Parliamentary Papers (1867-8), xxxii, Appendix iii.

them condemned by the French consuls there. President Washington was determined that the United States should not be embroiled in the war. Under pressure from the British government, he propounded the theory, still novel then, that a neutral state had a duty to prevent its subjects from enlisting in the service of a belligerent. The United States government brought an action for breach of what it contended was a common law crime, that is a crime not founded upon a statute but upon the general judge-made law. In *United States* v. *Henfield* (1793) (Wharton's State Trials 49), the accused was indicted at common law for disturbing the peace by privateering. Chief Justice Hay held that a citizen who, without the authority of the nation to which he belongs, takes a hostile part with either belligerent against the other, thereby violates his duty and the laws of his country and is indictable at common law. Every citizen has a duty to observe his country's international obligations. The jury had no sympathy with this, though, and failed to convict. There were many in the United States who supported the French cause, not only out of political sympathy with the revolution and republican aspirations, but because France had been their ally in the War of Independence and there was no love lost for the British, whose most recent affront had been the conscription of British subjects who had emigrated to America. The Americans understandably objected to what they considered to be the compulsory pressing into the British service in a British war of Americans whose allegiance was to the United States. Washington's bill met stiff opposition, but Jefferson, its principal opponent, was in retirement at the time of its discussion. It passed the Senate on the casting vote of the Vice-President. The Foreign Enlistment Act 1795 was the first legislation of its kind passed with the expressed aim of protecting the neutrality of the state. It was improved and made permanent in 1818.

The First British Foreign Enlistment Act

By a treaty with Spain of 1814, Britain had undertaken to prevent British subjects supporting the insurgents in the Spanish colonies of South America in their struggle for independence. The British government issued a proclamation in 1817 forbidding the fitting-out of expeditions to assist the forces seeking independence. The need for a British counterpart of the United States Foreign Enlistment Act was clear. For the first time, Britain was a neutral in a great maritime war and needed legislation relating to the provision of ships to the belligerents. Sir William Blackstone, a writer on the common law of England of the highest authority, had been of the opinion that it was a crime at common law, that is quite apart from any statute, to enter the service of a foreign state without the consent of the Crown.[7] But the legislation of George II had increased the offence from the misdemeanour it was at common law to a felony, punishable by death. Introducing the bill on 13 May 1819,[8] the Attorney-General expressed its purpose as:

to reduce the penalty from a felony to a misdemeanour, and to make the law equally applicable to acknowledged and to unacknowledged powers. Enlisting in the service of those persons who had assumed to themselves the powers of government (whether they were justifiable or not in assuming those powers he should not inquire, because he wished to avoid the political discussion of such a question), was a violation of that neutrality which this country professed to observe ... It was important to the country that the law should decide, that no man should have a right to enlist in foreign service.

The Attorney-General repeated himself many times and ended hopefully but lamely by saying that he did not expect any objection to the bill and that all the bill would do was already covered by the common law anyway.

But there were many in Parliament who for one reason or another would not support the bill. Sir James Mackintosh led the opposition. He pointed out that the penalty of death prescribed by the existing legislation was 'revolting to humanity, and which, therefore, now could never be inflicted'. The bill should be entitled 'a bill for preventing British subjects from lending their assistance to the South American cause'. He suggested an ingenious explanation for the distinction in the existing legislation between serving in the forces of an 'acknowledged' and an 'unacknowl-

7. The passage in Blackstone is Sir W. Blackstone, *Commentaries on the Laws of England*, IV, 122 (many editions). It says that even to receive a pension from a foreign prince without leave is a misdemeanour.
8. The debate on the 1819 Act is in *Hansard*, 13 May 1819, cc. 362–74; 3 June 1819, cc. 867–910; 10 June 1819, cc. 1084–118.

edged' power. Those who fight for an unacknowledged power are likely to find their own punishment without the processes of law, as they are not if captured entitled to be treated as prisoners of war and must suffer the fate of the rebels for whom they fight.

Castlereagh sought to disarm by abandoning the dissimulation of his Attorney-General and acknowledging the immediate political purpose of the bill. It sought to give the government the power needed to enforce the proclamation of neutrality:

And was it not a breach of that proclamation, when not only individuals whom perhaps it would not have been impossible to restrain, not only officers in small numbers went out to join the insurgent corps, but when there was a regular organization of troops, when regiments regularly formed left this country, when ships of war were prepared in our ports, and transports were chartered to carry out troops and ammunition? It was to prevent this that the present bill was brought in ...

When asked whether he intended to send a fleet to bring back the '5,000, perhaps nearly 10,000, persons from this country engaged in the naval and military forces of the insurgent states', he pointed out that the legislation was not intended to be retrospective.

In its passage through Parliament, the arguments for and against the bill were multifarious. It was despicable to bow to pressure from the unspeakable Spanish tyrant. The South Americans would win anyway. The penalty under the old Acts was too severe and for this reason they had become a dead letter. They were not a dead letter and some of those convicted of offences under them had been hanged. They did not still apply because they were passed to deal with immediate and temporary dangers. They were on the contrary of general application, as a careful consideration of their provenance showed. They were necessary because it was manifestly unfair that those who enlisted in the forces of legitimate governments, such as that of Ferdinand of Spain's, should be subject to the death penalty, whereas those who went to fight for the insurgents committed no offence. It was ridiculous to say that British officers fighting as mercenaries in Ferdinand's army were subject to any restriction when two of them in full dress Spanish uniform had been formally bidden farewell at the Prince Regent's levee the week before. The common law already made enlisting a crime and so there was nothing much new in the bill. If so, then why bother? Because there would then be law to prevent as well as punish. The mercenaries were fighting for liberty. No, for gain. There were 'many gallant soldiers who had fought the battles of the country' and 'in a great proportion paupers on their parishes', and 'British officers were subsisting on a miserable pittance'. How much cheaper then to let another paymaster support them! Moreover it would get a dangerous element out of the country, to do their mischief elsewhere. The bill would be 'converting this boasted land of freedom into a great prison; and engendering much discontent and dissatisfaction at home, which had better be allowed to effervesce abroad'. Grotius and Puffendorf, Vattel and Bynkershoek were quoted as authorities for the freedom to kill for hire, but the real arguments for the opposition were beautifully presented by a Mr Douglas:

In our present commercial distress, while our trade was in a state of stagnation, and our manufacturers were suffering almost intolerable hardships from the want of sale for the produce of their industry, Providence seemed to have opened to us the markets of South America – a country of immense extent, and of unlimited wealth, whose resources would grow with the growth of its independence, and in a short time enable it to purchase and consume whatever we could export for its use ... let the House consider what might be the consequences of rejecting a union with states, which from that rejection might be thrown into the arms of the North American republic, and thus compose along with it an alliance of incalculable strength ... to employ all its energies against the trade and power of this country from ancient jealousy or contemned friendship.

We should therefore allow those who had bled in the service of their own country and were now out of work and a burden on the parish to 'acquire additional experience in the new world and to promote the progress of human happiness and freedom ... They would be taught in the same school with our Raleighs and Essexes' and so on. The many British mercenaries who had fought in foreign armies and navies through the centuries, and the many foreigners who had fought in the British forces, were used as precedents. But it was the petition of Liverpool merchants who were doing well out of the war, and the interesting information that there was an annual trade with Buenos Aires alone worth £2 million, while all the trade with Spain was worth no more than £400,000, that showed where the interest lay. Crafty Castlereagh was astute to take the point:

> He was afraid that the hon. member had obtained his information, which was altogether unfounded, from *other* merchants [a dig at his bourgeois opposition], who had forgotten the British mercantile character in their occupation as agents for those colonies. In their uniting commerce and war, the merchants were not acting in a manner worthy of an honest and high-minded people, and the trade of the nation itself was compromised.

Castlereagh could command the votes and the Act was passed. It remained the law for just over fifty years.

The Background of the Foreign Enlistment Act 1870

Having got the legislation it wanted,[9] the government appears to have used it more against ships than mercenaries.[10] It was not used

9. The Act is the Foreign Enlistment Act 1819, 59 Geo. III c. 69.
10. Most of the decisions of this Act are noted in *English & Empire Digest* 15, Part xvi, sub-section 2, 875–8, under the heading 'Foreign Enlistment':

R. v. *Granatelli* (1849) 7 State Trials N. S. 979

Two Sicilies (*King*) v. *Willcox* (1850) 1 Sim. N. S. 301; 7 State Trials N. S. 1049; 14 Jur. 751; 61 E.R. 116; *sub nom. Two Sicilies* (*King*) v. *Peninsular & Oriental Steam Packet Co.* 19 L. J. Ch. 488; *sub nom. The Bombay* 6 L. Y. 165

Ex p. Crawshay (1860) 3 L. T. 320; 24 J. P. 805; *sub nom. Ex p. Crawshay* v. *Langley* 8 Cox C. C. 356

R. v. *Jones & Highat* (1864) 4 F. & F. 25

R. v. *Rumble* (1864) 4 F. & F. 175

A.-G. v. *Sillem* (1864) 2 H. & C. 431; 3 F. & F. 646; 159 E.R. 178; *sub nom. A.-G.* v. *Sillem, The Alexandra Case* 33 L. J. Ex. 92; 10 Jur. N. S. 262; 12 W. R. 257; *sub nom. R.* v. *Sillem* 3 New Rep. 299; 11 L. T. 223; 2 Mar. L. C. 100

R. v. *Corbett* (1865) 4 F. & F. 555

Re Grazebrook, Ex p. Chavasse (1865) 4 De G. J. & Sm. 655; 6 New Rep. 6; 34 L. J. Bcy. 17; 12 L. T. 249; 11 Jur. N. S. 400; 13 W.R. 627; 2 Mar. L. C. 197; 46 E. R. 1072

Burton v. *Pinkerton* (1867) L. R. 2 Exch 340; 36 L. J. Ex. 137; 16 L. T. 419; 31 J. P. 615; 15 W. R. 1139; 2 Mar. L. C. 494

R. v. *Carlin, The Salvador* (1870) L. R. 3 P. C. 218; 6 Moo. P. C. C. N. S. 509; 39 L. J. Adm. 33; 23 L. T. 203; 3 Mar. L. C. 479; 16 E. R. 818.

immediately and in 1823 there was a motion before the House for its repeal. Canning was eloquent in opposing the motion and it was defeated. In 1827 the government sent a warship and some gunboats to intercept a fleet of ships which, though ostensibly bound for Brazil, was intended to interfere in Spanish affairs, but in 1835 an Order in Council licensed the formation of the Spanish Legion under Sir De Lacy Evans to fight for Isabella of Spain. In 1846 the government seized and declared forfeit three ships being fitted out to sail against the government of Ecuador, but in 1847 the government declared itself powerless to prevent British subjects in Portugal enlisting in the revolutionary forces, because the acts complained of had been committed outside the jurisdiction. It considered prosecuting a Mr Hislop, who returned to England, but decided the evidence was too weak against him. In 1862, an Order in Council licensed Captain Osborn and Mr Lay to enter the service of the Emperor of China and fit out ships and recruit mercenaries. This licence was in 1863 extended to all military officers in Her Majesty's service.

The British government's reluctance to curb the activities of recruiters was not shared by some foreign governments, who were prepared to use a prosecution under the Foreign Enlistment Act 1819 as a deterrent. In 1849, the Sicilian Minister in London, on behalf of the King of the Two Sicilies, brought a private prosecution against Prince Granatelli and others, supporters of the provisional government which had been set up at Palermo. There were three charges: the enlisting of soldiers, the enlisting of sailors, and the fitting-out of a ship, the last, according to the judge, being the most material. In the words of the prosecution:

The object of the Act was to prevent persons in this country from equipping vessels or enlisting men with hostile purpose against any friendly state. It was unnecessary to dwell upon the policy of the law in question, because it was impossible to conceive anything more likely to disturb the relations between friendly states than for persons to equip vessels, and make hostile demonstrations in one country against another. The Minister of His Majesty the King of the Two Sicilies had therefore felt it his duty to institute the present prosecution against the defendants, and if the facts which would be laid before the jury did not bring them within the scope of the Act, it was a dead letter, and the sooner it was removed from the Statute-book the better. During the past year nearly the whole of the states of the Continent had been disturbed by revolutionary movements; many of the governments of these states had been shaken to their foundations, and all had been severely disturbed.

The prosecution said it had no doubt the jury would do its duty. But the jury did not see it that way, especially after the judge had expressed the opinion not that the law was doubtful or did not apply but that the offence was 'certainly no further immoral and improper than as being a violation of an Act of Parliament'. The 'dangerous revolutionaries' were duly acquitted, *R.* v. *Granatelli* (1849) (7 State Trials New Series 979).

Another private prosecution which failed, that time because the prosecutor used the wrong technical procedure, was an attempt to prosecute a newspaper proprietor for advertising for volunteers to fight for Garibaldi's army (*Ex p. Crawshay* (1860), 3 Law Times 320). But most interesting of all is a case which has been generally ignored, a successful private prosecution, brought on behalf of the Tsar of Russia, against a recruiter for the army of Garibaldi to fight for Polish freedom. In *R.* v. *Styles*, reported only in *The Times* 12 and 19 August and 24 September 1863,[11] Baron Brunnow, the Russian ambassador, obtained a warrant at Bow Street for the arrest of a Lieutenant Styles, 'who was enlisting men for service in the Polish insurrection'. Styles was committed for trial, and at the Old Bailey pleaded guilty and was released on his own recognizances, having undertaken not to continue his recruiting. Here was a successful private prosecution, having the desired effect of preventing further recruitment, after the British government had declined to prosecute.

By this time the Foreign Enlistment Act 1819 had been brought back to public attention by the outbreak of the American Civil War, recognized as war by a proclamation of neutrality by the British government in 1861.[12] Eight recruiters were prosecuted by

11. *R.* v. *Styles* (1863), *The Times*, 12 August 1863, p. 11; 19 August 1863, p. 10; and 24 September 1863, p. 9.
12. A full account of the international legal aspects of the American Civil War is Q. Wright, 'The American Civil War (1861–65)' in R. A. Falk, ed., *The International Law of Civil War*, Johns Hopkins Press, Baltimore, 1971,

the British government for enlisting men to serve in Confederate ships. Of these, two were acquitted, though the evidence against them was very strong; two were convicted and sentenced to pay fines of £50 each; one pleaded guilty and was released on recognizances of £150 and three were convicted and released on recognizances. But there was money to be made in building and fitting out ships for the Confederates. English shipbuilders were foremost in the world. Why should they not take advantage of the opportunities? The shipbuilders had their men in Parliament and there were many others there, indeed the majority, who were in sympathy with the Confederates.

In 1861, a Confederate ship for the first time entered a British port and the United States protested. Though the British government replied that there could be no objection to such an entry, it later forbade any belligerent cruiser or privateer to bring its prize into any British port. This prohibition did not apply to merchant ships, which were even allowed to load arms. Warships could stay in a British port for no more than twenty-four hours and the supplies they could take on were restricted. The United States protested in vain against Confederate warships being victualled and merchantmen shipping arms but the call for the application of the Foreign Enlistment Act 1819 to stop the building of warships for the Confederates was more successful.

In 1861, the United States complained that the *Peerless* had been fitted out in Canada as a privateer for the Confederates. They informed the British government that United States ships had been ordered to seize her. Threats were exchanged but were lost in the embarrassment which followed the discovery that it was for the United States themselves and not the Confederates that the *Peerless* had been fitted out. There had been an unfortunate failure of communication between the Navy department and the State department. In 1862, Liverpool shipbuilders were completing cruisers for the Confederates. The Foreign Minister found out and tried to stop the *Alabama* leaving port, but she escaped and

---

30–109. An older treatment from a British point of view is M. Bernard, *Historical Account of the Neutrality of Great Britain during the American Civil War*, Longmans, 1870; see pp. 361, 362 for prosecutions.

took on arms and a Confederate captain and crew in the Azores. The *Alabama* was not the only one, and the United States threatened war if any more were let slip. This led to the detention of armoured rams being built in Birkenhead. The British government were apprehensive about the compensation they would have to pay and the political consequences of further connivance or negligence. They were right to be, because an international tribunal after the war awarded $15,500,000 to the United States for the direct damage caused by the British negligence in letting the *Alabama* leave port.

In 1864, a prosecution brought against a shipbuilder failed because it was held that the mere building of a ship was not within the statute.[13] It was necessary to prove that the ship had been equipped. On appeal by the Crown the four judges divided equally and the appeal failed. There were other cases too which showed the judges' reluctance to convict. The government was concerned and in 1867 set up a Royal Commission to inquire into the laws available for the enforcement of neutrality to bring them 'into full conformity with our international obligations'. The Commission reported without delay,[14] but it was not their report which precipitated the Foreign Enlistment Act, which was not passed until 1870. It was the outbreak of the Franco-Prussian war.

13. *A.-G.* v. *Sillem*; see n. 10, p. 184.
14. In 1868.

13 The Foreign Enlistment Act 1870 and the Diplock Report

It was Lord Halifax who explained the haste and the timing of the passage of the Foreign Enlistment Act.[1]

The Bill repealed the existing law, re-enacting it with such improvements as experience had shown to be desirable. It prohibited subjects of Her Majesty, without licence from the Crown, from taking part in hostilities between two countries with which Her Majesty was on friendly terms. He need not adduce arguments to show how unjustifiable and monstrous it would be for British subjects to take part in hostilities, when the avowed policy of the Government was that of perfect neutrality; but it was a question not of International but of Municipal Law – not between their country and foreign countries, but between the Crown and the subjects of the Crown. A similar law existed in the United States; while on the Continent Governments were able to prevent their subjects from violating neutrality. The principal objects of the Bill were to prohibit any subjects from inducing others to enlist in the service of a belligerent Power, and from fitting out, equipping, or arming any vessel for such service. During the American War the powers of the Government in this matter were found to be insufficient ... This defect would be removed by the present Bill, which was based on the Report of a Commission presided over by the late Lord Cranworth, and composed of other distinguished men. It was no disrespect to them that the Report had not been sooner carried out, for matters of great importance had occupied the attention of Parliament during the last two years; but the pressure of circumstances had now necessitated the passing of a Bill with unusual rapidity.

A writer in the *Law Journal* at the time deplored the government's surrender to pressure from the Prussian government: 'The moment that Parliament extends the scope of our municipal law

1. For the debates on the 1870 Act, see *Hansard*, 1 August 1870, cc. 1365–81; 3 August 1870, cc. 1502–13; 4 August 1870, cc. 1550–56; 5 August 1870, cc. 1592, 1593; 8 August 1870, cc. 1676–80.

in favour of what is called neutrality, it invites belligerents to insist on the execution of that law with the utmost vigour.' But, changing direction in the middle of his argument, he suggested that the law did not go far enough and echoed the speeches of some Members of Parliament in calling for a ban on the sale of all armaments. 'Let us give up the trade. But do not let us go on playing the Pharisee and mocking morality by saying that it is right to sell these instruments of destruction today and wrong to do so tomorrow.' He had no more success than those who argue against arms sales today.

The new Act differed in effect from the old in two ways, in addition to the improvement of the sections dealing with ships and jurisdiction. It made a slight change to include any British subject in its prohibition of enlisting. The earlier legislation had referred to any natural-born British subject. More important, it prohibited service in the forces of a foreign state 'at war with any foreign state at peace with Her Majesty'. There was no such phrase in the earlier Acts. It is clear from the debates in Parliament that this insertion was in no way meant to restrict the application of the Act or to exclude unrecognized states. Its purpose was to stress that the intention of the Act was to protect neutrality.

The first case after the 1870 Act concerned events that had taken place before it, the struggle for freedom in Cuba against Spanish domination. In *R.* v. *Carlin, The Salvador* (1870) (L.R. 3 P.C. 218), the Privy Council was concerned to point out that the insurgents had the characteristics of a body of people, part of the province or people of Cuba, and it was on the very point that that was sufficient to bring them within the earlier Act that they reversed the decision of the court below.

The Application of the Foreign Enlistment Act 1870

The courts greeted the new Act with the same lack of enthusiasm as its forerunners.[2] They were quickly called on to apply it in pros-

2. Reported decisions on the 1870 Act are:
 The International (1871) L. R. 3 A. & E. 321; 40 L. J. Adm. 1; 23 L. T. 787; 3 Mar. L. C. 523
 Dyke v. *Elliott, The Gauntlet* (1872) L. R. 4 P. C. 184; 8 Moo. P. C. C. N. S.

ecutions of those who were fitting out ships for use in the Franco-Prussian War. Because only those cases are reported which contain interesting points of law, the law reports represent the odd, not the normal, but in the few cases decided at the end of the last century there is little relish for this legislation, which may have appeared to the judges of the time as a serious restriction of England's commercial destiny. A tug sent to tow a prize for a belligerent state was not surprisingly held to be employed in the naval service of a foreign state and thereby infringing the act (*Dyke* v. *Elliot, The Gauntlet* (1872), L.R. 4 P.C. 148). But a ship laying a submarine telegraph cable for the French government did not break the law (*The International* (1871), L.R. 3 A. & E. 321).

In 1876, it was necessary for the Law Officers of the Crown to advise that the Governor of the Bahamas should be told that the Foreign Enlistment Act 1870 applied to the insurgents in Cuba even though they had not been recognized as belligerents:

> In obedience to Your Lordship's commands we have the honor to Report
>
> *That* in our opinion the Attorney General of the Colony has not given due weight to the Interpretation Clause s.30 of the Foreign Enlistment Act 1870.
>
> If therefore the 'Amazona' is in the employment or intended to be employed in the service of the Insurgents in Cuba, although those Insurgents may not be in the strict sense of the word 'belligerents' the case is brought within the statute. The case of the 'Salvador' though under the former Foreign Enlistment Act, was decided upon words almost if not quite the same with the words in the 30th section of the Act of 1870; and is a clear authority upon the point that as in the 4th section of the Act of 1870 the Insurgents are a 'Foreign State' at war with a Foreign State at peace with Her Majesty.

In *R.* v. *Sandoval* (1887) (56 Law Times 526), it was held sufficient

428; 26 L. T. 45; 20 W. R. 497; 1 Asp. M. L. C. 211; 17 E. R. 373; *sub nom.* *R.* v. *Elliott* 41 L. J. Adm. 65

   R. v. *Sandoval* (1887) 56 L. T. 526; 51 J. P. 709; 35 W. R. 500; 3 T. L. R. 411; 16 Cox C. C. 206

   R. v. *Jameson* [1896] 2 Q. B. 425; 65 L. J. M. C. 218; 75 L. T. 77; 60 J. P. 662; 12 T. L. R. 551; 18 Cox C. C. 392

   U.S.A. v. *Pelly* (1899) 47 W.R. 332; 15 T. L. R. 166; 43 Sol. Jo. 224; 4 Com. Cas. 100

that Krupp guns should be purchased in England and shipped to a foreign port, knowing that there they would be used in fighting a friendly foreign state, in this case Venezuela. The most celebrated case arose from the Jameson raid.[3] In *R. v. Jameson* [1896] (2 Q.B. 425), preliminary points of a purely technical nature were taken by the defence against the form of the indictment. The court disallowed them and neither the facts nor the interpretation of the Act were discussed. But an anonymous writer of the editorial comment in the *Law Journal* exhibits the current opinion:

There is a disposition to assert that the Foreign Enlistment Act applies only when war is actually on foot. But this opinion arose among those who read the preamble to the statute without going on to study carefully its history and its sections and definitions or the only case decided under it (*R. v. Sandoval*). Venezuela was not at war when Sandoval fitted out his ships ... the definition of 'foreign state' in the Act is advisedly drawn to include such operations ... the National Reform Committee [Jameson's political force] and its supporters were within the act and preparing or levying war against the Boer section of the population.

The writer welcomed the conviction of the accused and their decision not to appeal as of 'political and international importance, as it saves the country from the humiliating position of having to confess that Charterland is outside Her Majesty's dominions and the Foreign Enlistment Act inadequate to punish British subjects conducting raids, from whatever motives into friendly, if vassal, States.' The point was that, for a conviction, it must be proved that Jameson had made war against a *foreign*

3. Leander Starr Jameson was a friend of Cecil Rhodes. At the end of 1895, Jameson, Rhodes and the Uitlander leaders in Johannesburg were plotting to overthrow the Transvaal government which opposed Rhodes's scheme to bring the whole of southern Africa under British rule. Jameson jumped the gun and invaded the Transvaal with 500 men on 29 December 1895. On 2 January he was forced to surrender to the Boers. He was subsequently tried in England with five of his officers for offences under the Foreign Enlistment Act 1870, and sentenced to fifteen months' imprisonment, but served only six. The raid was a serious embarrassment to the British government and to Rhodes, but Jameson remained his friend and ally and returned to political office, until ill health caused him to retire to England in 1912. He was knighted in 1909, and died in 1917.

state, and the British government had no wish to acknowledge the independence of its 'vassal'.

U.S.A. v. *Pelly* (1899) (47 Weekly Reports 332) was not a criminal prosecution at all. The United States government had contracted to buy a warship from an English shipbuilder and had paid a deposit. It was prevented from enforcing the contract or recovering the deposit because further performance of the contract became illegal under the 1870 Act. The contract provided for the deposit to be forfeit in those circumstances. The English court held directly that the contract became illegal when hostilities between the United States and Spain began, not three days later when the British government declared Britain to be neutral.

There appear to have been no further prosecutions. At least there are no more cases reported. The next occasion for the Act to be considered was the Spanish Civil War.

The Spanish Civil War[4]

The question immediately arose of the distinction between mercenaries and volunteers. No one went to fight for the Republic for money. There was no evidence presented in Parliament of any volunteer for Franco's forces who went on principle and not for money, but there no doubt were some. Debates in Parliament, whatever their expressed arguments might be, were between the supporters of the Spanish government and the supporters of the fascist rebels, between left and right. But the irony was that the

4. For the Spanish Civil War see A. D. McNair, 'Law Relating to the Civil War in Spain' (1937), 53 *Law Quarterly Review* 471 and A. V. W. Thomas and A. J. Thomas Jr, 'International Legal Aspects of the Civil War in Spain' in Falk, op. cit., 111–78. Debates on the British volunteers in the Spanish Civil War are in *Hansard*, 18 December 1936, cc. 2793, 2794; 19 January 1937, cc. 30, 31 [Mr Cocks: 'Three cheers for the International Brigade!'] and 97–101, 111, 112; 122; 135–7; 160; 167, 168; and 11 February 1937, c. 560. By March 1939 there were weightier matters in Europe to be debated and the House was more concerned with helping refugees and returning volunteers. There were protests against public money being spent on the repatriation of law-breakers. D. N. Pritt on 7 March 1939 (cc. 1991, 1992) said: 'No Englishman is breaking the law if he enlists in the forces of a foreign state if he chooses to do so!' Debate followed, but events in Czechoslovakia overwhelmed it.

reactionary forces were for once rebelling against the legal government of progressives. The Labour Party was unwilling to debate the issues on political principle and found itself burdened with the task of arguing in just the terms used by the representatives of the middle class for over a century, and forced to support the larger argument against the control of mercenaries. It was natural that the conservatives, by now the political representatives of the bourgeois interests they had opposed in 1819, should nevertheless use the old arguments in favour of preventing enlistment in a foreign army.

On 10 January 1937, the Foreign Office issued a public warning calling attention 'to the fact that the Foreign Enlistment Act 1870, and in particular sections 4 and 5, are applicable in the case of the present conflict in Spain'. This was eleven months before *de facto* recognition of Franco's regime. There was no equivocation there. The intention was to deter the volunteers, for reasons which may be said to be the government's support for Franco or a concern to protect the ill-advised from the serious consequences of their actions. The warning rightly declared that it was an offence for a British subject to serve in any of the forces of either party or to leave the King's dominions for this purpose, or for any person in the United Kingdom to induce British subjects to do either of these things.

In a lecture in the University of Oxford in that year, Professor A. D. McNair, perhaps Britain's most prestigious international lawyer, said:

There is no doubt that both the Spanish Government and General Franco's Government are 'foreign States' for the purpose of the Act. The words that trouble me a little are 'at war'. Can it be held by a British Court that there is a 'war' in Spain when our Government has declined to grant recognition of belligerency and reiterates that it has granted belligerent rights to neither side? This is a question of English criminal law, not of international law ... So I do not feel called upon to express a positive opinion and will only venture the following observations:

(a) On the question whether His Majesty himself is in a state of war or of peace with another power the statement of the Executive is conclusive.

(b) It is reasonable to infer that a Declaration of Neutrality issued by the Executive would bind an English Court to hold that there was an international war in existence or a war that has become such for us as a result of our recognition of belligerency.

(c) I can see nothing in the relevant sections of the statute which requires a Court to hold that a civil war cannot be a war within the meaning of sections 4 and 5 unless His Majesty has accorded recognition of belligerency; that is an international act having, it is true, certain domestic repercussions, but I can see no reason why it should be essential before an English municipal Court can hold that a state of war exists; from the point of view of the mischief aimed at by the statute it seems to me quite as objectionable that British subjects should be participating in a foreign civil war in which we have not granted recognition of belligerency as in one in which we have.

(d) It is simply a matter of the construction of the word 'war' occurring in a statute; that statute expressly includes civil strife within its aim, as appears from the definition of 'foreign State', and if a judge upon hearing evidence as to the facts should come to the conclusion that there is a 'war' in Spain to which these sections applied, he would seem to me to be giving effect to the plain meaning of the word, and I cannot see any justification for displacing the plain meaning by implying after it in cases of civil war the expression 'in which His Majesty has granted recognition of belligerency to a rebel Government'.

(e) The American decision in *The Three Friends* (1897) 166 U.S.1 is worth noting; there the Supreme Court applied the section prohibiting the fitting out of ships 'to cruise or commit hostilities' to a state of insurgency not recognized as belligerency, which was 'war in a material sense' though not 'in a legal sense'; the Court said: 'We see no justification for importing into section 5283 words which it does not contain and which would make its operation depend upon the recognition of belligerency.'

(f) On the whole, I do not recommend anyone to test by personal experience the view of the law expressed in the warning issued by the Foreign Office.

But of all the thousands who went to fight in the International Brigade and otherwise, not one was prosecuted in England, though there were prosecutions in other European countries. The reasons are not obvious. Of course, no one made money by recruiting them. It may well be that those who would have rejoiced to see the survivors of the International Brigade punished were silenced by the rush of events, at least for the duration of the Second World War.

The Diplock Report[5]

When it became obvious to the British government that it would have to do something about the public concern at the activities of the mercenaries in Angola, who were defeated, killed and captured by the People's Republic of Angola or slaughtered by one another, the tired old stratagem of setting up a committee to provide an excuse for inactivity was employed and has served its purpose. The government appointed politicians who could be trusted to produce the kind of recommendations which the government wanted: one of the Law Lords and a conservative Member of Parliament from each side of the House. They held no public hearings, they seem to have done no research, they seem to have found it easy to present a picture of the present law which allowed them to make recommendations for its alteration based on an undeveloped political morality.

The Committee reported in August, when it was far too late to do anything about the mercenaries in Angola, and its Report is worthy of careful analysis, not for its quality but because the government will no doubt try to use it as the basis for legislation which will put back the law a couple of centuries.

The Report of the Committee of Privy Counsellors appointed to inquire into the recruitment of mercenaries, Cmnd 6569, reinforces the myth that the present legislation is outdated and obscure, and that the government was wise not to attempt a prosecution. About the language of the Act the Committee says:

The fact that it is a penal statute has two consequences. The first is that it falls to be construed with strict regard to the statutory language used. It is not permissible for courts of law to extend the definitions of statutory offences by analogy in order to deal with new situations which they regard as equally reprehensible ...

5. There has been little criticism of the Diplock Report in the press. Chris Mullin in *Tribune* followed earlier informative and challenging articles with 'Mercenaries: no effective change from Diplock Report', 6 August 1976. A mild reproof of the Report is D. Roebuck, 'The Diplock Report on Mercenaries', *New Statesman*, 13 August 1976, 202, 203.

The statutory language . . . is adapted to conditions as they existed in 1870 as regards relations between sovereign states, the kinds of armed conflict that had taken place in foreign territory during the previous decades and the means of transport and of waging war that were then available. The immense changes in those conditions which have taken place in the last hundred years and particularly since World War II have resulted in there being important omissions from the Act and a number of obscurities in the statutory language affecting most of the ingredients of the offences. These make the application of the Act to United Kingdom citizens who participate in a particular internal conflict in a foreign state a matter of grave legal doubt and the commission of an offence almost incapable of satisfactory proof.

We have seen that the opinions of the courts and of the law officers of the Crown were that an internal conflict in a foreign state was included in the scope of the Act and that, far from it being necessary to extend the definition of a foreign state, the interpretation section of the Act was more than sufficient. But the Privy Counsellors do not like what the interpretation section forces upon them. They cannot deny its meaning directly and so they must obfuscate the point by suggesting an even more impossible construction – that the meaning is restricted to a state *recognized* by the British government – and admitting that such a construction is wrong. No one but the Committee had suggested such a construction. The argument was dead once the 1819 Act was passed. How then were they to overcome the plain words? They say that it would be 'unsuitable' to apply the Act as it stands.

The expanded definition of 'foreign state' prevents its being confined to a government that is recognized by HM Government as the *de jure* sovereign government over a particular area. It is, and was no doubt intended by the draftsman to be, broad enough to make it a criminal offence to enlist in armed forces raised by rival governments in a civil war . . . But the questions whether and, if so, when the Act becomes applicable to particular cases of internal struggles for power between rival factions within a state in the varied circumstances in which struggles may arise today, are capable of raising so many doubts as to make this part of the Act unsuitable, in our opinion, to continue to be used as a penal statute.

In this paragraph for the first time the real point of the Committee's work is made plain. 'Unsuitable' is a giveaway word and shows that they are, in that passage at least, talking not of legal but of political difficulties. The meaning of the present Act is plain – only too plain. It catches very neatly mercenaries such as those in Angola and their recruiters in England, and for reasons which have become clear that is the last thing the government wants to do anything about. Even less do the Opposition want to restrict anyone who will fight the opponents of colonialism. The judge is not supposed to have political views, so at best two: nil with one abstention!

The Committee goes on to make much of the words 'at war' in sections 4 and 5 of the Act. It is suggested that only entities entitled to be recognized in international law as exercising belligerent rights can be 'at war'. While there is certainly something in this argument, it is countered by the argument that the Act clearly defines the entities as including 'any part of any people'. Any prosecution would argue that the words are clear. They would have the not inconsiderable authority of Lord McNair, not usually considered a radical, to support them. But the Committee make no mention of that. Instead, they make the totally unsupported and unsupportable assertion:

> In a prosecution for illegal enlistment or recruitment under the Act it would thus be necessary to prove that HM Government had recognized the persons on whose behalf the armed force was raised and the opponents against whom they were fighting as being *de facto* or *de jure* governments ...

The cases decided on the Act, its forerunners and its US counterparts do not support such an interpretation.

The second difficulty that the Committee foresaw is that of proof.

> The effectiveness of a penal statute depends upon the likelihood that, upon a trial in the United Kingdom of a person accused of an offence under the Act, the prosecution will be in a position to prove by admissible evidence the existence of each and every ingredient of the offence and to do so with that degree of certainty that is required for the conviction of a criminal offence ...

> The prosecution would be confronted by evidential difficulties in proving what the accused had in fact done in the foreign country, with sufficient particularity to justify a conviction for having enlisted in a

particular armed force. This would require oral evidence from eye-witnesses of his conduct as they had observed it in the confusion likely to be prevalent in the kind of conflict in which the services of mercenaries are sought.

These would be other mercenaries who would be privileged against self-incrimination. But the offence does not require any acts to be done abroad. The crime is not fighting as a mercenary but *enlisting* or *recruiting* in Britain or leaving to enlist abroad, all offences which are totally performed within the jurisdiction of the courts. Sir Geoffrey de Freitas, a member of the Committee, said to a television interviewer that it was too bad if things were done abroad that the government did not like. It was outside its power to control them. But enlistment and recruitment are crimes under the Act if done in Britain. For example, all the Angola mercenaries enlisted and were recruited in England and many have confessed as much to the police and said so openly to newsmen and television interviewers. All the British mercenaries at the trial in Luanda were proved to have enlisted in England. Difficulties of proof of acts abroad are quite irrelevant and should have appeared so to the experienced members of the Committee. One of the objections to *any* law against enlistment is said by them to be:

The chances of convicting the accused would depend not so much on his actual guilt as on his exceptional bad luck in there being available to the prosecution in his case sufficient evidence to convict him on his trial in this country.

What an argument! If it were serious it would be equally cogent against customs dodgers, currency swindlers, importers of rabid dogs and the perpetrators of most of the crimes in the calendar. Most convictions in some kinds of crime depend on the 'exceptional bad luck' of the criminal, as studies of unreported and unpunished crime show, from rape to speeding.

It is strange that an Act so impossible to apply, even where the government sees a serious threat to democracy if it isn't, should be described in the standard legal textbook without comment. *Russell on Crime* mentions no complexities or difficulties of application.[6] In a letter to *The Times* on 13 February 1976,

6. *Russell on Crime*, 12th edn, by J. W. Cecil, Turner Stevens, 1964.

Colonel G. I. A. D. Draper, the leading authority in England on this part of the law, wrote:

> The wide definition . . . shows that Parliament was going way beyond the technical meanings of 'state', 'government' and 'war'. The words used in the Act of 1870 give little support to the view you cite from Archbold's *Criminal Pleading* that the Act does not extend to enlistment in the government or rebel forces during a civil war in a foreign state at peace with Her Majesty. In the early stages of the Spanish Civil War 1936–1939, HMG expressed a view quite at variance with that cited from *Archbold*.[7]

In an article which was not directly concerned with this subject at all,[8] Professor Glanville Williams, England's leading scholar of the criminal law, said in passing: 'The Foreign Enlistment Act 1870 is a model of draftsmanship. The question of jurisdiction under the internal law (as it was understood in 1870) was very much in the mind of the framers of this Act.' As we have seen, the Foreign Office itself said the Act would apply to those who enlisted in the Spanish Civil War. So did the Home Office. But then most of those volunteers were not mercenaries at all. There were a few who signed on for the fascists and Carlists. But those who fought against Franco did not fight for money but belief in freedom and democracy. No wonder the British government warned them. What could have inhibited the government from warning those whom it knew to be off for Angola? What new legal insight or experience caused the government's advisers to change their opinion of the efficacy of the Act?

7. The standard practitioners' manual is T. R. Fitzwalter Butler and S. Mitchell, eds., *Archbold's Pleading, Evidence and Practice in Criminal Cases*, 38th edition, Sweet & Maxwell, 1973. In section 3092 at page 1213 the unsupported and erroneous statement appears: 'The provisions of this Act do not extend to enlistment in the Government or rebel forces during a civil war in a foreign state at peace with Her Majesty.' It is a bold gesture to quarrel with authority as respected as Archbold but Archbold's unsupported dogma cannot stand against a decision of an English court. See *R.* v. *Sandoval* cited above and Professor Colonel G. I. A. D. Draper's letter in *The Times*, 13 February 1976.

8. Professor Glanville Williams's article is G. Williams, 'The Venue and Ambit of the Criminal Law' (1965) 81 *Law Quarterly Review* 276, 395, 518 (3 parts) at 471.

The Diplock Committee said that it was the practical difficulties of proving what happened abroad which explained why there had never been a prosecution, let alone a conviction, under the Act. As there is no need to prove that anything happened abroad, this explanation will not do. It was also suggested by the government and *The Times* that without a warning the Act would not apply. That is equally fallacious. The Act has certainly been applied by the courts when no warning has been given. It is true that it was usually the shipbuilding provisions which were enforced, but it can hardly be suggested that without a warning some sections of the Act are in force but other sections are not.

The Report goes on to say:

A handful of prosecutions had been brought under the Act of 1819 which it replaced, but these all arose under provisions relating to the employment of ships in belligerent service or the fitting out of naval or military expeditions.

We have shown how untrue that statement is. We have discovered by simple and obvious research methods that there were at least nine prosecutions under the 1819 Act, for *recruiting*. Mountague Bernard's well-known book on the American Civil War tells of eight prosecutions. The same information is in the Report of the Royal Commission on the Neutrality Laws. The conviction of Lieutenant Styles is in *The Times* and can be traced quite simply through the cases referred to in a basic tool of legal research, the *English and Empire Digest*, under the heading 'Foreign Enlistment Act'.

What a study of the cases decided on the Acts shows is not that it is impossible to get a conviction but that their application depends upon the political will of the government of the day and its opinion of the political motivation of the force which the mercenaries or volunteers are going to support.

The Diplock Committee's Proposals

The Report concludes that it is impossible to distinguish between a mercenary and a genuine volunteer according to their motives, and suggests the following definition: 'any person who serves voluntarily and for pay[9] in some armed force other than that of Her Majesty in the right of the United Kingdom'. It does not seek to make being a mercenary a crime. On the contrary, it says that to prevent a citizen accepting service as a mercenary is a restriction on his personal freedom which could only be justified on the grounds of public interest. The Committee advises that the provisions of the 1870 Act are obscure and unworkable and should be repealed. Enlistment as a mercenary should cease to be an offence and service abroad as one should not be made criminal. The only legislation should be to give the government the power, though significantly not the responsibility, to prohibit recruitment within the United Kingdom if it saw fit, in relation to specified armed forces which it had previously stipulated as unsupportable. Then when the government had decided that the political colour of the mercenaries' boss was sufficiently unpleasant, it should have power not only to stop advertisements but the publication of addresses from which information about recruiting could be obtained. This last is a necessary refinement, as was shown by the advertisements masquerading as news items which appeared in the English press on behalf of Banks and Hall.

There will be great pressure on the government to pass legislation in the form suggested by the Report. It is, of course, based on the premise that the present legislation is unworkable, a premise we have shown to be false. Why would a committee of senior politicians, Sir Derek Walker-Smith, a Tory MP, Sir Geoffrey de Freitas, a Labour MP, and Lord Diplock, a judicial member of the House of Lords, seek to free enlistment as a mercenary from the criminal odium and sanctions it has attracted in England for centuries?

A political ideology which sets up as a freedom to be protected the right to be a hired killer in a foreign war, above the rights of the people of other countries to order their affairs without such intrusion, is an ideology which should be regarded with contempt. When it leads to the suppression of history and the twisting of law it is exposed for what it is. The whole report is subject to the same

9. This won't quite do. Many mercenaries would enlist without pay, just for the chance of loot. See, for an example, Butcher in Chapter 11. 'For gain' would be an obvious but not completely satisfactory improvement.

slant. It seeks to be pragmatic and becomes divorced from reality. One would think from the comments of the Committee that the struggle of the people of Africa for freedom from colonial exploitation was some kind of game. The use of mercenaries by oppressors of all kinds is growing. The best that the Committee can recommend is a reduction in their control.

It is important to remember the circumstances in which the Committee was set up and the way in which it has worked. The government, under the stress of the revelation that the British mercenaries had not confined themselves to slaughtering black foreigners but had started on one another, hurriedly sought a way of avoiding embarrassing questions. It set up a committee which had neither the power nor the responsibility it needed. It did not seek independent advice. It held no public hearings. It could not compel the testimony of Banks and his competitors in the recruiting trade. It did not listen to the colourful and informative stories which the returned mercenaries were so keen to tell to the press. It did not seek the great bulk of evidence collected by the Angolan court. It produced a Report which, however weak in its law and unimaginative in its morality, has done just the job which the government wanted. Not only has the very existence of the Committee made it possible for all questions in Parliament to be fobbed off with the answer that a committee was looking into the matter, not only will its misinterpretation of the law allow the government an excuse for not prosecuting the mercenaries who returned, who could have told embarrassing stories of official complicity; it has recommended and therefore legitimated the abolition of the age-old crime of enlisting as a mercenary, for centuries considered necessary, at least to have on the statute book if not to be enforced, for the sake of Britain's reputation among the nations of the world.

The Government's Present Policy

The overt policy of the present government towards enlistment and recruitment for Angola was quoted at the start of Chapter 12. Statements such as that by Mr Roy Jenkins, the Home Secretary; the obfuscations of Mr Harold Wilson, the Prime Minister at that time; the acts of those whom one would expect to carry out government policy, the police who allowed bail jumpers and violent wanted criminals to leave, and the immigration officials who speeded their passage; the approval of Opposition spokesmen like Mr Reginald Maudling and Mr Julian Amery of the mercenary trade; the humbug of the Diplock Committee, which considered that restrictions on enlistment would be a serious inroad into personal freedom – of hired killers to ply their trade – all may not add up to convincing evidence that the government was concerned to encourage recruiting. The reader must make up his own mind. What is incontrovertible is that John Banks broadcasts regularly on both BBC and commercial television, announcing that he is still recruiting, for Angola and elsewhere; that mercenaries are still leaving England in considerable numbers to go to Africa, to the Lebanon and elsewhere to commit murder and cause destruction in struggles in which they have no legitimate concern; that the illegal Smith régime in Zimbabwe recruits quite openly in England and that throughout Africa the British government's inaction reinforces the people's conviction that Britain is conniving in the use of mercenaries to protect for a little while longer its privileges and its opportunities for exploitation.

14 Revolutionary Justice

The International Commission

In early May 1976, the Ministry of Justice of the People's Republic of Angola invited about fifty men and women from all over the world, almost all of them lawyers, to meet in Luanda and form an International Commission of Inquiry on Mercenaries, to consider the past and present activities of mercenaries and to suggest ways in which their future recruitment and use could be stopped. Some were chosen by their governments but many were there as individuals. The Western press were understandably eager to find out the Angolan government's criterion for selection, particularly of the members from non-socialist countries. When it became clear that they had been chosen for their record of objectivity, professional reputation and concern for peace and human rights, equally understandably the Western press lost interest and said nothing. It is worth while though to illustrate not only the standing of the members but their diverse backgrounds.

Sixteen African countries, seven from Western Europe, the German Democratic Republic and the USSR, USA and Canada, six from Latin America, three Arab countries, with Vietnam from Asia and Australia from Oceania, made up a broadly representative international body. There were three Ministers of Justice, and two Attorney-Generals, fifteen judges and ten practising lawyers, ten professors of law and three other academics, two ambassadors, a policeman and four writers. With a great Russian international lawyer, a veteran of Nuremberg, sat a famous American trial lawyer, recently honoured by HM the Queen. With a former judge of a Dutch War Crimes Court sat judges from Canada, Cuba, Mozambique, Nigeria, Tanzania and South Yemen. Professors of Law from Australia, Belgium, Germany, Italy, Portugal and Vietnam. Ministers of Justice from Africa, Latin America and the Middle East.

All the members of the Commission were given every opportunity to observe the trial of the thirteen British and American mercenaries with which the meeting of the Commission had been timed to coincide. All the evidence and papers were open to their inspection.

The Commission set up a committee to consider the trial's fairness. Its members were practising lawyers and experts in criminal procedure. After some days of deliberation and consideration of a number of drafts, they reported to a Plenary Session, which adopted the following Declaration. It was drafted in French and the English translation is not quite idiomatic.

DECLARATION ON THE COMPLIANCE OF ANGOLAN PROCEDURAL LAW WITH THE UNIVERSAL PRINCIPLES GUARANTEEING RESPECT FOR THE RIGHT TO DEFENCE

I. The effective consecration of respect for the rights of defence demands, according to principles common to different juridical systems, the observance of the following rules:

(a) the defendant has a right to know the charges that are being made against him;

(b) the defendant has a right to examine the case file;

(c) the defendant has a right to question witnesses for the prosecution;

(d) the defendant has a right to be heard;

(e) the defendant has a right to present his own witnesses;

(f) the defendant has a right to be assisted by counsel;

(g) the trial must be public.

II. An analysis by the International Commission of Inquiry of Law 7/76 of 1 May, which creates the People's Revolutionary Court, and lays down the procedural norms which govern the Court, shows that the above-mentioned principles referring to the right of defence have been fully respected. In fact:

(a) sub-paragraph (a) of Article 12 in conjunction with Article 10 of the Angolan Law states that the defendant is obligatorily notified of the charges against him, namely, a brief statement of the punishable acts, an indication of the laws and rules which were violated and the demand for application of the corresponding penalties;

(b) sub-paragraph (c) of Article 12 consecrates the right of the defendant, through his counsel, to have access to and freely consult the case file during an eight-day period;

(c) No. 2 of Article 23 of the Angolan Law provides for the right of the defendant to question the witnesses for the prosecution;

(d) the right of the defendant to be heard is guaranteed by Articles 20, 22 (nos. 1 and 2), 24 and 25 (no. 1), all from the above mentioned Law 7/76;

(e) Article 12 sub-paragraph (d) and Article 23 No. 1 stipulate that defendant may present his own witnesses and that these shall be heard;

(f) the right to be assisted by counsel is effectively guaranteed by Article 12, sub-paragraph (b) and by Article 13, not only by the right which the defendant has of naming a defence counsel of his own choice up to the day of the trial, but also by the obligation of the Court to name an official defence counsel in the notice of charges;

(g) finally, Article 15 No. 1 prescribes that the trial is public.

III. The principle *nullum crimen sine lege*, according to which no fact is considered a crime and therefore punishable without a pre-existing law declaring it as such, is a principle which is recognized by the different juridical systems and is consecrated in the Constitutional Law of the People's Republic of Angola and reaffirmed in Law 7/76 of 1 May, which creates the People's Revolutionary Court. It is respected by the indictment presented in the present case as it is based on internal law and on the norms and principles of international law that the People's Republic of Angola, as a sovereign State, decided to make its own.

Luanda, 12 June 1976

This declaration was based on a study of Angolan law and the trial documents made before the trial started. It could not deal with the fairness of the conduct of the proceedings. Because the Commission was determined that nothing it did should be alleged to have influenced the court in any way – not that there was any reason to fear for the court's independence – it was resolved that the Declaration should not be published nor its import revealed in any way, until after the trial was over. When the hearing was concluded, though before judgement was pronounced, the Commission published the following statement:

FINAL STATEMENT AND VERIFICATION OF THE FAIRNESS OF THE PROCEDURE OF THE TRIAL IN ACCORD WITH THE CRITERIA PREVIOUSLY LAID DOWN

Having attended and observed all sessions of the trial of the mercenaries before the People's Revolutionary Court, the International Commission of Inquiry on Mercenaries is satisfied that the trial has been fair and conducted with dignity and solemnity. The Commission is further convinced that all rules of procedure have been interpreted in favour of or extended in favour of observing the rights of the defendants.

Luanda, 19 June 1976

What the Commission carefully did not do was to express a view on whether the decision of the court was right, on the law and on the evidence. It considered that to do so would have been to usurp the function of the court itself. If the Commission had decided to consider the correctness of the verdict, it would have had to stay in session until after the judgement was pronounced, which was impossible. No doubt there will be published in many countries in many languages, by members of the Commission as well as others, critical evaluations of the trial as a whole, which will include considerations of the evidence presented and the law applied and the severity of the sentences. Such assessments can be left to the individual judgements of legal scholars. What the Commission did state clearly was that the rights of the defence had been carefully and completely protected. This was an opinion shared by the defence counsel. Mr Cesner, the American who defended two of his three compatriots, Grillo preferring to keep his Angolan lawyer, said: 'I believe the principal aim has been to conduct a fair trial. It should be noted that the Tribunal has very carefully considered the facts and circumstances.' Mr Stanbrooke, one of the British lawyers, said: 'This is an historic trial, of historic importance to the problem of mercenarism . . . I hail the illustrious People's Prosecutor who presented the case with great fairness.' Another British lawyer, Mr Kerrigan, said: 'I have been very grateful to the Tribunal and to the Ministry of Justice for all their careful co-operation, including access to my client at all hours. In this tribunal you have shown every courtesy to the defence and every co-operation in meeting our requests. By this you have shown the value you place on the rule of law.' Perhaps most convincing of all is the final statement of Derek Barker, one of the executed mercenaries: 'I thank the lawyers for having appeared for me at this fair trial.'

The trial is important for a number of reasons. It shows to mercenaries and potential mercenaries that they run the risk of capture and punishment. The evidence and the way it was presented served to educate the accused, the Angolan public and, through television and newspapers, the whole world about the sordid nature of the mercenary's trade. It shattered once and for all the myth of the 'Soldier of Fortune', with its catalogue of sadism and butchery, racism and stupidity, military incompetence and vaunting vainglory, lies and cheating and plain unmistakable cowardice and desertion of mates. The leaders: Callan, the kicked-out private who liked to be called colonel, who liked to kill the defenceless, a brutal bully with a big gun, whose rage when he saw signs that some of his precious 'men' were not taking him seriously led him to slaughter them, who swaggered in court and claimed the responsibility of the Commanding Officer, but who, when he saw his own death approaching, tried to pretend he was mad. Copeland, like one of his own victims, whining for mercy and running in panic from his own execution at the hands of Holden Roberto's dogsbody, Nick Hall. McKenzie, hard and bitter, with enough sense to realize that the massacre of the mercenaries meant the end for him, cleverly spotting the holes in the prosecution witnesses' evidence, and greatly concerned with Callan to prevent some secret emerging during the trial, drawing on the sustenance from Callan that their special relationship gave him; the man who had done Callan's killing at Callan's whim, still afraid, like all bullies' henchmen, that the bully would turn on him in the end.

But the trial was much more than a deterrent. It contrasted the lowest level of human development, the man who kills for money or pleasure, with the strength and decency of the Angolan peasant. The excuse put forward by the British and American lawyers was that their clients were the wretched products of a corrupt and exploitative capitalist system. They stressed repeatedly the shortcomings of their own countries, the unemployment, the lack of education, the alienation which produced the hapless creatures, doomed to unfulfilling emotional lives, lightened only by gambling and drink and violence. It was extraordinary how enthusiastic some of the lawyers became in describing and illustrating the decadence of the West.[1] It was strange to see the contrast with the

1. The *International Bulletin*, 18 June 1976, reported Ed. Arthur, a mercenary at that time standing for election as county sheriff in his home state of Ohio,

witnesses, the soldiers and the judges. The responses of João Antonio were described in Chapter 8. Perhaps the most interesting insight into the difference between the Angolan and the British way of looking at things came when counsel, trying to show that his client might not have been threatening João Antonio, said that just because a gun was pointed at him, it did not mean a threat. It might have been used to indicate direction. João Antonio smiled and shook his head slightly in disbelief: 'You might do that to an animal, but not to a man.'

The very new government of the People's Republic of Angola showed by the trial the maturity of its institutions, particularly its system of justice. No trial could have been conducted with greater humanity. Throughout, the presiding judge spoke to the accused in quiet and friendly tones. There was no pomp, no distance placed between him and the men in the dock. He relied entirely upon his own natural dignity and warmth.

But there was no doubt who was in control, as the following exchange shows.

PEOPLE'S PROSECUTOR (to talkative witness): Comrade, please, answer the question and don't digress!

WITNESS: Excuse me, Comrade Prosecutor, but I thought I was in the People's Revolutionary Tribunal, not the old fascist court, and I could speak my mind and tell the whole truth as I saw it.

This brought a murmur of encouragement from the public in court. The witness got even more cheeky with counsel for the defence. The presiding judge was gentle but firm. 'It is true that this is not a fascist court. If it were, you would not be fooling about. It is also true that a great man once said that truth is revolutionary. But a lot of people have died, there has been destruction and tragedy. So, if you will allow me, Comrade, please talk about things with respect.' There was no need for a further intervention. At one stage it became clear that a witness was making up a story as he

---

as saying that he headed a group which financed the American lawyer at the trial, Robert Cesner. Cesner, said Arthur, was a man 'who had the ability to go into a communist country and look 'em straight in the eye and say "You people are full of crap".' Mr Cesner was, on the contrary, properly respectful.

went on, embroidering it to impress the court. After the lunch-time recess the presiding judge announced that the previous witness had been arrested and would face trial on charges of perjury. The court was made up of six judges, one of them an auxiliary. The presiding judge was Attorney-General of Angola, and a very experienced and respected member of the legal profession. The others were a member of the Angolan Women's Movement, two soldiers and two administrators. Three of the six were legally qualified.

The lengths to which the court was prepared to go in its attempts to secure the rights of the defence were shown when the British lawyers turned up on the third day of the trial. Articles 12 and 13 of the Law No. 7/76, the Code of Criminal Procedure, taken together provide that the defendant shall have the right to nominate his own counsel, but that he cannot change from counsel appointed by the court to counsel of his own choice once the day of the trial has arrived. This point was taken, as it had to be, by the People's Prosecutor. The court adjourned and deliberated. In spite of the clear statutory provision and the lack of any discretion placed in the court by the statute, the court held that a substitution of counsel would be allowed. It could see no harm to the proceedings and the rights of the defence must be protected even beyond the statutory limit.

More important than the interesting new procedures at the trial, many of which were in any case not as new as they seemed to British lawyers but the traditional ways of all civil-law countries, that is those countries which do not take their legal tradition from England; and more important than the lessons learned from the clash of racist neo-colonial cultures with the realities and aspirations of the 'new man' being created in Angola; there are lessons to be learned about the ways mercenaries are employed, the ways they behave and the ways they can be overcome. A great deal of information was produced at the trial, a trial which, it must be remembered, was from the start intended to produce the truth about mercenary activities in Angola as well as finding the guilt or innocence of the accused. Much more is now known about the undercover activities of the British and US governments. Angola has experience and techniques which are available for all of Africa to use in its struggle for freedom. All oppressed people of the world have reason to be grateful to the people of Angola for their example in the severe but measured justice meted out to the mercenaries.

The sentences were as follows: Costas Georgia (alias 'Colonel' Callan), Andrew Gordon McKenzie, John Derek Barker and Daniel Gearhart sentenced to death. Gustavo Grillo, Kevin Marchant and Michael Wiseman, each thirty years; John Lawlor, Colin Evans and Cecil Fortuin, each twenty-four years; Gary Acker, Malcolm McIntyre and John Nammock each sixteen years. The executions were carried out by firing squad on 10 July 1976.

It is hoped that all other countries will take as seriously as Angola the threat to peace presented by the use of mercenaries. Every country needs clear legislative prohibition of all kinds of mercenary activity, effective judicial administration, but most of all the unequivocal political intention to stop mercenaries that has been exhibited in Angola.

15 The National Laws

Perhaps it is not surprising that national laws show great diversity in their treatment of the problem of mercenaries. The legal systems of the world are varied both in form and technique. Different countries have different needs. Some countries are much more likely to provide recruiting grounds for mercenaries than others and there the need for effective legal sanctions is immediate. But all countries share the need for strict legislation against enlistment and recruiting. While the experience of comparative lawyers has shown that law works better if each country develops the legal techniques most appropriate for its own conditions, the political decision to have efficient laws and to apply them effectively needs to be taken everywhere.

Political exigencies prevent leisurely scholarship. We would have liked to have been able to consider, if not the laws of all countries, at least a representative selection. But problems of communication, time and limited space in the book have caused us to restrict our description to those countries whose laws were readily accessible.[1] The law in Britain has been considered in earlier chapters. In this chapter we deal with the laws of countries which have produced mercenaries and still provide many of the mercenaries operating today: the United States, the British Commonwealth, Belgium, France and Sweden.

The United States

When the history of the Foreign Enlistment Acts was dealt with in Chapter 12, it was shown that the United States under the

1. It is believed that there is other research being presently done, some of it of a comprehensive kind. Since we completed our manuscript we have discovered the existence of a doctoral thesis by L. David, recently presented to the University of Nice, on the legal problems of mercenaries and volunteers.

guidance of George Washington passed the first legislation concerned to control the enlistment of citizens of one country in the army of another, hoping in that way to ensure that international relations should not be put in jeopardy. Earlier statutes in England had not, at least overtly, been concerned with the more refined notions of neutrality then becoming accepted. It was this early law which shaped not only the later statutes of Britain but the present law in the United States, which is found in the United States Code and the decisions of the courts upon it. There is no doubt of the validity of the prohibitions; the United States government has not pretended that the legislation is obscure or difficult of application and it was said in March 1976 by those in authority that investigations were being made on which to base prosecutions if evidence were to become available.

It was in March 1976 that Robert L. Keuch, Acting Deputy Assistant Attorney General, Criminal Division, gave evidence before the Subcommittee on International Resources, Food and Energy of the Committee on International Relations of the House of Representatives.[2] Citing 'longstanding Justice Department policy' as the reason for his refusal to 'comment specifically on current investigative efforts', he assured the subcommittee that the Criminal Division 'has been aware of numerous allegations regarding recruitment efforts and is conducting appropriate investigations'. Rather more efficient investigations in Luanda produced a mass of evidence against the American recruiters, which is available to the United States authorities, but no prosecutions have been brought.

Provisions relating to the prohibition and punishment of acts likely to prejudice the United States in its international relations are grouped together in the United States Code. Section 959 of Title 18, headed 'Enlistment in foreign service', says:

(a) Whoever, within the United States, enlists or enters himself, or hires or retains another to enlist or enter himself, or to go beyond the jurisdiction of the United States with intent to be enlisted or entered in the service of any foreign prince, state, colony, district or people as a

2. We have a copy of the testimony of Mr Keuch dated 10 March 1976 and issued by the Department of Justice, Washington.

soldier or as a marine or seaman on board any vessel of war, letter of
marque, or privateer, shall be fined not more than $1,000 or imprisoned
not more than three years, or both.

Subsection (b) exempts citizens who enlist in the army of an ally
of the United States in time of war and subsection (c) citizens of
foreign states transiently in the United States. It should be noted
that the section prohibits the enlistment and recruitment of any
person as a soldier, marine or seaman in the service of a foreign
country or people, quite widely described. There is no requirement
that the foreign state be 'at war'. It would be possible to construe
the term 'soldier' narrowly to exclude 'civilian advisers' but not
the mercenaries in Angola. An informal engagement with no more
than the prospect of advancement or payment in the future was
held to be sufficient in 1920 in *Gayon* v. *McCarthy*.[3] The surrounding sections deal with other matters similarly relevant to neutrality
or good relations with foreign states. Section 956 is headed
'Conspiracy to injure property of foreign government' and
provides that

If two or more persons within the jurisdiction of the United States
conspire to injure or destroy specific property situated in a foreign
country and belonging to a foreign government ... or any railroad,
canal, bridge ... and if one or more such persons commits an act within
the jurisdiction ... to effect the object ... each ... shall be fined not
more than $5,000 or imprisoned not more than three years, or both.

Section 957 makes it an offence to possess property or papers, in
aid of a foreign government, to be used in violating any penal
statute or treaty. Section 958 makes it an offence to accept or
exercise a commission to serve a foreign state in war against a state
at peace with the United States. Section 960 deals with expeditions
against a foreign friendly nation.

There is also a provision in the Immigration and Nationality
Act section 349, which takes United States nationality away from a
person who is found guilty of 'entering, or serving in, the armed

3. *Gayon* v. *McCarthy* (1920) 252 U.S. 171 concerns the recruitment of a
sailor, recently retired from the US navy, and unemployed, in the force
raised by Felix Diaz against the government of Mexico.

forces of a foreign state' without prior authority. This provision is incorporated in Title 8 of the United States Code, section 1481 (a) (3). The Supreme Court, however, has held that Congress cannot take away citizenship merely by legislation to that effect. To do so would be unconstitutional. In 1967, it held in *Afroyim* v. *Rusk*[4] that there must be evidence that the offender had voluntarily abandoned his citizenship. The nature of the act committed could provide that evidence. In that case, the act which infringed the Code was not serving in a foreign army, but voting in a foreign election. Afroyim was Polish-born, a naturalized citizen of the United States, who had gone to Israel and voted in elections for the Knesset. It was held by a bare majority of five judges to four that that act was not of itself sufficient unequivocal evidence of an intention to abandon United States citizenship. This was a departure from earlier authority and it is possible that it would not be followed in less poignant circumstances. The Supreme Court is not bound by its own decisions. Moreover, there is conflicting authority in a case whose facts are much more analogous to those which concern us.

In *United States ex rel. Marks* v. *Esperdy*,[5] the decision of the Second Circuit of the United States Court of Appeals was upheld by the Supreme Court in 1967. Herman F. Marks was a United States citizen, born in Milwaukee. He went to Cuba in 1958 to join Fidel Castro in the Sierra Maestra. After the victory he continued to serve as a captain, in charge of La Cabana, the military prison in Havana. After disagreements he returned to the United States in July 1960 and was arrested and charged with unlawfully attempting to enter the United States as an illegal immigrant. It was alleged that he was an alien, who lost his citizenship under section 1481, having served in a foreign force. The Supreme Court held that he had voluntarily joined up with the revolutionary forces and thereby chosen to abandon his citizenship. It will be interesting to see whether the United States government will be as astute as to

4. *Afroyim* v. *Rusk* (1967) 387 U.S. 253 was noted in 112 U. Pa. L. Rev. 761 and 31 Fordham L. Rev. 373.
5. *U.S. ex rel. Marks* v. *Esperdy* (1963) 315 F. 2d 673, affirmed 84 S. Ct. 1224; 377 U.S. 214; 12 L. Ed. 2d 292; rehearing denied 84 S. Ct. 1904, 377 U.S. 1010; 12 L. Ed. 2d 1059.

charge Bufkin and Lobo del Sol and the others who served the FNLA or are now with Smith's army in Rhodesia.

Title 22 of the United States Code, section 612, requires agents of foreign states to register. Any registered agent who carries on recruiting activities without reporting them commits an offence under section 618 (a) (2). Any person who represents the interests of a foreign principal breaches section 611 (c) (1) (iv) and, if he pays out money for a foreign principal, is brought within the Act by section 611 (c) (1) (iii).

The British Commonwealth

For the most part, the countries which were within the dominion of the British Crown in 1870 became subject to the Foreign Enlistment Act.[6] Section 2 applied the Act to all the dominions of Her Majesty but, by section 3, the Act was to be proclaimed in every British possession by the governor immediately he received notice of its passing, and came into operation there only when proclaimed. It was certainly assumed in the British Parliament at the time of the Spanish Civil War that the Act was in force throughout the Commonwealth, as appears from *Hansard* Volume 320 column 1010. Moreover, it has been held that the Act applies to all British subjects wherever they may be and to foreigners throughout the Queen's dominions (*R.* v. *Jameson* [1896] 2 Q.B. 425). It applies in Northern Ireland and the Northern Ireland Parliament has been expressly deprived of power to legislate on foreign enlistment by the Government of Ireland Act 1920 section 4 (2). It is interesting to note (and could become important to remember) that the Republic of Ireland is not a foreign country, and therefore not a 'foreign state', according to section 2 of the Ireland Act 1949.

6. Section 2 of the Foreign Enlistment Act 1870 provides: 'This Act shall extend to all the dominions of Her Majesty, including the adjacent territorial waters.' Section 3: 'This Act shall be proclaimed in every British possession by the governor thereof as soon as may be after he receives notice of this Act and shall come into operation in that British possession on the day of such proclamation, and the time at which this Act comes into operation in any place is, as respects such place, in this Act referred to as the commencement of this Act.'

As new territories fell under British rule, the Act was proclaimed, sometimes belatedly, in them; for example in Papua in 1898 and in 1906 in Ashanti, Fiji, Orange River Colony and Transvaal. But at about the same time there was passed in a number of colonies legislation of a similar but interestingly different kind.[7]

In the Bahamas, Bermuda, British Honduras (now Belize), Cayman Island, Gibraltar, Grenada, Hong Kong, Jamaica, Mauritius, St Helena, Singapore and Straits Settlements for example (for this list is illustrative and not exhaustive) there is legislation which provides for the representative of the Crown – Governor, Governor-General or whatever – to permit or prohibit all forms of recruiting. If he makes an order prohibiting recruitment, any person who induces or attempts to induce another to take employment of any kind, not just military, in the service of a foreign state, very widely defined, commits a misdemeanour and may be punished by imprisonment and fine. What is interesting about all this colonial legislation is that the British government, very soon after the passing of the Foreign Enlistment Act 1870, decided that it was not sufficient for the colonies, to which it had been applied, and in some places passed legislation of potentially much wider scope relating to recruiting. Yet at the same time, in other colonies, the Foreign Enlistment Act was still being proclaimed. The new and wider legislation did not necessarily affect the application of the Foreign Enlistment Act 1870, which applied *in addition* where not expressly or implicitly repealed. In the British Honduras, section 7 of the new Act expressly preserved the application of the Foreign Enlistment Act 1870.

A comprehensive study of the whole of the British Empire and later the Commonwealth, as they waxed and waned, is neither

7. For the colonial legislation see: Bahamas, Penal Code s. 443; Bermuda, Foreign Recruiting Act 1874; British Honduras (Belize), Foreign Enlistment Ordinance; Cayman Islands, Foreign Recruiting Law c. 57; Gibraltar, Foreign Recruiting Ordinance 1877; Grenada, Foreign Recruiting Law 1875; Hong Kong, Ordinance No. 1 of 1874; Jamaica, Foreign Recruiting Law c. 133; Mauritius, Penal Code (Supplementary) 1945 ss. 10–14; St Helena, Ordinance c. 99 (1876); Singapore, Foreign Recruitment Act 1875; Straits Settlements, Foreign Recruitment Ordinance 1875. The Western Australian Foreign Recruiting Act 1874 is similar but restricted to recruiting for military service (section 3).

possible nor necessary in this book, but it seems clear that for many parts of the Commonwealth the Foreign Enlistment Act was the only law on mercenaries and still is.[8] But many countries, in Africa in particular, as they won independence passed new Penal Codes or Criminal Codes, in which they attempted to comprehend a full statement of the principles of their criminal law.[9] Although in Rhodesia and Nigeria it is true that the Foreign Enlistment Act 1870 still applies, in the Gambia, Ghana, Kenya, Malawi, Tanzania, Uganda, Zambia and Zanzibar there are codes which have replaced it. They usually provide that a person commits an offence who, without the President's licence, prepares a naval or military expedition against a friendly state; or who, being a citizen of the Republic, accepts a commission or engagement in the service of a foreign state at war with a friendly state, or whether citizen or not, induces another to do so; or who goes on board a vessel with a view to quitting the country to accept a commission or engagement abroad. There are also provisions relating to owners and builders of ships.

It is also of interest that Canada passed new legislation at the time of the Spanish Civil War. The Canadian Foreign Enlistment Act 1937 differs from the 1870 Act scarcely at all. There is the same definition of a 'foreign state', but a new definition of 'armed

8. It would appear that the Foreign Enlistment Act still applies to Antigua, Australia, British Solomon Islands, Brunei, Cyprus, Dominica, Fiji, Gilbert and Ellice Islands, Leeward Islands, Malaysia, Montserrat, New Zealand, Saint Christopher, Nevis and Anguilla, Saint Lucia, the Seychelles, Sierra Leone, Tonga, Trinidad and Tobago, Turks and Caicos Islands and the Virgin Islands.

9. The legislation in the countries with new laws is: The Gambia, Criminal Code s. 61; Ghana, Foreign Enlistment Act 1961 (which, passed in the light of the experiences of the Congo, makes it a first degree felony, punishable by life imprisonment, to accept or induce any engagement in the military service of any other *country*); Kenya, Penal Code s. 68; Malawi, Penal Code s. 62; Tanzania, Penal Code s. 65; Uganda, Penal Code s. 52; Zambia, Penal Code s. 72; Zanzibar, Penal Code s. 53. The law in Rhodesia is governed by the Act c. 116 of 1904 ss. 3–28, which incorporates the Foreign Enlistment Act 1870. In Nigeria, the Foreign Enlistment Act 1870 applies, see C. O. Madarikan and T. Akinola Aguda, *Brett and McLean's The Criminal Law and Procedure of the Six Southern States of Nigeria*, 2nd edn, Sweet & Maxwell, 1974. We are grateful to Mr Justice Nyalali of the Supreme Court of Tanzania for his help on the law in East Africa.

forces' which does not appear in the 1870 Act and includes combatants and non-combatants but excludes those doing medical and humanitarian work if under the control of the Canadian Red Cross or another recognized Canadian humanitarian society. The provisions relating to means of conveyance are extended to include air transport. A number of cases under the British Act of 1819 had held that it applied to Canada, but showed no enthusiasm for enforcing its provisions, and happily accepted an opportunity to avoid it on technical grounds.[10]

It is not only in the countries which have taken their legal system from England that there is legislation dealing specifically with recruitment. Other countries of Western Europe have seen the same need and legislated to fill it.

Belgium

The law in Belgium[11] illustrates well the need for clear and comprehensive legislation. Though there are laws against recruitment they have not proved effective. The Penal Code prohibits and punishes the recruitment of civilians to serve in a foreign army without licence of the Crown.[12]

Article 135 ter [Law of 15 June 1951 art. 99]. Anyone who recruits any person or incites or takes engagement of any person for profit in a foreign army or force, by gifts, payment, promises, threats, abuses of authority or power, shall be punished by imprisonment of from eight days to six months.

Exceptions from the prohibition of recruitment by gifts, payments and promises may be proclaimed by the King.

10. The Canadian cases on the British Act of 1819, arising out of the American Civil War, were *In re John Smith* (1864) 10 U.C.L.J. O.S. 247; *R.* v. *Schram et al.* and *R.* v. *Anderson et al.* (1863–4) 14 U.C.C.P. 318; *Re Martin* (1864) 3 Practice Reports (Ontario) 298; 10 U.C.L.J. O.S. 130.
11. We are grateful to Professor Paulette Pierson-Mathy for providing us with the information on which this section is based.
12. *Article 135 ter* [loi 15 juin 1951, art. 99]: Sera puni d'un emprisonnement de huit jours à six mois celui qui, par dons, rémunérations, promesses, menaces, abus d'autorité ou de pouvoir, aura recruté des hommes ou aura provoqué ou recueilli des engagements d'homme au profit d'une armée ou d'une troupe étrangère. Des dérogations à l'interdiction de recrutement par dons, rémunérations, promesses, peuvent être édictés par le Roi.

Article 135[13] quater provides that it is an aggravation of the offence if the recruit is a minor and article 135 quinquer[14] that an attempt to recruit carries the same penalties as the act itself.[15] There is also a much older provision, in article 123,[16] that is of more general application: 'Whoever by hostile actions not approved by the government exposes the State to hostilities on the part of a foreign power, shall be punished by imprisonment of from five to ten years and, if hostilities result, by imprisonment of from ten to fifteen years.' This provision, though, has never been applied to recruiters.

There is no prohibition of individual enlistment in the Penal Code, but there was special temporary legislation to deal with volunteers for the Spanish Civil War. By a *loi de circonstance* of 11 June 1937,[17] Parliament forbade not only recruitment for profit but also the departure or transit of anyone going to serve in

13. *Article 135 quater* [loi 23 juin 1961, article unique]: Est puni d'un emprisonnement d'un mois à un an et d'une amende de mille francs à dix mille francs, ou d'une de ces peines seulement, celui qui obtient un engagement à servir dans une armée ou une troupe étrangère, d'un mineur non autorisé à cet effet par ses parents, son tuteur ou son curateur.
14. *Article 135 quinquer* [loi 23 juin 1961, article unique]: La tentative de commettre les délits prévus aux art. 135 ter et 135 quater sera punie des mêmes peines.
15. It is noteworthy that these provisions were incorporated in the Code by a Law passed on 31 December 1936, at the start of the Spanish Civil War.
    An Arrêt of the Second Chamber of 18 October 1937 held that the crime of recruiting is committed by one who transports persons recruited elsewhere through Belgium, who gives them food and lodging and pays the cost of their travel. It was held that the law was clear and not restricted to recruits of Belgian nationality. The purpose of the law, the court said, was to protect Belgium from the reprisals which other countries might take if Belgium were to allow the recruitment, even of foreigners, within that country.
16. *Article 123* provides: Quiconque, par des actions hostiles non approuvées par le gouvernement, aura exposé l'État à des hostilités de la part d'une puissance étrangère, sera puni de la détention de cinq à dix ans, et si des hostilités s'en sont suivies, de la détention de dix à quinze ans.
17. Loi 11 Juin 1937. *Article 1er.* Sont interdits en Belgique: (a) le recrutement et les actes de nature à provoquer ou à faciliter le recrutement de personnes autres que celles des nationaux espagnols au profit d'une troupe ou d'une armée en Espagne ou dans les possessions espagnoles, y compris les zones d'influences espagnoles au Maroc; (b) le départ et le transit de

Spain, subject to a penalty of imprisonment of up to six months.

There were many Belgian mercenaries in the Congo conflict but no general legislation, temporary or otherwise, to stop them. The government took some steps to discourage them, by withdrawing the passports of a number of former mercenaries or limiting their validity to countries outside Africa or making Belgians who wanted passports or visas for Katanga sign an undertaking not to serve in a foreign force. These measures were not of much effect. When the United Nations Security Council adopted Resolution s/161 of 21 February 1961, requiring member states to take energetic measures to prevent the departure of mercenaries and to refuse them passage, the Belgian Minister of Justice gave instructions that both Belgians and foreigners should be prevented from leaving to enlist in an armed force in the Congo. Many still went.[18]

When the influx of mercenaries into Angola took them through Brussels in January 1976, there was no law effective to stop them. Nearly all of them were British nationals and there was no law which caught them. A socialist Member of Parliament, Monsieur E. Glinne, tried to introduce legislation which would 'ensure the non-intervention of Belgians and foreigners residing in or passing through Belgium in the civil war in Angola'. Events moved too quickly for the legislation to be passed. It would have revived the legislation of 11 June 1937 replacing references to Spain with 'the territory over which Portugal ceased to exercise its responsibilities on 11 November 1975'.

---

personnes autres que celles de nationaux espagnols pour servir dans une armée ou une troupe visée à l'alinéa précédent.

Article 2 Le Roi est autorisé à prendre par arrêté délibéré en Conseil des Ministres, toutes dispositions nécessaires pour l'exécution d'accords internationaux en vue d'assurer la non-intervention des pays contractant et des personnes y résidant dans la guerre civile espagnole.

Article 3 Les infractions à l'article 1er et aux arrêtés pris en vertu de l'article 2 sont punies d'un emprisonnement de huit jours à six mois.

18. In a note to the Secretary-General of the United Nations dated 17 February 1961, the Belgian government said: 'Tout individu, belge ou étranger, recruté comme militaire par une personne privée, devra être refoulé vers l'intérieur du pays s'il est démontré qu'il a l'intention de quitter le royaume pour rejoindre une des armées opérant ou en voie de formation dans l'ex-Congo.'

'Major' Roden, one of the Angolan mercenaries who returned to England, tells the following tale. A Belgian called André Blavier, who said he had been a mercenary in the Congo and had been in the Belgian army, was recruited by Banks for an expedition to Zambia to fight the Smith régime in Rhodesia. There is no way of knowing whether there was ever such a deal, but it certainly never got further than the expensive and drunken recruiting meeting in the Skyline Hotel at Heathrow airport, on 25 and 26 July 1975. 'Lieutenant' Blavier was in England in January 1976 and travelled with the party which left on 30 January. As we saw earlier, according to Roden, Blavier, 'who had been edgy ever since the party arrived [in Brussels], was detained by men in plain clothes' who can be presumed to be Belgian policemen.

It is important to remember that Blavier was an ex-serviceman. In Belgium, men who are no longer on active service remain until the age of forty-five in the category of 'militaires en congés illimités', or 'soldiers on indefinite leave'. They are subject to call-up in certain circumstances. If they do not respond to their call-up within fifteen days in peacetime or three days in wartime, under article 45 of the Military Penal Code they can be declared deserters.[19]

This law was applied in the Spanish Civil War. Moreover, a ministerial regulation requires such men to obtain the authorization of the Minister of National Defence before joining a foreign force.[20] There was obviously sufficient law for the men in plain clothes to quote to 'Lieutenant' Blavier to dissuade him from continuing his journey to Angola.

19. The Military Penal Code provides: *Article 45* Est déclaré déserteur: tout sous-officier, caporal, brigadier ou soldat . . . en congé qui ne sera pas rentré à son corps, en temps de guerre trois jours, en temps de paix quinze jours . . . après la date fixée par son ordre de rappel.
20. The arrêté ministériel of 20 February 1961 provided: *Article 5* Il est interdit au militaire en congé illimité de contracter un engagement dans une armée étrangère sans autorisation du ministre de la Défense nationale.

France[21]

The only French law which applies to mercenaries is found in article 85 of the Penal Code[22]:

Whoever in French territory in time of peace shall recruit soldiers on behalf of a foreign power, shall be punished by imprisonment of from one to five years and to a fine of 3,000 to 30,000 francs.

So far as we can discover, this article has never been the subject of a prosecution. It is interesting to note also that not even the minimum and maximum fines have been altered. The crime is classified as an injury to the safety of the State and, as an *atteinte à la sûreté de l'État*, an offence under art. 85 is tried by the special court, the *Cour de Sûreté de l'État*, which has its own procedure,[23] lacking many of the safeguards normally provided for the accused. The commentary in the *Encyclopédie Dalloz*[24] says that the crime is committed by anyone, French or foreign, who on French territory in time of peace recruits civilians or soldiers for a foreign force. Unlike other provisions of this part of the Code, the offence is committed even if the foreign power is not at war with France.

Many of the mercenaries now fighting in the Lebanon are French and some were no doubt recruited in France. Either this apparently widely drafted law is not wide enough, or there is not sufficient concern for the evils of mercenarism to put it into practice.

Sweden[25]

It has been a crime in Sweden since the nineteenth century to

21. We are grateful to Mme Gisèle Halimi, avocat à la Cour, for documents, information and elucidation.
22. *Code Penal*, Dalloz, 1974–5 edn: Art. 85. Sera puni d'un emprisonnement de un à cinq ans et d'une amende de 3,000F à 30,000F quiconque, en temps de paix, enrôlera des soldats pour le compte d'une puissance étrangère, en territoire français.
23. See *Répertoire de Droit Pénal et de Procedure Pénale*, mise à jour 1975 (2e edn) under 'Atteintes à la sûreté de l'État'.
24. Under 'Atteintes à la sûreté de l'État', Chapter 3, paragraphs 48–53.
25. We are grateful to Professor Lars Rudebeck for providing us with the information on which this section is based. It is on the replies to his ques-

recruit for a foreign force without the King's permission. As in Britain, this legislation was first intended to keep able-bodied men at home. More recently its purpose has been to protect Sweden's neutrality. In 1909, Sweden ratified the Hague Convention of 1907, according to article 4 of which it is forbidden to organize fighting forces or to open recruiting offices on the territory of a neutral power. Article 6, however, provides that a neutral power has no responsibility to stop individuals leaving the country to enlist in a foreign army. Swedish law also stops short of prohibiting enlistment.

In 1918, the Prime Minister stated in Parliament that the government would not allow fighting forces to be organized in Sweden to take part in the civil war in Finland. Individuals were allowed to leave to take part in the war. In 1919, the Foreign Minister made a similar statement with regard to the Baltic states. The problem arose again during the Spanish Civil War. Like Britain and the United States and most of the countries of Western Europe other than the fascists, the Swedish social-democrat government adopted a policy of non-intervention. The existing legislation prohibiting recruiting in Sweden was not considered sufficient to stop Swedish citizens from volunteering for the International Brigade. A special law was passed on 5 March 1937, later extended to 28 February 1939, when it expired. This special law made it a crime for a Swedish citizen to enlist for armed service in Spain, or to recruit or otherwise induce people to do so. By a special decision of the Swedish government, the volunteers who got back at the end of the war were not prosecuted.

And so, from 1939 onwards, the only law in force was that which prohibited recruiting in Sweden. During the Second World War this was circumvented by making sure that the recruitment was legally accomplished outside Sweden. The future recruits were encouraged to leave Sweden and sign their contracts once outside the country. In 1948, new legislation was passed to stop these

tions addressed to the chief public prosecutor that we have based our statement that there has been no prosecution since 1948. See also N. Beckman, C. Holmberg, B. Hult and I. Strahl, *Brottsbalken jämte förklaringar* (Swedish Criminal Law with Explanations), vol. 2, 3rd edn, Norstedt & Söner, Stockholm, 1973, pp. 340–43.

loopholes. The law, still in substance the 1948 law, is now set out in:

Swedish Criminal Code chapter 19:12 [law 1974/565]
Anyone who in this country, without permission of the government, recruits any person for foreign armed service or other comparable service or who induces any person to leave the country unlawfully in order to take up such service shall be sentenced for unlawful recruiting to payment of a fine or to imprisonment for not more than six months or, if the country is at war, to imprisonment of not more than two years.

It is noteworthy that enlistment is still no crime and that the crime is restricted to recruiters, and in addition those who induce if the recruits leave unlawfully. It is not normally unlawful to leave the country in peacetime if a valid passport is held. Moreover, by chapter 19:16 [law 1974/565] of the Criminal Code, the public prosecutor needs the special permission of the government to bring a prosecution based on chapter 19:12. It is not surprising that the chief public prosecutor for the whole country has stated that since 1948 the law on this subject has not been invoked. It is certain that Swedish pilots flew for the Biafran side in the civil war in Nigeria and there have been rumours that there were Swedish pilots flying transports for the FNLA early in 1976.

The Special Problem of Rhodesia

One of the more obvious howlers in the Diplock Report is the suggestion that because the Foreign Enlistment Act 1870 refers to service in the forces of a foreign state, and because Rhodesia is still legally a part of the Queen's dominions, therefore enlistment for the forces of Ian Smith is not caught by the Act.[26] It is at least

26. Paragraph 32 deals with Rhodesia. It rightly points out that the 1870 Act does not deal with enlistment in the forces of other dominions. The Act provides that the force must be outside the Queen's dominions. This would apply, says the Committee, even in a Commonwealth country which had adopted a Republican constitution. No doubt. But an unwise assumption follows. 'The Act would have no application to service in the army or air force of the regime in Southern Rhodesia, since this still remains, *de jure*, a Crown colony.' But the *regime* is not a Crown colony! In any case, a force in rebellion against the Crown, such as that in Rhodesia, is dealt with by other legislation. It is still an offence punishable by death to serve in that force against Her Majesty.

arguable, however, that the army of the illegal régime in Salisbury, which is in rebellion against the Crown, is no longer the army of one of the Queen's dominions at all, but a rebel force. Such an army might well be a 'foreign force' within the Act.

It does not much matter whether the recruiters for Rhodesia can be prosecuted for offences against the Foreign Enlistment Act. Nor is it necessary here to inquire into possible charges of conspiracy to murder and commit lesser crimes, which might well prove as successful against the recruiters for Rhodesia as they could against those for Angola. What is incontestable is that the recruiters for Rhodesia break the provisions of an Order in Council, the United Nations Sanctions Order No. 2, 29 May 1968. That Order, made under the Southern Rhodesia Act 1965, and approved as an Order in Council by the House of Commons on 15 July and by the House of Lords on 18 July 1968, makes it an offence to publicize opportunities for employment in Rhodesia *of any kind*, not just military.

What powerful forces are at work to stop the British police bringing to justice those who are giving assistance in this way to rebels in revolt against the Crown? Surely it would be unwise to imagine that they are so strong that the British government is not really in charge of the matter at all! Perhaps it is the technical problem of the lack of evidence for a successful prosecution. As the authorities are bound to use that excuse anyway, we should consider its merits.

In the *Panorama* programme on BBC TV on 19 July 1976 there were interesting interviews with some of the people in Britain closely involved in the support of the rebel régime, with some of those who had been recruited, with Robert Hughes, a Member of Parliament well known for his opposition to racist régimes in Africa, and with Colonel G. I. A. D. Draper, an expert in international law who teaches at the University of Sussex. The story of McCarthy, the deserter from Smith's army, and the other recruits is told in Chapter 10. It was revealed that Teilan, the recruiter in Germany, had been successfully prosecuted in West Germany. If the West German government has the will to prosecute, to carry out its duty to the United Nations, it seems strange that the British government should not do the same, especially when the recruits go to fight in a rebel army. The friends of Smith interviewed on the television programme were naturally shy of confessing directly the facts of their crimes before an audience of millions, though it is arguable that even the guarded statements they made are prima facie evidence of their offences. The interview with one of the recruiters which has become a standard part of such programmes was this time with Aspin, the bungling braggart who will do anything for money but does nothing well. He said enough to convict himself:

This morning again we received another fifty letters from potential recruits who specifically say they would like to go to Rhodesia to fight ... It's my intention to send men out [to Namibia] ... If at the end of their tour of duty they decide to go to ... Rhodesia that's entirely up to them ... Is anything strictly legal?

The answer to that is that it doesn't matter whether it is legal or not if you know you are not going to be prosecuted! We found no difficulty in getting a transcript of the programme from the BBC. The police can do the same. Perhaps it is asking a bit too much of Scotland Yard to read the *Morning Star* every day, but they had brought to their notice by the *Guardian* and other papers the *Star*'s scoop on G. R. Ward, Smith's man in Portsmouth. What could be plainer evidence of the commission of an offence under the Sanctions Order than the following letter:

Dear Sir,
Owing to the fact that recruitment of mercenaries will soon stop. And seeing that you have shown an interest in this line of work. I am enclosing a blue card that may be of interest to you.

NOT MERCENARY WORK

If you do not wish to use it, please return it. If you know of someone who would like one, please ask them to write to me, asking for a blue card and enclosing a stamped addressed envelope.
If you or others wish similar cards send a S.A.E.
You may also let others see this letter.

Yours faithfully,
G. R. Ward.

The blue card referred to in the letter read:

NOTE
PLEASE WRITE
FOR
REINFORCED
INFORMATION

NAME OF SERVICE
HEADQUARTERS
PRIVATE BAG 7721
CAUSEWAY
SALISBURY, RHODESIA

Whether or not those who go to fight in Rhodesia come within an acceptable definition of mercenaries, whether or not the Foreign Enlistment Act 1870 applies, the inactivity, to use as complimentary term as possible, of the British police, illustrates an important truth about all the law described in this chapter: if a government lacks either the political will to enforce its laws or effective control of law enforcement, then the laws which exist on paper provide neither a protection for the people nor a deterrent to the lawless.

16 An International Fight Against an International Threat

The Background

It has been stressed that the only effective way of stopping the enlistment and recruitment of mercenaries is for each country to have laws which clearly prohibit those activities and an unequivocal political will to enforce them. The early history of the recognition by governments that their duties as neutrals required them to suppress the recruitment of mercenaries is described in Chapter 12. It was because governments believed that it was in their interests to remain neutral and that mercenaries might prejudice their neutrality that they passed the modern laws against enlisting and recruiting. Indeed, in some countries the only legislation relevant to mercenaries has been that which makes it an offence to do anything which may prejudice relations with a foreign country.[1]

To encourage the enactment of laws fostering neutrality in this way, international organizations since the start of this century have drafted conventions of one kind or another to provide guidelines or authoritative pronouncements on international law and practice.[2] Although with the creation of the United Nations Organization, neutrality is no longer seen as the goal for which

1. There are many examples given in F. Deak and P. C. Jessup, eds., *A Collection of Neutrality Laws, Regulations and Treaties of Various Countries*, Greenwood Press (Reprint), Westport, Connecticut, 1974. See e.g. pp. 75, 76 for Bolivia, Penal Code 1834 art. 160 and Military Penal Code 1903 art. 96.

The crudeness of the morality of the early natural lawyers is well but not deliberately illustrated in E. B. F. Midgley, *The Natural Law Tradition and the Theory of International Relations*, Paul Elek, 1975, pp. 121–3 and the notes on p. 473. The analogy is there referred to between the mercenary unsure of whether his killing is, in the situation in which he finds himself, moral according to the divine law and the husband who, unsure of the legality of his marriage, is diffident about making love to his wife!

2. The first seems to be The Hague Convention, 1907, art. 4.

nations should strive, but rather collective security, the urge to outlaw mercenaries which produced article 4 of the Hague Convention of 1907 has grown, and is now more powerfully expressed in recent resolutions of the UN and OAU.

Although in international law a state has no duty to prevent its citizens enlisting as individuals in a foreign war or insurrection, the recognized laws of neutrality require every state to refrain from helping rebels and to stop military expeditions leaving its territory to assist the rebel forces. Once it is recognized that there is a state of belligerency, article 4 of the Hague Convention of 1907 applies: 'Corps of combatants cannot be formed nor recruiting offices opened on the territory of a neutral power in the interests of the belligerents.'

This convention applies only to belligerents. The recognition of belligerency was a difficult problem even in an international war; in civil strife it has become intractable. Although the Geneva Conventions of 1949 extended to civil wars the basic humanitarian provisions of the Hague Conventions, protecting noncombatants and prohibiting murder, mutilation and torture, the taking of hostages, outrages against personal dignity, and also protecting certain rights of proper criminal procedure, they did not apply the prohibition of recruiting to civil wars.

The United Nations and the Congo[3]

The problem of mercenaries became acute during the fighting in the Congo. In 1961, Tshombe had 500 white mercenaries from Europe and South Africa fighting for the secessionist cause in Katanga. The UN Security Council on 21 February 1961 passed a resolution[4] urging 'that measures be taken for the immediate withdrawal and evacuation from the Congo of all Belgian and other foreign military and paramilitary personnel and political advisers not under the United Nations Command, and mercen-

3. The problems of international law and the Congo hostilities are discussed in D. W. Monemar, 'The Postindependence War in the Congo' in R. A. Falk, *The International Law of Civil War*, Johns Hopkins Press, Baltimore, 1971; and in R. Simmonds, *Legal Problems Arising from the United Nations Military Operations in the Congo*, Martinus Nijhoff, The Hague, 1968.
4. U.N. Doc. 5/4741 of 1961.

aries'. On 24 November 1961[5] a further resolution authorized the use of whatever force was necessary to carry out this decision. The United Nations force in the Congo launched 'Operation Rumpunch' to expel the mercenaries and 273 were repatriated in August 1961, but there were still 237 there in November. Though the embassies of the Western countries who had nationals serving as mercenaries in Tshombe's army undertook to get them out, they made little attempt to fulfil their promises. Some passports were withdrawn for a while, or endorsed 'Not Valid for the Congo', but this had little effect. Belgium, whose duplicity and determination not to give up colonial power were largely responsible for the fighting, professed to have no power to stop its citizens being mercenaries, except under the statutes which allowed the government to control the movements of reservists 'on unlimited leave'.[6]

Later United Nations Initiatives

The United Nations has condemned mercenaries on a number of occasions. On 20 December 1968, the General Assembly declared[7]

that the practice of using mercenaries against movements for national liberation and independence is punishable as a criminal act and that the mercenaries themselves are outlaws, and calls upon the Governments of all countries to enact legislation declaring the recruitment, financing and training of mercenaries in their territory to be a punishable offence and prohibiting their nationals from serving as mercenaries.

Declarations of the General Assembly in December 1969 and December 1970,[8] and a resolution of the Security Council on mercenaries in the Republic of Guinea, were followed by a general condemnation on 12 December 1973:[9]

5. The use of mercenaries by colonial and racist régimes against the national liberation movements struggling for their freedom and in-

---

5. U.N. Doc. 5/5002 of 1961.
6. The relevant Belgian law is described in Chapter 15.
7. U.N. Doc. S/2465 (xxiii) Implementation of the Declaration on the Granting of Independence to Colonial Countries and Peoples.
8. Resolution 289 (1970) of 23 November 1970.
9. U.N. Doc. 3103 (xxviii), 12 December 1973.

dependence from the yoke of colonialism and alien domination is considered to be a criminal act and the mercenaries should accordingly be punished as criminals.

The Organization of African Unity

The Organization of African Unity has also been active in condemning mercenaries and encouraging legislation to suppress them. As early as the time of the Congo fighting, the Council of Ministers expressed its abhorrence and appealed to the Democratic Republic of the Congo to stop the recruitment of mercenaries and expel those on its territory.[10]

At its Fourth Ordinary Session in Kinshasa in September 1967, the Assembly of Heads of State and Government expressed further condemnation of the aggression of mercenaries and, after calling upon Member States of the OAU and also the United Nations for support, made an urgent appeal[11]

to all states of the world to enact laws declaring the recruitment and training of mercenaries in their territories a punishable crime and deterring their citizens from enlisting as mercenaries.

When in 1970 the Republic of Guinea was threatened by the Portuguese forces, which included mercenaries from other countries, the Council of Ministers passed a resolution condemning mercenaries and asking the Administrative Secretary General to prepare a draft Convention to outlaw mercenaries and unmask their activities in Africa.[12] An even more elaborate Declaration was made by the meeting of Heads of State and Government in Addis Ababa in June 1971.[13]

The OAU's most important contribution, however, was the Report of its Committee of Experts, charged with drafting a Convention on Mercenaries. This Report, presented to the Nineteenth Ordinary Session of the Council of Ministers at Rabat in June 1972,[14] has influenced all subsequent thinking on the

10. OAU Doc. ECM/Res. 55 (III), Addis Ababa, 10 September 1964.
11. AHG/Res. 49 (IV), September 1967.
12. OAU Doc. ECM/Res. 17 (VII), December 1970 (Lagos).
13. OAU Doc. CM/St. 6 (XVII), Addis Ababa, 21 to 23 June 1971.
14. OAU Doc. CM/1/33/Ref. 1, Rabat, June 1972.

international control of mercenaries and determined many of the arguments presented at the International Commission of Inquiry in Luanda. It is worth quoting at length from the Convention which it suggested:

OAU CONVENTION FOR THE ELIMINATION OF MERCENARIES IN AFRICA[15]

PREAMBLE

We Heads of State and Government of Member States of the Organization of African Unity,

Considering the grave threat which the activities of mercenaries represent to the independence, sovereignty, territorial integrity and harmonious development of Member States of OAU,

Considering that total solidarity and co-operation between Member States are indispensable for putting an end, once and for all, to the subversive activities of mercenaries in Africa,

Decided to take all necessary measures to eradicate from the African continent the scourge that the mercenary system represents. We agree on the following:

ARTICLE ONE

Under the present Convention a 'mercenary' is classified as anyone who, not a national of the state against which his actions are directed, is employed, enrols or links himself willingly to a person, group or organization whose aim is:

(a) to overthrow by force of arms or by any other means the government of that Member State of the Organization of African Unity;

(b) to undermine the independence, territorial integrity or normal working of the institutions of the said State;

(c) to block by any means the activities of any liberation movement recognized by the Organization of African Unity.

ARTICLE TWO
Offence

1. The actions of a mercenary, in the meaning of Article One of the present Convention, constitute offences considered as crimes against the peace and security of Africa and punishable as such.

2. Anyone who recruits or takes part in the recruitment of a mercenary, or in training, or in financing his activities or who gives him protection, commits a crime in the meaning of paragraph I of this article.

15. OAU Doc. CM/433/Rev. L, Annex 1.

ARTICLE THREE
Duties of State

The Member States of the Organization of African Unity, signatories to the present Convention, undertake to take all necessary measures to eradicate from the African continent the activities of mercenaries.

To this end, each State undertakes particularly:

(a) to prevent their nationals or foreigners living in their territory from committing any of the offences defined in Article Two of the present Convention;

(b) to prevent the entry to or the passage through their territory of any mercenary or equipment intended for their use;

(c) to forbid in their territory any activity by organizations or individuals who employ mercenaries against the African States Members of the Organization of African Unity;

(d) to communicate to other Member States of the Organization of African Unity any information, as soon as it comes to their knowledge, relating to the activities of mercenaries in Africa;

(e) to forbid on their territory the recruitment, training or equipping of mercenaries or the financing of their activities;

(f) to take as soon as possible all necessary legislative measures for the implementation of the present Convention.

ARTICLE FOUR
Sanctions

Every contracting State undertakes to impose severe penalties for offences defined in Article Two of the present Convention.

ARTICLE FIVE
Competence

Every contracting State undertakes to take the measures necessary to punish any individual found in its territory who has committed one of the offences defined in Article Two of the present Convention, if he does not hand him over to the State against which the offence has been committed or would have been committed.

ARTICLE SIX
Offences calling for extradition

In accordance with the provisions of Article Seven of the present Convention, the offences defined in Article Two above should be considered as offences calling for extradition.

Extradition

1. A request for extradition cannot be rejected, unless the State from which it is sought undertakes to prosecute the offender in accordance with the provisions of Article Five of the present Convention.

2. When a national is the subject of the request for extradition, the State from which it is sought must, if it refuses, undertake prosecution of the offence committed.

3. If, in accordance with sections 1 and 2 of this Article, prosecution is undertaken, the State from which extradition is sought will notify the outcome of such prosecution to the state seeking extradition and to any other interested Member State of the Organization of African Unity.

4. A state will be regarded as an interested party for the outcome of a prosecution as defined in section 3 of this Article if the offence has some connection with its territory or militates against its interests.

[Articles 8 to 11 are formal.]

The Luanda Convention

The International Commission of Inquiry on Mercenaries, sitting in Luanda in June 1976, recognized that the creation, elaboration and enforcement of new and existing international law had not only legal but political significance. In the struggle, usually a long-drawn-out struggle, to get a new Convention signed and ratified, the debates in all the national and international bodies, and the detailed criticism of the drafts, inform the public, arouse argument and enliven public opinion.

The members of the Commission who sat on the committee charged with drafting a new Convention on Mercenaries were for the most part lawyers with experience in international law. The meetings were lively and long, and the Convention which was finally accepted by the whole of the Commission had been through many drafts.

Creating a definition of a crime which will withstand the assault of an intelligent and experienced defence lawyer is never an easy matter. Getting a committee to do it makes it almost impossible. Only endless patience and goodwill produced the definition in the draft set out below. Once it had been decided that a definition must contain all of the following four elements, not just the first three, the rest of the draft was straightforward. The four elements are:

He fights in a foreign country;

he does not fight as a soldier of his own country;

he fights for personal profit, whether or not he also has some ideological motivation;

the purpose for which he fights is to interfere with a people's right to self-determination.

The draft which follows here is offered by the Commission as a stimulus to international discussion and action.

DRAFT CONVENTION ON THE PREVENTION AND SUPPRESSION OF MERCENARISM

PREAMBLE

The High Contracting Parties

Seriously concerned at the use of mercenaries in armed conflicts with the aim of opposing by armed force the process of national liberation from racist colonial and neo-colonial domination;

Considering that the crime of mercenarism is part of a process of perpetuating by force of arms racist colonial or neo-colonial domination over a people or State;

Considering the resolutions of the United Nations (Res. 2395 (XXIIX), 2465 (XXXXX), 2548 (XXIV) and 3103 (XXVIII) of the General Assembly and of the Organization of African Unity (ECM/Res. 5 (III), 1964; AHG/Res. 49 (IV), 1967; ECM/Res. 17 (VII), 1970, and OAU Declaration on the Activities of Mercenaries in Africa CM/St. 9 (XVII)), which have denounced the use in these armed conflicts of mercenaries as a criminal act, and mercenaries as criminals, and which have urged States to take forceful measures to prevent the organization, recruitment and movement on their territory of mercenaries, and to bring to justice the authors of this crime and their accomplices;

Considering that the resolutions of the UN and the OAU and the statements of attitude and the practice of a growing number of States are indicative of the development of new rules of international law making mercenarism an international crime;

Convinced of the need to codify in a single text and to develop progressively the rules of international law which have developed in order to prevent and suppress mercenarism, the High Contracting Parties are convinced of the following matters:

ARTICLE ONE
Definition

The crime of mercenarism is committed by the individual, group or association, representatives of state and the State itself which, with the aim of opposing by armed violence a process of self-determination, practises any of the following acts:

(a) organizes, finances, supplies, equips, trains, promotes, supports or employs in any way military forces consisting of or including persons who are not nationals of the country where they are going to act, for personal gain, through the payment of a salary or any other kind of material recompense;

(b) enlists, enrols or tries to enrol in the said forces;

(c) allows the activities mentioned in paragraph (a) to be carried out in any territory under its jurisdiction or in any place under its control or affords facilities for transit, transport or other operations of the abovementioned forces.

ARTICLE TWO

The fact of assuming command over mercenaries or giving orders may be considered as an aggravating circumstance.

ARTICLE THREE

1. When the representative of a State is responsible by virtue of the foregoing provisions for acts or omissions declared by the foregoing provisions to be criminal, he shall be punished for such an act or omission.

2. When a State is responsible by virtue of the foregoing provisions for acts or omissions declared by the foregoing provisions to be criminal, any other State may invoke such responsibility:

(a) in its relations with the State responsible, and

(b) before competent international organizations.

ARTICLE FOUR

Mercenaries are not lawful combatants. If captured they are not entitled to prisoner of war status.

ARTICLE FIVE

Crimes of mercenaries and other crimes for which mercenaries can be responsible

A mercenary bears responsibility both for being a mercenary and for any other crime committed by him as such.

ARTICLE SIX

National legislation

Each contracting State shall enact all legislative and other measures necessary to implement fully the provisions of the present Convention.

ARTICLE SEVEN
Jurisdiction

Each contracting State undertakes to bring to trial and to punish any individual found in its territory who has committed the crime defined in Art. 1 of the present Convention, unless it hands him over to the State against which the crime has been committed or would have been committed.

ARTICLE EIGHT
Extradition

1. Any State in whose territory the crime of mercenarism has been committed or of which the persons accused of the crimes defined in Art. 1 are nationals, can make a request for extradition to the State holding the persons accused.

2. The crimes defined in Art. 1 being deemed to be common crimes, they are not covered by national legislation excluding extradition for political offences.

3. When a request for extradition is made by any of the States referred to in para. 1, the State from which extradition is sought must, if it refuses, undertake prosecution of the offence committed.

4. If, in accordance with paras. 1–3 of this article, prosecution is undertaken, the State in which it takes place shall notify the outcome of such prosecution to the State which had sought or granted extradition.

ARTICLE NINE
Judicial guarantees

Every person or group brought to trial for the crime set out in Art. 1 is entitled to all the essential guarantees of a fair and proper trial. These guarantees include:

the right of the defendant to get acquainted in his native language with all the materials of the criminal case initiated against him, the right to give any explanation regarding the charges against him, the right to participate in the preliminary investigation of the evidence and during the trial in his native language, the right to have the services of an advocate, or defend himself if he prefers, the right to give by himself or through an advocate testimony in his defence, to demand that his witnesses be summoned and participate in their investigation as well as in the investigation of witnesses for the prosecution.

ARTICLE TEN
Mutual assistance for criminal proceedings

The Contracting Parties shall afford one another the greatest measure of assistance in connection with criminal proceedings brought in respect of any of the crimes defined in Art. 1 of this Convention.

ARTICLE ELEVEN
Duty of States to ensure effective punishment

Each contracting State shall take all administrative and judicial measures necessary to establish effective criminal punishment for persons and groups guilty of crimes set out in Art. 1 of this Convention. In particular, the State where a trial takes place shall ensure that effective and adequate punishment shall be meted out to the guilty.

ARTICLE TWELVE
Settlement of disputes

Any disputes relating to the interpretation or application of the present Convention shall be settled either by negotiation or by any International Tribunal or Arbitrator accepted by all the Parties concerned.

The Secretariat of the International Commission of Inquiry remains in Luanda. It has taken the responsibility for bringing this draft Convention before the appropriate bodies and for winning international support for it.

It should be remembered that the purpose of this draft Convention is to stimulate discussion, not to stifle it. It was on this understanding that agreement was possible among a group whose ideas of definition were so often widely different. It is unlikely that some Western countries will support a definition which concerns itself so forthrightly with those who serve in anti-liberation forces to the exclusion of all others. There is obviously a need at this moment to stop recruiting of French right-wing students and ex-Angolan mercenaries for service in the Lebanon; yet it might be hard to persuade an English or American court that the fighting there is directly concerned with the Palestinian or Lebanese people's right to self-determination. Nevertheless, the Luanda Draft should prove the stimulus for the international legislation on which enforceable national laws will be based.